Quentin & Flora

President Theodore Roosevelt and his sons, Ted, Archie, Quentin, and Kermit, 1904.

Quentin and Flora

A Roosevelt and a Vanderbilt
in Love during the Great War

by Chip Bishop

Author of
The Lion and the Journalist
The Unlikely Friendship

of Theodore Roosevelt

and Joseph Bucklin Bishop

To the memory of Charles and Eugenie Bishop, my father and mother, whose wartime romance blossomed into 50 years together.

Contents

I knew Quentin as a child, and one could easily discover in the child the man that he would be. Millions of long lives will have been forgotten when his memory will still be fresh among us as in his own country.

Jean Jules Jusserand
French Ambassador to the United States
During the Great War

Introduction

During that suffocating late August of 1909, a moist stillness blanketed the flat French terrain, 130 kilometers northeast of Paris. In defiance of mid-summer's oppressive heat, hordes of inquisitive spectators turned out, many in their extravagant Edwardian fashions, to gaze skyward at the most celebrated athletes of the time. Twenty-two pioneer pilots, mostly French, along with their 38 archetype aéroplanes, had been drawn to the first international Reims Air Meet—La Grande Semaine de l'Aviation de la Champagne—by a 200,000-franc purse offered by New York Herald playboy publisher James Gordon Bennett, Jr. The daring young men in their flying machines soared and dived, competing to be the highest and fastest fliers in the world. Cheering fans gasped as wispy contrails painted the sky.

Gripping the slatted safety fence along the airfield's rim, a sandy-haired 11-year-old American boy watched the performance with head up, eyes open wide, and mouth agape. Quentin Roosevelt reveled in the show, displaying at once awe and exhilaration. The youngest and favored son of recently-retired U.S. President Theodore Roosevelt was there by happenstance, winding up the season with Edith, his mother, the former first lady.

"You don't know how pretty it was to see all the *aéroplanes* sailing at a time," Quentin later wrote to a school chum. "At one time there were four in the air. It was the prettiest thing I ever saw." Recalling his favorite, a monoplane called the *Antoinette*, Quentin likened it to "a big bird in the air." He observed, "It does not wiggle at all, and goes very fast."[1]

Less than a decade later, as a young aviator, he would wing into another summer sky, above a patch of France, not 20 miles from Reims, which was inhabited by warring Germans. Exposed in his open-air cockpit, outfitted in goggles and an American Air Service uniform, and flanked by twin machine guns on his wings, Quentin would race in mortal pursuit of the enemy Boche.

1

One

The Dance

Moonlight danced on the fluttering sea as the richly-dressed couples strolled arm in arm to the edge of the cliff. They allowed their gazes to fall across Sheep Point Cove and then onto Rhode Island Sound and the dark woodlands of Middletown that lay beyond. By the conclusion of supper around midnight, the warmth of the August evening had been chilled by the damp ocean breeze. In defense, ladies nestled tightly into their shawls, and their gentlemen escorts fast buttoned their tailcoats.

The evening had been a proper affair, *the* event of the 1916 Newport season. The entire summer colony, it seemed, had responded with eagerness to the engraved invitation from Mr. and Mrs. Harry Payne Whitney of Newport and New York. Their guests' presence had been requested for the evening of August 4, at a dance to mark the coming out of their elder daughter, Flora Payne Whitney, just turned 19, at The Reefs - the Whitney "cottage" on Bellevue Avenue.

The house stood somewhat inelegantly between the ornate Rosecliff to the north, built for a Nevada silver heiress, and Beechwood, occupied in summers by Mr. and Mrs. John Jacob Astor before he went down with the *Titanic* four years earlier. The Reefs was one of Newport's oldest showplaces. It had been built before the Civil War as an Italianate villa and had passed to the Whitneys in 1896, the most recent addition to a roster of homes stretching from the Adirondacks to Aiken, South Carolina. Like its more stately neighbors, The Reefs bore a formal stucco exterior but had a singularly choppy construct of gables, a clock-type tower, a veranda, and free-standing chimneys set off by gaudy awnings. Some in the Newport colony sniffed that it resembled an aging train depot. Yet all would agree that The Reefs was an entirely proper setting for a young debutante to be presented to society at a time of transition from Edwardian posh to Woodrow Wilson stiff.

An elegant new ballroom, colored in hues of blue and yellow, had been appended in haste to the main building. When planning began for the dance in March, Flora's father had ordered workmen to labor around the clock to ensure that the ballroom would be ready by summer. Within 90 hectic days, the room was finished, allowing craftsmen to install a spacious parquet floor, sparkling crystal chandeliers, and similarly grand finishing touches. During construction, Flora's mother, Gertrude, supervised further elaborations and drew up an expansive guest list suitable for the debut of Cornelius Vanderbilt's great-great-granddaughter.

If you had attended the dance, you would have mixed with nearly 500 men and women, many of whose names and stations were familiar from the newspapers: Rhode Island Governor and Mrs. Robert Livingston Beeckman, Russian Ambassador and Mrs. George Bakhmeteff, and the Rockefellers, Pells, and Morgans. The Spanish ambassador was on hand, as was the Marquis de Polignac from France. All had come to welcome Flora formally into their grand circle and to pay tribute to the Whitneys and Vanderbilts, two of America's foremost families. Their forebears, everyone knew, were pioneers in American industry and transportation during the 18th and 19th centuries.

Growing up in the Vanderbilt and Whitney estates Flora was nurtured by a French governess because her parents traveled the world frequently, often to distant and exotic places. At about age six she began to understand her father's passion for riding, horse racing, and polo, and to appreciate her mother's talent for sculpture and collecting contemporary American art. The family's elegant lifestyle would later prompt Cole Porter to pen the verse:

> You're the top!
> You're the Tower of Babel
> You're the top!
> You're the Whitney stable.[2]

Inheriting her mother's stark facial features, Flora was almost— but not quite—pretty. Her wide-set hazel eyes, fluted mouth, and prominent brows ruled an otherwise sweet and narrow face. But when she smiled under floppy curls set to either side of her face—in the style of the day—it all seemed to come together with charm and smartness.

Her cousin, the actress Beatrice Straight, recalled that Flora "was encouraged by her brilliant mother . . . whom she adored to develop into an amazing woman in her own right, a woman of great purpose and style."[3] But first, Gertrude Vanderbilt Whitney would have to present her daughter to society, according to the imperatives of the era.

Even with the addition of the fashionable ballroom, the Whitney cottage simply was not spacious enough to seat 500 for a formal dinner. Flora's guests fanned out to dinner parties at assorted locations in the Newport colony, as was the practice. When the multitudes arrived later at the dance, Flora and her mother, attired with contemporary seasonal dash and permed hair, stood to receive them. According to *The New York Times*, the tall and lanky Gertrude "wore a costume of black with jet trimmings, and Miss Whitney wore white with silver trimmings."[4] The net-like foundations of their dresses backed long and draping jet beads, said to be the work of French peasants, designed to individualize a lady's frock. Surely the beads glittered radiantly on mother and daughter in the brilliant reflected light of the ballroom.

Once Gertrude had extended her hand to each approaching guest, she turned to present her daughter. Flora shook hands and delivered the obligatory, "How do you do?" before the guest passed by. If there was no one in line at the moment, Gertrude could pause to engage a guest in polite small talk, perhaps commenting on how enchanting a lady's dress was. Flora, in turn, was likely to learn from the chatter that her costume was "simply divine."

In her left hand, Flora would have held a small spray of flowers, likely a trendy bouquet of gardenias or lilies-of-the-valley, set in lace paper and tied with a satin ribbon. Since it was customary for guests to send bouquets to the debutante, the ballroom was surely festooned with hundreds of them, ensuring a colorful and fragrant milieu.

B. H. Friedman, Gertrude Vanderbilt Whitney's biographer, observed the moment: "The smell of the sea mixes with that of flowers, perfumes, colognes, cigarettes and dark Havana cigars. Cultivated voices, laughter, the popping of champagne corks, and the clink of ice mix with the sound of music, as couples dance . . ."[5]

Despite her palpable success at high-end entertaining among the Social Register crowd, Gertrude did not relish the duty. She understood that it was obligatory for someone of her station, but she felt to her core that she had much more to tender. She had notable artistic ability, ambition, and a determination to rise above the expected role of a Vanderbilt or Whitney wife during the Gilded Age.

As Conrad's Orchestra and the Hawaiian Band played on past midnight, most in the party retired for a casual supper in the dining room or beneath the huge illuminated tent on the lawn. Nancy Perkins Lancaster, Flora's school pal, remembered that they "danced till sunrise and bathed in the ocean"[6] before finally retiring.

Varieties of roses from the estate's conservatories adorned the tables. Flora's stood in the center of the dining room, safeguarded by a bevy of young women, her favored friends. The seat next to Flora was reserved for her escort, the young man whose bouquet she likely had held in the receiving line. As the evening wore on, Flora and her escort danced with élan. His name was Quentin. At 18, he was handsomely husky, shorter rather than tall, with thin, straw colored hair. With Flora on his arm, and in formal black tie attire, he exuded an easy charm and perpetual smile that showcased a prominent and oddly familiar set of fine teeth. Some of the more observant guests thought that he resembled the young Theodore Roosevelt minus the spectacles and moustache. Indeed, Quentin *was* the youngest son of the retired 26th president of the United States who was often identified at the time as "the most famous man in the world."

Quentin may have overstayed his welcome at The Reefs. He apologized later in a note to Gertrude for committing "the cardinal sin of staying in Newport for more than three days." Nonetheless, he and Flora savored each other's company in the days following the dance; they had a particularly fine time motoring in her luxurious Scripps-Booth roadster along Newport's scenic Ocean Drive.

Many older guests remembered Quentin from his years as "a child of the nation." During his father's tenure in the White House, between 1901 and 1909, the boy shone in the public spotlight as no presidential child had for decades, perhaps ever. Reporters and photographers succumbed to Quentin's rambunctious nature and playful antics. In consequence, the newspaper-reading public consumed every word printed about him and often clipped his photos for their scrapbooks. Occasionally, outlandish pranks by Quentin and his public school chums—known endearingly as the White House Gang—made it into the press. In turn, the misdeeds brought down on Quentin a half-hearted presidential reprimand and still further public appreciation for the adventures of son and father.

At 12, Quentin would be sent off to the Groton School in Massachusetts for academic preparation as his three brothers had been before him. Out of the public glare, he settled in to achieve honor grades, an unremarkable stint on the football squad, and a turn or two on the stage. The boy's singular talent for prose and poetry caught his advisors' attention and earned Quentin standing on the editorial board of the school's newspaper, *The Grotonian*, in his final year. In that role and later as press editor, he directed the production of the weekly four-pager, and contributed thoughtful articles and editorials. Upon graduation, continuing the Roosevelt tradition, it was off to Harvard in the fall of 1915.

At the time of the 1916 Newport dance, Quentin and Flora had known each other for about a year. Their families were well acquainted from New York social events. Quentin and Flora had corresponded regularly between his freshman dorm and whichever seasonal home she happened to be occupying. A cache of letters at Harvard's Houghton Library reveals that early on, they were in a ring of friends—Timmy, Clara, Jimmy, Pat, Doug and Helen—that socialized at school gatherings and parties, often in Cambridge. In February of that year, Quentin had sent Flora a card that unmistakably characterized their relationship as platonic.

By April, Quentin was struggling to understand what Flora meant to him. He had begun to address her with her pet name, "Foufie," used by others in the family. "I am trying to make up my mind about you," he admitted. "I don't know exactly how much to say to you for the simple reason that I've not quite decided how 'safe' you are."[7]

Just ten days before the dance, it seemed that Flora hadn't decided on an escort. "Is it O.K. if I come to Newport on the 5th?" Quentin wrote. "Cousin Adele says you are having a dance on the 6th. If so, I suppose, of course, that I'm not expected, so please let me know."[8] Quentin had the dates mixed up but he was plainly fishing for an invitation. To a 21st century reader of their letters, Quentin and Flora's relationship seemed at the time to be cloaked in caution and uncertainty.

Quentin had spent most of the summer of 1916—and the previous one—in olive garb at the urging of his father. The winds of war were raging across Europe as Germany and others of the Central Powers fought the Allies, led by Great Britain, France and Russia. While President Wilson labored to find "peace in our time," ex-President Roosevelt stubbornly demanded that the U.S. intervene on behalf of the Allies and prepare its young men militarily. In consequence, there would be no summer break for Quentin and his brothers. They trained daily in the hot and damp of a civilian officers' readiness camp in Plattsburgh, N.Y.

As Quentin was to learn, being a son of Theodore Roosevelt was no easy duty. In fact, it was a full-time job. T. R. demanded the most of himself in his professional and personal lives, and he expected no less from his offspring. His standards were above high, and he anticipated allegiance from his sons, even for some of his more radical views. As the youngest and most promising of the Roosevelt brood, Quentin faced extraordinary expectations.

Two

Quintus

The newborn arrived unexpectedly on the Friday before Thanksgiving 1897 in Washington, D.C. Some who wore the blue during the War Between the States recalled November 19 as the anniversary date of Mr. Lincoln's address on the Gettysburg battlefield. But to Theodore Roosevelt and his wife, Edith Kermit Roosevelt, the early birth of Quentin was a celebratory event to be sure, yet with a feeling of conclusiveness. Quentin would be the last child of their sprawling brood which, at the time, counted Ted, age 10; Kermit, 8; Ethel, 6; and Archie, 3½. And of course there was the defiant older daughter they called Sister, née Alice, 13, the child of T. R. and the late Alice Hathaway Lee.

"By the aid of my bicycle, I just got the Doctor and Nurse in time," Theodore reported of the birth to his sister Anna, called Bamie. "Edith is doing well. . . . We are very glad and much relieved."[9]

Derived from the Latin *Quintus*, Quentin was a seldom-bestowed male name meaning "the fifth." It was chosen by the Roosevelts to honor their fifth born and also the memory of Edith's grandfather, Isaac Quentin Carow. Perhaps because of the significance of his given name, Quentin was spared a middle one. Yet in his toddler years, he would not escape his father's endearing pet monikers, "Quenty-quee" and "Quenikins," in conversation and letters.

With a pleasantly plain face, blue-grey eyes and thin, dark brown hair, Edith Roosevelt cherished her roles as loving wife and mother. They were fulfilling and finite, she believed. With adults, Edith could be reserved and standoffish but with Theodore and the children, "Mother" was relentlessly calming. One of the family's close friends explained that "the chief ambition of Mr. and Mrs. Roosevelt was not to rear a brilliant family but to keep the children like other children, unspoiled by their father's distinction, and to bring them up simply and to fit them to be womanly women and manly men."[10] The family had domestic help of course, but each evening when it came time to tuck the children into bed, Edith insisted that she do it.

"Quentin is the merriest, jolliest baby imaginable," she would soon inscribe in her baby journal, allowing, nonetheless, that "Archie, by no means, approves of Quentin." Edith probably sighed with relief as she added, "The others love him."[11]

For his part, Theodore hurried to preserve the Roosevelt tradition by enrolling tiny Quentin in the Groton School within two hours of his birth. There, in the countryside northwest of Boston, under the Episcopalian tutelage of austere Rev. Endicott Peabody, Quentin would learn his lessons and receive a gentleman's polish.

Edith seemed to rebound normally from childbirth, relishing the trappings of the Christmas holidays with Quentin at her breast. But as the rank cold of the Washington January set in, she was felled suddenly by a flu-like grippe. Some of the children were hastily dispatched to relatives; Quentin's at-home care was assumed by the family's long-time Irish nurse, Mame, the venerable Mary D. Ledwith. As Quentin passed his four-month birthday, Theodore could report that Edith was "crawling back to life."

If that weren't enough, Ted, the oldest son, was plagued with debilitating "nervous headaches," prompted, said doctors, by his father's demand for superior scholarly and physical achievement. Chastened, Theodore let up on Ted, relaxing his expectation that his namesake "be all the things I would like to have been and wasn't."[12] The incident was an early and predictive symptom of Theodore's unduly-high demands on his children. It would manifest itself most consequentially for Quentin and his brothers in the years leading up to the Great War.

Improbability aptly describes the breathtaking story of Theodore Roosevelt's life and his public ascent. Born in Manhattan to a well-to-do mercantile family just before the Civil War, he was schooled at home. Prodded by his father to overcome his asthmatic condition with vigorous exercise, "Teedie" gradually conquered the affliction; he was able to enter Harvard in 1876 as a strapping amateur boxer.

Following graduation—and on his 22nd birthday—he married a college sweetheart, Alice Hathaway Lee, a shy, diminutive beauty from Chestnut Hill, Massachusetts. On February 12, 1884, their daughter, Alice, was born. But within hours, tragedy struck. Roosevelt's wife had failed to rally from childbirth and lay slipping away in the family's midtown brownstone. Two days later, she was dead from kidney disease. On the same day, in the same house, Theodore's mother, Mittie, succumbed, at age 46, to typhoid fever. For Theodore Roosevelt, it was a horrific Valentine's Day. He informed his diary, "The light has gone out of my life."

Two years later, following a failed campaign for mayor of New York City, Theodore sailed for London to marry the waiting Edith Kermit Carow to whom he had been secretly engaged. She had been a presence throughout his life, first as his sister Corinne's childhood playmate and later, as his own off-and-on special friend. Since his first wife's death, the relationship with Edith had matured and deepened.

In 1898, soon after the U.S. declared war on Spain, Theodore felt compelled to put on a uniform and fight in Cuba. He quit a senior Navy government post and began to recruit a volunteer regiment of western horsemen, riflemen, and Harvard pals to support the regular army. The legendary Rough Riders were born. Yet, in the forefront of his mind was the matter of a wife and six young children. Would he—could he—appear to be deserting them to fulfill his lust for battle? "It was my one chance to do something for my country and for my family," Theodore later recalled. "I know that I would have turned from my wife's deathbed to have answered the call."[13]

Quentin, at eight months, would often pass his waking hours on the shady piazza that wrapped Sagamore Hill, the family's imposing Victorian mansion at Oyster Bay, Long Island. Under the fretful care of Mame, he was now teething, rolling from side to side and crawling toward his siblings who played noisily in the front yard. If Quentin missed his absent father's cuddle, it was not apparent to the tall and stately governess. Nearing 70, Mame had tended to all the Roosevelt children, starting with Ted. In fact, as a young woman, she had cared for a young Edith and won her family's everlasting confidence.

Six-months-old Quentin.

(Courtesy of the Theodore Roosevelt Birthplace National Historic Site and the Theodore Roosevelt Center at Dickinson State University.)

A sideways glance at Mame, rocking in the shadowy refraction of the late afternoon sun, revealed a still-handsome woman behind rimless glasses, her light hair stretched sternly into a bun. Despite the summer day's warmth, Mame's household gown descended past her ankles. Though fashioned of cool white cotton, it bore a high, stern collar. You imagined that she had been attractive in her youth, yet apparently had turned away suitors and elected instead to live the life of a spinster. Seemingly, her affections were reserved solely for the Roosevelt family. Mame adored the angelic Quentin, perhaps realizing that he would be the last of her trusts.

With her husband at war, Edith waited anxiously at home for letters; she read the screaming newspaper headlines with apprehension. "Rough Riders Face Hostile Fire!" "Americans Fall as Roosevelt Narrowly Escapes Spanish Bullet!" "Roosevelt Leads Charge Up San Juan Hill." He was, in the war for American hegemony and Cuban liberation, a fearless and genuine American hero, saluted by his men and the enthralled nation for uncommon courage and bravery.

Within hours of mustering out of service, the captor of San Juan Hill was approached to stand for governor of New York in the fall. Roosevelt accepted the Republican nod, launched a vigorous whistle-stop campaign tour, and marched on to a narrow but clear victory in November.

The family, including 13-month-old Quentin and Mame in tow, transitioned with some trepidation to their new home, the Executive Mansion in Albany. At the state capitol, Governor Roosevelt engaged in political fisticuffs with organizational chieftains who resisted his efforts to fight corruption. At home, Edith tempered the mischievous will of the children. Sylvia Jukes Morris, Edith's biographer, recalled that, "One warm spring night, as Edith entertained a fashionable crowd in the executive drawing room, she was appalled to smell a powerful zoological odor rafting up from downstairs. Investigation disclosed that it represented the accumulated winter droppings of several dozen pet rabbits, hamsters and guinea pigs which the children housed in the cellar."[14]

As time went on, Roosevelt's clashes with state Republican Party bosses grew so contentious that talk soon turned to ways of getting rid of the governor. That meant "kicking him upstairs," far away from Albany. The "upstairs" they had in mind was the open vice presidential slot on President William McKinley's 1900 re-election ticket.

Amid enthusiastic shouts of "We want Teddy" at the national Republican convention, delegates propelled the president and Roosevelt into the general election with near-unanimous backing. As was the custom, McKinley restricted his campaign appearances to handshaking at home. But young Roosevelt, by some authority's count, tirelessly stumped more than 21,000 train miles in more than half the states. On Election Day, the McKinley-Roosevelt team won handily, triumphing almost 2-1 in the Electoral College.

In early January, Roosevelt headed off to Colorado on an extended hunting trip. Edith was left behind to plan yet another family move and, with Mame, to manage the children's active lives. Edith wrote to her husband almost daily. "I wish you could have heard Quentin saying his prayers tonight," she jotted. "With a most serious intent little face, he suddenly intoned them as if he were in a cathedral."[15] But all was not wistful. "Quentin had a real tantrum tonight," she disclosed 24 hours later. "After putting him in the closet and slapping him on the hand, I had to carry him away to my room and keep him until he became quiet. . . . Then he lay on my lap with his eyes tight shut and his elbow crooked over them and refused on any terms to go back to 'bad old Mame' and his supper."[16]

Quentin and Mary Ledwith, his nurse, about 1900.

(570.R67q – 003, Theodore Roosevelt
Collection, Houghton Library, Harvard University)

In the next day's letter, Edith revealed that Quentin had been rushed to the hospital to have surgery. "He is all right but of course he has had a hard afternoon, constantly vomiting as the result of the ether." It seems that Quentin had developed an abscess in an ear as a consequence of a cold. His mother told her husband that she had comforted him with a tale of T. R.'s shooting of a mountain lion in the West. She signed off, "Many kisses, darling. E."[17]

Theodore Roosevelt was vice president barely six months when McKinley was gunned down by an anarchist during a public reception in Buffalo, N.Y. On vacation in the Adirondacks with Edith and the children, Roosevelt rushed to the president's side. After lingering for eight days, McKinley succumbed to his wounds, and a stunned Theodore Roosevelt hurriedly took the historic oath of office. At 42 years, 10 months and 16 days, he was—and still is— the youngest president in U.S. history. Quentin Roosevelt, not yet four, was of course incapable of comprehending his looming fate, a child destined to grow up amid the razzle-dazzle of the Roosevelt White House.

Three

Rich Little Girl

In the tony town of Fulham on the north bank of the Thames, an American heiress, just days away from her 12th birthday, stares in wonder at the unfolding scene. Thoroughbred men and their thoroughbred ponies, saddled together, are engaging in a storied polo match for the legendary Westchester Cup. It is the summer of 1909, and while ex-President Theodore Roosevelt is on safari in Africa, young Flora Payne Whitney is visiting the exclusive Hurlingham Club with her family. She is not certain which fascinates her more—the attractive young polo players or their noble mounts. She watches the swift action on the field: ponies shifting their gallop, sensing the sway of their riders who lean side-to-side while swinging mallets at a small white ball on the green turf. It's a rapid yet intricate field dance.

"Polo is the most difficult game on earth," wrote Nelson W. Aldrich, Jr. in *Old Money*. "The man on horseback is a primal image of command and self-command, grace and power united." Polo requires, he said, "the horsemanship of Genghis Khan, the anticipatory sense of a hockey player and the hand-eye coordination of a pool shark."[18]

The coveted Westchester Cup had been in British hands since 1876 but now Flora's father, Harry Payne Whitney, and his Meadow Brook Big Four were winning the best of three matches and reclaiming the trophy for America. The capture didn't happen by chance. Harry had determined a few years earlier to use some of his vast wealth to acquire "the finest string of polo ponies ever collected" and to rear them at his famed Whitney Stables at Old Westbury on Long Island. It was, after all, the largest and finest private stable in the world. Since it is the quality of the competing horse that ranks above all in international polo, Harry had more than 100 steeds shipped to England to ensure superior equestrian reserves for the Westchester Cup match.

Soon after their historic triumph, Harry, Flora, and her mother Gertrude departed their rented castle at Oakley Court to be presented, along with the rest of the Big Four, to King Edward VII of Great Britain. Being in the company of the high and mighty on a world stage was nothing special to the Whitneys. Their station and social standing virtually demanded it.

Harry had the required pedigree: family roots back to the time of William the Conqueror, generations of increasingly-prosperous ancestors in America, birth in gilded Manhattan, schooling at Groton, Skull and Bones at Yale, and law at Columbia. Now at 37 and in the prime of his life, Harry walked proudly at "medium height and with a lithe sturdiness and healthful tan acquired from living in the open air."[19] Indeed, he was one of America's richest men, having inherited more than $24 million (almost $605 million in today's dollars) from his father, New York industrialist and real estate tycoon William C. Whitney, a one-time secretary of the Navy under President Grover Cleveland. A shrewd financier, Harry would inflate that fortune many times over in his own right. But he also opted for the life of a dashing, high-profile sportsman, not only in polo but in yachting, show dogs, and thoroughbred racing. The drawing rooms of Old Westbury were crowded with silver loving cups and oil paintings of fabled champions, among them *Regret* which, in 1915, became the first filly to win the Kentucky Derby, and *Whiskery*, the 1927 Derby victor.

Inheriting his Democratic politics from his father, Harry projected a personal magnetism and disarming friendliness, as well as a willingness to share his fortune with the less fortunate—ideal qualities for an aspiring public servant. Hoping to entice Harry's interest in high office, mining executive and friend John Hays Hammond once told him, "You could even beat Teddy [Roosevelt] if you would go into politics."[20] But Harry's passion lay not with the ballot but with the bridle and lash.

As he walked among his stables, Harry often would be in the company of Flora, teaching her gamesmanship along with the tenets of the mock royal lifestyle. She relished "living in her father's heaven." But around the same time, she began to apply her innate curiosity to people and activities that attracted her. As she grew to womanhood, Flora would learn to ride and train her own horses. Also of interest were the heralded high-stakes poker games at Cady Hill House, her father's upstate New York retreat in Saratoga Springs. Years later, Flora's son, Whitney Tower, would note, "So well did Ma learn her poker lessons at Harry's table that later in life, she was often the only lady invited to traditional men's games in New York."[21]

It was in the late winter of 1896 when Harry intensified a "desperate flirtation" he had been having with the charming and energetic young woman who would become his wife and Flora's mother. If his family fortune was vast, it blushed in contrast to hers. Twenty-one-year-old Gertrude Vanderbilt, tall, dark-haired, and stately, was an heiress to uncounted riches and opulence, the great-granddaughter of the legendary shipping and rail tycoon, Commodore Cornelius Vanderbilt.

In February of that year, Harry was invited to join Gertrude and her parents on the Vanderbilt family's private railroad car. With an abundance of attendants and steamer trunks, they set out from New York for the warmth and luxury of Palm Beach. Later, on a sun-drenched hotel piazza in Florida, after days of self-revealing conversation and hand-holding, Harry and Gertrude nuzzled in a hushed corner. Harry stared deeply into her large green eyes and asked, "Gertrude, shall we have an understanding?" The ensuing dialogue leaps from the pages of Gertrude's journal.

"Oh, Harry," she whispered breathlessly in response.

"Taking my poor ugly hand," Gertrude remembered, "he kissed it over and over again . . . saying, 'No, no Gertrude—it can't be. Oh, no, Gertrude.'" It was rapturous.

During the train ride home, Gertrude recorded another incident when Harry leaned forward and pulled her hands to his. "Kiss me," he asked. As she silently cherished the moment, Harry kissed her sensuously, sealing their commitment.

As an "available" Vanderbilt daughter, Gertrude had been warned by her grandmother that men would woo her mainly to gain wealth. Now, with Harry—who didn't need her money—she felt genuinely loved and desired.

Gertrude had grown up in Manhattan, profoundly privileged and surrounded by parents and siblings who had evolved into "custodians" of the family riches. When she was three, the family began to inhabit an imposing French Renaissance château along midtown Fifth Avenue, the setting for lavish dinners and balls that earned the Vanderbilts prominence on New York's Social Register. B. H. Friedman, Gertrude's biographer, ventured that her emerging identity was grounded not only in her family's Dutch Protestant heritage (akin to the Roosevelts') but also in the energy and drive of her father, grandfather, and great-grandfather. From the beginning, she had wrestled with the challenge of being a Vanderbilt and had longed to break out of the confines that traditionally defined wealthy women of the era. "There were lots of things I could not do because I was Miss Vanderbilt," she recalled.[22] But, of course, there was Harry.

In a white satin dress and her mother's veil, Gertrude Vanderbilt wed Harry Payne Whitney on August 25, 1896 at The Breakers, her grandparents' Newport mansion. *The New York Times*, in its coverage of the premier event in that summer outpost, gushed at the "cascades of fine asparagus and maidenhair ferns, white lilies, hydrangea, pink and white roses and white gladioli" arrayed about the manor. An intimate grouping of family and friends dined sumptuously with imported china and silver, and drank from fountains of sparkling champagne served in the finest crystal. As Flora Miller Biddle, Gertrude's granddaughter, later recalled, "These two young people seemed to have the world before them."[23]

As a child, Gertrude had been taught to appreciate art in all its types. Growing up, she had dabbled in drawing and small-scale clay modeling, but her breakthrough moment came as a sculptor early in the new century on one of her many trips to Paris. Through introductory lessons *en salon*, visits to *le Louvre* and *la Sainte-Chapelle*, and ultimately Versailles, Gertrude was moved to passion by the force of artistic expression. Upon returning home, she experienced acute appreciation for the magnificent works on display at The Breakers. Her granddaughter later observed, "Sculpture would allow her to express her emotions, would give her a certain freedom and would enable her to compete in a milieu where women had some chance of success."[24] Sculpture and the assemblage of works by undiscovered American painters indeed would come to rule her later life, as she moved resolutely between the complementary roles of artist and patron.

When Flora Payne Whitney was born July 29, 1897, *The New York Times* reported that she would be named Alice in honor of her maternal grandmother. But it was Harry's mother, Flora, upon whom the honor was bestowed. Baby Flora entered a generation that was "virtually the last in which members of society were the heroes and heroines of American fantasy."[25] Popular magazines of the era were just as likely to devote their photogravure to the moneyed class as they were to famous politicians or athletes. From the beginning, the spotlight shone on Flora and her younger siblings, Cornelius (called Sonny), and Barbara.

"There is no prettier child in all Newport at present than little Flora Whitney," *The New York Times* fawned in a society dispatch in the summer of 1899. "Flora would bring joy to the heart of a portrait painter, for her coloring and features are perfect. She has sunny hair which falls from under her fluffy white hat in soft ringlets. Her expressive hazel eyes are shaded by long brown lashes . . . her eyebrows, curved and dark, would have been the inspiration of a poem had this little maiden lived in ancient Roman days."[26] She was, indeed, an American princess.

Writer Brendan Gill cited another emblem of the lives of the rich. "Money talks and sometimes money shouts, but the most cultured voice that money possesses is the silent one of architecture." And young Flora thrived in an atmosphere of grand homes that bespoke of her destiny as a child of luxury. Her first home, at 2 West 57th Street in Manhattan, was an ivy-covered castle of gables and turrets on a prominent corner lot, a wedding gift to her parents from William C. Whitney. When Flora was 12, the family moved into 54 grandiose rooms at 871 Fifth Avenue. With the interior designed by McKim, Meade and White, the mansion was furnished with more than 900 pieces of art and furniture that had belonged to Harry's father. There, Flora would grow up in surroundings that included gilded door frames, a dining room covered from baseboard to ceiling with early Italian paintings, and a coffered ceiling brought from a palace in Genoa.

Flora and her brother, Sonny, at a family wedding in 1905.

(Courtesy Flora Miller Biddle.)

In off times the family would retreat to Old Westbury, 630 acres of dwellings, woods, and meadows with special outbuildings for tennis and exercise. Alternatively, the clan would embark for its rambling estate in Aiken, South Carolina where Joye Cottage sat at the aptly-named intersection of Easy Street and Whiskey Road. The Aiken property has long since passed out of the family and the New York homes are gone, symbols of when, as Gill noted, "the rich worked hard at their pleasures." But they were Flora's cherished growing-up habitats, venues of much joy, culture, and learning— and bases from which, later on and undisturbed in her bedroom, she would commence a notable three-year string of correspondence with her friend, Quentin Roosevelt.

Taken together, the expansive homes, the nurses, governesses and footmen, the lavish dinners and parties, and the routine excursions to England and the Continent encompassed the "gilded cage" in which young Flora blossomed. It happened, in the later words of her daughter, Flora, "with all the material comforts, surrounded by protective adults, unaware of the many forms of suffering that exist almost everywhere in the world."[27]

Yet as impeccably as she was molded, the handiwork was not altogether perfect. When Flora was five, she was a subject of a bizarre letter written to Harry by Gertrude when, according to B. H. Friedman, Gertrude was "increasingly confined, nauseated and depressed." During her pregnancy with Flora's sister, Barbara, Gertrude was convinced that she was going to die, so she wrote out her final commands. "For heaven's sake, remember that Flora is horribly sensitive. Give her lots of love, and bring her up to be strong and good. She has the possibilities of lots of unhappiness in her, poor little tot . . . guard against these tendencies."[28] Friedman reported that Gertrude neglected to sign the letter. It remained sealed and unsent for the rest of her life.[29]

Four

Dismal No More

The children's dolls in the nursery at Sagamore Hill were orderly arrayed on the bed, each bearing an unfamiliar black armband. "For President McKinley," explained Quentin, not yet four in late September 1901. The spacious Roosevelt home on Long Island was stirring with frenzied activity as Edith organized the family's move into the Executive Mansion in Washington [it was not yet known as the White House]. Her husband, the nation's new president, was in Canton, Ohio for McKinley's gravesite services, so it fell to the new first lady to determine how to shoehorn Theodore, herself and the six children, along with a governess, into the family living quarters on the second floor of the mansion.

Earlier in Washington, following McKinley's ceremonies, Edith offered to extend her personal condolences to Mrs. McKinley but the widow was too distraught to see her. That heightened Edith's perception that, under the shroud of assassination, the Executive Mansion was the "gloomiest place" she had ever been in. ". . . The horror of it hangs over me, and I am never without fear for Theodore," she wrote to her sister, Emily.[30] Rallying during the train trip home to Sagamore Hill, Edith concluded that the best way to overcome her dread was to fill the dismal old place with her children and their toys and animals.

On September 27, 1901, President Roosevelt waved enthusiastically from the North Portico as a line of carriages and moving trucks delivered Edith, the older children, their belongings, and a menagerie of creatures that galloped, flew, and crawled. In short order "the mother flung open the windows and let the warm September air into the dowdy Victorian rooms," Roosevelt biographer Hermann Hagedorn observed. Edith further made the place her own by exiling the drab horsehair furniture to the attic.

The immediate challenge was to adapt the mansion's cramped living quarters to the needs of a bustling family of eight. Living space was further limited by the location of the president's office on the same floor (the Oval Office was not built until 1909). With imagination and shared sacrifice, the Roosevelt family was temporarily accommodated into five bedrooms and just two bathrooms. One small bedroom, adjacent to Edith and Theodore's room and overlooking the South Lawn, was reserved for Quentin and his brother, Archie, both of whom had not yet come from Sagamore Hill. Hagedorn reported, "When the job was completed, she [Edith] dropped, went to bed and, for the better part of two days, slept the 'heavy sleep of exhaustion.'"[31]

Edith Kermit Roosevelt with Archie, left, and Quentin at the White House, probably in 1902.

(545—013, Theodore Roosevelt Collection, Houghton Library, Harvard University.)

By mid-October, Archie and Quentin, the two youngest, had arrived at the mansion and begun exploring the many hidden places that offered tempting venues for play and mischief. Outside, the once-quiet South Lawn was transformed into a hive of activity by paddling ducks in the fountain, a grazing pony, and a gaggle of bicycle-riding children. The permanent staff, trained to adjust smoothly to new tenants, had to stretch their memory back a generation to the Garfield days to recall a time when children romped with such gaiety.

Visitors to the Executive Mansion were among the first victims of the *joie de vivre*. White House historian William Seale told the story: "Tourists in the somber East Room were startled when the littlest Roosevelt, Quentin, burst up like a jack-in-the-box from one of the palm vases sunk in the center of circular divans, to audible giggles from fellow conspirators hiding behind the curtains."[32]

Occasionally, the country's business was interrupted by children and pets. "This morning, Quentin and Black Jack [a terrier] have been unwilling to leave me for any length of time," Theodore wrote to his son, Ted, who was away at school. "Black Jack simply lies curled up in a chair, but as Quentin is the most conversational, he has added an element of harassing difficulty to my effort to answer my accumulated correspondence."[33]

Roosevelt inventoried some of the mansion's other non-human residents in a letter to Joel Chandler Harris, creator of *Uncle Remus*, the children's favorite author,". . . Sailor Boy, the Chesapeake Dog, and Eli, a most gorgeous macaw with a bill I think could bite through boilerplate, and who crawls all over Ted, and whom I view with dark suspicion; and Jonathan, the piebald rat, of most friendly and affectionate nature; and the flying squirrel; and two kangaroo rats—not to speak of Archie's pony, Algonquin, who is the most absolute pet of them all."[34]

As the new century advanced, the Executive Mansion by the Potomac was indeed a frenzied place, full of youthful vigor, enthusiasm and surprises. Edith may have been taxed to her limit but the nation could not help but be enthralled with newspaper accounts of the goings-on. Her mail was top-heavy with inquiries about her plans for the children's schooling. "You can't think how much anxiety pervades the country about the children's education," she wrote to her husband. "I screen letters from school tutors every day."[35]

Edith and Theodore concluded, as fall commenced, that sons Kermit and Archie would be best served by exposure to local children in the Washington public schools. Ted was at Groton, Ethel attended boarding school elsewhere in the city, and "exceedingly pretty" Alice remained above it all, in relative isolation with Theodore's sister, Bamie, in Connecticut. That left Quentin, "the baby," to occupy himself during the day with picture books, toys and the animals. He was "a handful," T. R. observed.

"The cleverest of the six," Edith added.

Toward the end of 1901, the president issued an order officially changing the name of the Executive Mansion to the White House; around the same time, he and Edith began planning to refurbish the historic old building, not only to meet the family's considerable space needs but also to accommodate the mounting number of official receptions and dinners the Roosevelts were required to host. Privately, Mother and Father whispered that their home—the nation's home—was looking seedy, even tawdry. Rebuffing pleas by architects to "take it down, stone by stone," they instead decided on a wholesale renovation that would still require some parts of the building to be gutted to their frames. A new west wing would be added to accommodate the presidential offices. By June of 1902, architect Charles McKim wrote: "The house is torn to pieces. . . . Bedlam let loose does not compare with it."[36] The pervasive noise and dust sent Theodore fleeing to a temporary office adjacent to Lafayette Park, across from the White House; Edith and the children escaped with the menagerie to Sagamore Hill for the summer. The president would join them in July for the remainder of the season.

By November, the Roosevelts had returned to discover that "from the chaos of the demolition, the White House emerged transfigured." The president had a roomy new suite of offices apart from the bustling mansion, and the family quarters were now dressed with seven bedrooms and seven baths, and collections of fresh furnishings and carpet. Historian Seale said that the second floor "seemed as modern as a new hotel."

To celebrate, Theodore and Edith hosted a dinner for his two sisters and their husbands. As it happened, the date was September 22, which would have been the 70th birthday of the president's father, Thee. "I feel as if my father's hand were on my shoulder," he said at the table, "and as if there were a special blessing over the life I am to live here."[37] All was ready for Washington's official fall season—and the family's holiday celebrations.

"Yesterday was Thanksgiving, and we all went riding," the president wrote to Kermit, by now also attending Groton. "We had a three hours' scamper which was really great fun." But, Theodore relayed, the day was not without incident. "I have just had to descend with severity upon Quentin because he put the unfortunate Tom [the family cat] into the bathtub and then turned on the water. He didn't really mean harm."

Kermit must have felt homesick as he read from his father's letter. "After dinner we cleared away the table and danced. Mother looked just as pretty as a picture, and I had a lovely waltz with her."[38]

A month or so later, the president chronicled a White House Christmas to remember:

Yesterday morning at a quarter to seven, all the children were up and dressed and began to hammer at the door of their mother's and my room, in which their six stockings, all bulging out with queer angles and rotundities, were hanging from the fireplace. So their mother and I got up, shut the window, lit the fire, taking down the stockings of course, put on our wrappers and prepared to admit the children. . . . Then all the children came into our bed, and there they opened their stockings. Afterwards, we got dressed and took breakfast, and then all went into the library, where each child had a table set for his bigger presents. Quentin had a perfectly delightful electric railroad which had been rigged up for him by one of his friends, the White House electrician . . .[39]

There was a surprise in store for the president and the first lady, too. And while it fleetingly may have violated one of Theodore's tenets, the episode created a holiday story for the ages. At the time, Theodore Roosevelt shared a growing national opposition to stripping forests of fir and spruce trees for Christmas. It was deemed destructive and wasteful to a vital natural resource, so no holiday tree had graced the White House for the first two seasons of the Roosevelt presidency. The *Hartford Courant* perhaps spoke for him when it editorialized at the time, ". . . [T]he woods are being stripped and an altogether endless sacrifice is going on, not in obedience to any real need but just to meet the calls of an absurd fad."[40]

As an avid outdoorsman, conservationist, and the architect of the U.S. Forest Service, T. R. held the view that the cutting down of trees for Christmas was a prime example of deforestation for an unnecessary commercial cause. But his two young sons were not of the same mind. They liked Christmas trees and thought there should be a place for one in their home. Quentin, aided by Archie, identified a small tree on the White House grounds, took it down, and smuggled it into the big closet of his parents' bedroom. A White House tradesman later rigged lights for it. On Christmas morning, it was revealed. Without irritation or sentiment, the president later reported to a correspondent, "We all had a look at the tree, and each of us got a present off of it."[41] There is no evidence as to whether Quentin and Archie received a lecture from their father for the act. In time, it was said, the incident, along with advocacy from Forest Service Chief Gifford Pinchot, helped persuade the president that Christmas trees, if rightly harvested and replaced with extra saplings, were beneficial to woodlands.

Throughout the holidays Theodore Roosevelt had hobbled, favoring his left leg. For more than three months, the president had been recuperating from a severe gash to the shin suffered in a horrific traffic accident, and the aftereffects of two subsequent operations. On September 2 in Pittsfield, Massachusetts, on the last day of a two-week New England campaign tour, an accelerating trolley car had slammed into T. R.'s open-air carriage. The collision had sent Theodore and his official party flying. "President, governor and secretary hurled in different directions, like fragments of a bomb," historian Edmund Morris wrote.[42] The president landed on his face, minus his spectacles, a pant leg torn and a leg severely cut. Gingerly picking himself up, he angrily lit into the trolley driver, accusing him of losing control of his vehicle. But of greater concern to T. R. was the lifeless body lying nearby under the steel wheels of the overturned trolley. It was Big Bill. Brawny William Craig, an affable Scot, was the president's personal bodyguard, assigned to protect him from the fate that befell his predecessor. Craig had been riding in the front of the carriage next to the coachman and had taken the worst of the impact. Theodore is said to have muttered on the spot, "Poor Craig. How my children will feel."

When the president returned to the White House that evening, swollen and black and blue, he took on the task of telling Quentin, something he had been dreading all the way home. To Quentin, not yet five and without experience in human death—save for McKinley—it was devastating news. Big Bill had been a special pal, his adult companion around the White House when his parents were busy with official duties, and the man who had unfailingly read him the newspaper funnies each Sunday. His father's comforting words eased Quentin's immediate hurt, but the unexpected and violent loss of someone so dear left him emotionally wounded, unable to comprehend why on earth this would happen.

Fifteen years would intervene until Quentin once again would be confronted with the enigma of death; then it would have an eerie prescience. Then a pioneer American aviator serving in France during the Great War, Quentin unsealed a transoceanic letter from Flora postmarked from New Brunswick, Canada, July 31, 1917. She agonized about the toll of war: "Oh, Quentin," she asked, "why does it have to be? It isn't possible that it can be for any ultimate good that all the best people in the world have to be killed."[43]

Five

Malefactors of Great Wealth

Theodore Roosevelt had little appreciation for people of vast wealth, principally those who did not put their resources to work for the good of others. In 1895, around the time he was appointed police commissioner for the City of New York, he laid bare his viewpoint in *The Forum*, a leading opinion journal of the time:

> Too much cannot be said against the men of wealth who sacrifice everything to getting wealth. There is not in the world a more ignoble character than the mere money-getting American, insensible to every duty, regardless of every principle, bent only on amassing a fortune, and putting his fortune only to the basest uses—whether these uses be to speculate in stocks and wreck railroads himself, or to allow his son to lead a life of foolish and expensive idleness and gross debauchery, or to purchase some scoundrel of high social position, foreign or native, for his daughter. Such a man is only the more dangerous if he occasionally does some deed like founding a college or endowing a church, which makes those good people who are also foolish forget his real iniquity. These men are equally careless of the working men whom they oppress, and of the State, whose existence they imperil. There are not very many of them, but there are a very great number of men who approach more or less closely to the type, and, just in so far as they do so approach, they are curses to the country.[44]

It is not known whether Roosevelt had the Vanderbilts and Whitneys in mind when he wrote those heated words, but some of the male ancestors of Flora Payne Whitney could well have recognized something of themselves between the lines.

When Harry Payne Whitney, Flora's father, died of pneumonia at age 58 in October 1930, he was said to have built one of America's greatest fortunes. Bankrolled by his father who had made huge sums consolidating railroads, and his uncle, the tobacco and steel financier Oliver Hazard Payne, Harry earned his own reputation as a shrewd financier and capitalist. His profitable investments in oil, transportation, tobacco and especially, industrial and precious metals, amazed those critics who had dismissed him as a mere playboy polo player. In 1924, he had a brush with scandal when he was called to testify before a U.S. Senate committee investigating the Teapot Dome affair. Lawmakers wanted to know of Harry's role in the financing of a favorable lease of Navy oil reserve fields in Wyoming. He laid open his books in two separate hearings and escaped accusations of wrongdoing. His association with the widely publicized probe did, however, soil his reputation and deflate his portfolio for a while. But Harry rebounded successfully later in his life by developing abundantly productive copper and zinc mines in northern Canada. An accounting of Harry's estate, published by *The New York Times*, reported that it was valued at more than $71 million (nearly $1 billion in today's dollars).

During his lifetime, much of Harry Payne Whitney's money went to support a lavish lifestyle including multiple homes, far-reaching tours abroad and, of course, the polo ponies. To his credit, he did help sustain the Metropolitan Opera Company of New York and explorations of the American Museum of Natural History in Manhattan, whose co-founder was, coincidentally, the president's father.

Flora Payne Whitney's great-great-grandfather on her mother's side, Commodore Cornelius Vanderbilt, began his extraordinary career at age 16, ferrying vegetables on a small sailboat between Manhattan and Staten Island. By the time he died in 1877, he was said to be the second richest person in U.S. history, behind John D. Rockefeller. His $150 billion fortune, in current dollars, had been amassed during a lifetime in maritime shipping, real estate, and railroads. He may be best remembered for organizing the New York Central Railroad and building Manhattan's old Grand

Central Depot, a classic edifice that was replaced by Grand Central Terminal in 1913.

In a remarkable parallel with Theodore Roosevelt's later initiative to build the Panama Canal in Central America, Vanderbilt organized the Accessory Transit Company in the 1850s to transport Gold Rush travelers between San Francisco and New York via the jungles of Nicaragua. Envisioning the long-term payback of inter-oceanic travel through Central America by canal, the Commodore conspired with a young swashbuckler named William Walker and a band of his adventurers to seize control of Nicaragua. They succeeded for a while, until Walker covertly wrested control of Vanderbilt's assets. Another revolution, this one supported by Vanderbilt, toppled Walker and summarily disposed of him at the front end of a firing squad. Attempts to construct a canal in nearby Panama would be left to the French, who failed amid epidemics of malaria and yellow fever in the 1880s, and ultimately to Theodore Roosevelt who succeeded in the early 20th century.

In the mid-19th century, the Commodore entrusted his oldest son, William Henry, with the bankrupt Staten Island Railway. The younger Vanderbilt responded with a career in railroads and investments that would see him nearly double the value of his father's bequest.

A third-generation Vanderbilt, Cornelius II, inherited $70 million ($1.8 billion in today's dollars) and succeeded his father as head of the New York Central and associated rail lines in the 1880s. He and his wife, Alice Gwynne, built The Breakers, the grandiose summer home in Newport that embodied the family's sumptuous lifestyle. As we have seen, it was the extensive art collection at The Breakers that inspired Cornelius's younger sister Gertrude's calling as a sculptor and art patron.

In 1873, at age 79, the Commodore set aside $1 million to endow and build Vanderbilt University in Nashville. In those years of Reconstruction that followed the Civil War, he said he was determined to "strengthen the ties which should exist between all sections of our common country."[45] It would be the only major gift of the Commodore's lifetime.

In 1910, when ex-President Roosevelt returned to New York City from his African safari and subsequent tour of European capitals, 37-year-old Cornelius Vanderbilt III, chairman of the welcoming committee, joined him in a raucous street parade. The brother of Gertrude Vanderbilt Whitney and uncle to Flora Payne Whitney had a long-standing family association with the Roosevelts, based on their shared social circle.

A fifth-generation Vanderbilt, Cornelius IV—known as Neily Jr.—befriended T. R. as a child during the president's occasional visits to his parents' Fifth Avenue mansion. One time, the postman delivered an official-looking envelope to Neily with contents that read, "The President of the United States and Mrs. Roosevelt request the pleasure of your company at a White House luncheon." The following Saturday, 10-year-old Neily found himself enjoying the rare honor of a visit to the Lincoln Study, sitting across the desk from the president. Roosevelt saw the opportunity for a teaching moment.

"We men," decided T. R., "will have our food served here. We have important matters to discuss."

In his memoir, Neily recalled what had transpired: "It was a meal and a lesson in Lincolniana combined. Accentuating his words with an occasional tap on the desk with his fork, the president spoke earnestly and eloquently of "that strange figure from the plains of Illinois who spent many a sleepless night in this study, standing in front of that window on the right and staring into space over the leafless trees below and over the dark expanse of the Potomac beyond . . ." Young Vanderbilt later recalled that he was struck by "the passionate quality of [Roosevelt's] voice, the fiery pantomime of his odd, expressive face, and the sad whimsical smile with which he described his tragic predecessor."[46]

Nearly a decade later, before America had committed men to the Great War, Neily clashed with his mother over wartime service, and Theodore Roosevelt was called in to referee the family tiff. As Neily pleaded to join up "like every other friend of mine," Grace Vanderbilt responded with exasperation, "Folly, utter folly." Pointing out to Neily that he had never even left his house unescorted (for fear of kidnapping), she did agree to hear out T. R. on the matter. Neily rushed for a pen and paper to write to his old friend, now retired to Sagamore Hill, and a vocal proponent of American intervention.

By the time Roosevelt's reply arrived, Neily was in the Army. "Your dear mother . . . and I do not agree about you," Roosevelt wrote. "I am very proud of you; I sympathize absolutely with the course you are taking; I feel that you are doing exactly what, if you were my son, I would wish you to do." Urging his correspondent to "get into the fighting line," Roosevelt declared, "I am exceedingly glad that you do not wish to go to Washington to join the 'slicker-and-slacker' brigade." It was signed, "Your comrade, an old ex-colonel, Theodore Roosevelt." Mrs. Vanderbilt was said to comment, ". . . Which goes to prove that even a man of Theodore Roosevelt's genius can be wrong once in a while."[47]

The early 20th century Whitneys and Vanderbilts, with their ancestors' and their own riches invested in railroads, must have watched with trepidation in 1902 when President Roosevelt mounted a forceful legal assault on men who organized a trust to control the major rail lines in the west. Roosevelt was no enemy of business—he understood its indispensable role in economic growth and jobs—but he was wary of powerful industrial corporations and their overlords. Corporations were "artificial individuals," he thought, with the power to pray on the working man and the poor. "A riot of individualistic materialism" had produced enormous fortunes, Theodore observed, and ensuing court decisions had left the nation and the states impotent to deal with their big business excesses. Denouncing the "robber barons" of the era, the president concluded that "these men demanded for themselves immunity from governmental control which, if granted, would have been as wicked and foolish as immunity to the barons of the 12th century."[48]

Opportunity arose that spring when the Roosevelt administration raised its "Big Stick" and filed suit against three railroad moguls—J. P. Morgan, James J. Hill, and Edward H. Harriman—who had formed a new holding company to control four railroads operating west of Chicago. Their intent, the president believed, was to fix shipping rates and force competitors out of business, thereby manipulating a substantial part of the country's economy.

Their Northern Securities Company was accused of unscrupulous restraint of trade under the Sherman Anti-Trust Act that was enacted in 1890 to prohibit oppressive monopolies. At the time, Roosevelt said he did not favor government control of corporations, but he did believe it was incumbent upon Washington to regulate the worst of their practices.

The railroad barons fought back; Morgan even tried to cut a backroom deal, suggesting, in a White House meeting with the president, that he send "his man to my man, and they can fix it up."

"We don't want to fix it up," Roosevelt responded tersely. "We want to stop it."[49]

As the suit wound its way through federal courts, Congress moved at Roosevelt's insistence to create the Department of Commerce and Labor to further control the excesses of big business. Finally, in March 1904, the U.S. Supreme Court decided 5-4 in favor of the government (*Northern Securities Co. v. United States*) and ordered Northern Securities Company dissolved. This victory was followed by the Hepburn Act of 1906 which gave the Interstate Commerce Commission authority to set maximum railroad rates. It was an historic string of precedent-setting achievements for Theodore Roosevelt whose legacy would include a deserved reputation as a crusading "trust buster."

Surely the Vanderbilts and Whitneys followed these events with apprehension, fearing that government intervention would erode the control they had over their businesses—and fortunes. They acknowledged that through judicial action, legislation, and administrative regulation, Roosevelt had instituted federal authority on the overreach of big corporations. The families could take some comfort from the president's parallel view that, "When a railroad is managed fairly and honestly and when it renders a real and needed service, then the government must see that it is not so bedeviled as to make it impossible to run it at a profit."[50] Nonetheless, the episode certainly placed a chill on the Roosevelt-Vanderbilt-Whitney relationship, one that would persist into the next decade when their progeny tried valiantly to bring the families together through wedlock.

Six

Of Pillows and Grades

A n early sign of Quentin's rambunctiousness emerged at the end of October 1903, amid the splendor of the crisp and dry fall in Washington, D.C. It came as Edith sat at her White House desk, attending to routine correspondence. Amid the stack of letters laid out for her attention was a plain, square card marked "Board of Education of the District of Columbia." Unknowingly, the first lady had come face to face with her parental obligation to review Quentin's first report card.

She and Theodore had enrolled their youngest in first grade at a respectable public school a few blocks northwest of the White House. The Peter Force School was located at 1740 Massachusetts Avenue, amid the lustrous Victorian manors and relaxed country houses of Embassy Row. It would afford Quentin the basic "three R's." More important, the parents reasoned, a public school would give him daily exposure to a cauldron of children, not only from the neighborhood's privileged families but also from working class people that Theodore championed. After all, siblings Ted, Kermit, Ethel, and Archie had attended public schools early in their lives, and they had done well later in private schools.

"How do you get along with those common boys?" a society matron once asked Quentin.

Shaking his head quizzically, he responded, "I don't know what you mean. My father says there are only four kinds of boys: good boys and bad boys, and tall boys and short boys. That's all the kinds of boys there are."[51]

Quentin's teacher, Miss B. C. Bushman, had graded her student with marks that ranged from "fair" to "excellent." The son of Theodore Roosevelt received the expected "excellent" in grammar and language, a "good" in arithmetic and reading, and a "fair" in penmanship. But it was the humble "good" in deportment that stopped Edith's eye. She probably smiled, understanding that her soon-to-be-six-year-old probably deserved a more critical evaluation of his behavior. But what elementary schoolmarm could summon the courage to disparage the conduct of the son of the president of the United States? Undoubtedly Quentin's "good" in deportment was a bighearted and charitable apple from the teacher. As she penned "E. K. Roosevelt" to the report card in the space provided to the right of the grades, Edith surely had a twinkle in her eye, reflecting her affection for the "fine, bad little boy" of her brood.

The Force Elementary School, now demolished, was named in honor of the late Peter Force, mayor of Washington, D.C. when it was a government-chartered city. The three-story red brick building, set behind a wrought iron fence and a row of tall maples, had become shopworn in recent years. Rows of six-over-six paned windows let in just enough light to allow its interior to qualify as dingy. The floor boards sagged. The old furnace groaned. Yet the building was alive with young bodies half settled at ancient wooden desks or navigating narrow hallways, ever in restless motion.

The Force School, Quentin's first school, in Northwest Washington, D.C.

(Courtesy of the Historical Society of Washington, D.C.)

A classmate and friend, Earle Looker, would remember that young Quentin's "tow head was always mussed, his tie coming untied, his clothes being torn, his stockings refusing to stay up."[52] Certainly, Edith did not permit her son to leave home looking ragged. But as he grew, Quentin often engaged in rough play or got tangled in skirmishes with other boys while walking or riding his bike to school. "He was as irrepressible mentally as he was physically," Looker recalled, "and either way, there was no holding him down or back. He was active, alert, eager, bubbling over with ideas, strange words, humor and deeply-seated sentiment."[53]

One time in class, Quentin let a spitball fly from his homemade sling shot. Its intended target was a classmate standing up front, preparing to recite. "Q aimed at the back of his head," Looker recounted. "But Q's aim was poor, and the spitball went appallingly on, and caught the teacher full in the face." The following day, as "many small faces pressed little noses against the window panes," a carriage bearing the president of the United States drove up. In a moment, Theodore Roosevelt appeared in the classroom, carrying a large bouquet of flowers for the teacher. "I really had to come to offer my apology for Quentin's rude and thoughtless behavior," he announced. "I understand he did not make an altogether satisfactory apology to you. . . . And so, the least I could do, I thought, would be to come myself."[54] Quentin, it was said, sat in his seat, hushed, turning purple with embarrassment.

Disrespectful behavior was not the rule of every school day. "Quentin could say such funny things," remembered another teacher, Virginia J. Arnold, who shared a case in point with Edith many years later. "If the president is in his room, [at home], you must not look their [sic] way," Quentin declared. "You must wait until he is gone before you open that closed door. The president is having a pillow fight and must not be seen."[55]

It seems that intergenerational pillow clashes were rather commonplace at the White House. Around the time Quentin started school, Theodore wrote to his 14-year-old son, Kermit— who was at the Groton School—of an encounter that had occurred when he and the first lady had returned home from riding horses. ". . . Mother went upstairs first and was met by Archie and Quentin, each loaded with pillows, and whispering not to let me know that they were in ambush; then as I marched up to the top, they assailed me with shrieks and chuckles of delight, and then the pillow fight raged up and down the hall."[56]

Earlier, there was another White House row—with political consequences. "The other night, before the diplomatic dinner," the president reported to Kermit, "having about fifteen minutes to spare, I went into the nursery where the two small persons in pink 'tommies' [Quentin and Archie] instantly raced for the bed and threw themselves on it with ecstatic conviction that a romp was going to begin. I did not have the heart to disappoint them," Roosevelt allowed, "and the result was that my shirt got so mussed that I had to change it."[57]

The president was close to his younger sons, believing that Quentin, in particular, was showing early signs of brainpower and cleverness. To encourage him, Theodore often made en effort in early evenings, when he was not traveling, to spend time with him. "Archie and Quentin are just as cunning as they can be," he told Kermit. "If mother has a headache, I generally read to them or else tell them a story. They always clamor for the latter, and I always try to compromise on the former as I feel as though my powers of invention had completely given out."[58]

During a bitter February evening in 1904, the president was disturbed by a noise in the nursery. "I went in," he later reported, "and there were the two little boys in the firelight, sitting up in bed chuckling and trying, in turn, to repeat poems to each other." Theodore was welcomed into the nursery by his sons as "a boon companion," and settled in comfortably to read Quentin and Archie the concluding cantos of his favorite poem, Longfellow's epic, *The Saga of King Olaf.*[59]

Theodore Roosevelt, of course, had to be president and father at the same time. Once, while on tour in California, he hurried off a melancholy letter to Quentin: "Whenever I see a little boy brought to us by his father or mother to look at the procession as we pass by, I think of you and Archie and feel very homesick."[60]

Quentin would occasionally revel in the pomp that would attend formal presidential dinners at the White House. He knew that he couldn't take part, but he would sometimes inch halfway down the grand staircase in his pajamas to watch the start of the spectacle. He would secrete himself behind the narrow brass staffs of the handrail, his bright eyes wide with wonder. The president's military aides, in full dress uniforms and with gleaming ceremonial swords, would draw Quentin's attention as they prepared guests on the first floor for the entrance of the official party. William Seale painted this picture:

> Promptly at eight, just after the White House clocks had chimed, the blast of two trumpets and the rolling back of the iron gates at the foot of the grand stairway, announced the descent of the presidential party. It was a substantial procession, two abreast, against the background of pale stone and white plaster. . . . The pace was not slow but a healthy walk to music that kept those who had not practiced it shooting anxious glances at their feet lest they trip, and the whole line fall in like tin soldiers.[61]

Quentin watched with fascination as his father, elegant in black evening attire, descended the marble steps with his mother, glowing in full Edwardian splendor, at his side. Their arms were not joined; each navigated the staircase without using the handrail, their eyes fixed full ahead. As the party reached the transverse hall and entered the Green Room to receive their guests, Quentin would scurry breathlessly back to the nursery, eager to tell Archie of the magical scene he had witnessed.

Yet, as in every household, there were days when the Roosevelts were confronted with the usual trials of family life, such as when Quentin fell ill during his mother's absence. "Quentin's sickness was surely due to a riot in candy and ice cream with chocolate sauce," Theodore told Kermit. "He was a very sad bunny the next morning and spent a couple of days in bed."[62]

Or when the littlest angel crossed his father: "Last night I had to spank Quentin for having taken something that did not belong to him, and then not telling the truth about it," Theodore remembered. "[Quentin's sister] Ethel and Mother acted respectively as accuser and court of first resort and then brought him solemnly in to me for sentence and punishment—both retiring much agitated when the final catastrophe became imminent." The sentence was not recorded for posterity but Roosevelt allowed, "To-day, Quentin has been as cunning as possible. He perfectly understood that he had brought his fate on himself."[63]

Around this time, Quentin began to show the usual boyhood interest in sports—baseball in particular. Growing up, he would invite school chums to the White House where, with the help of a groundskeeper, a baseball diamond was sculpted into the lawn. Quentin and his neighborhood friends would engage in spirited pickup games which Theodore and Edith would sometimes watch from their second-floor windows. "I like to see Quentin practicing baseball," T. R. later told Archie. "It gives me hope that one of my boys will not take after his father in this respect, and will prove able to play the national game!"[64]

The oft-told story of a creature's escapade in the White House elevator is perhaps the best-loved Quentin tale of all. In the spring of 1903, his brother Archie was laid up in bed, a casualty of measles and whooping cough. With his parents away, five-and-a-half-year-old Quentin concocted a bold scheme to console him. Engaging White House coachman Charlie Lee in the conspiracy, Quentin led Algonquin, Archie's calico pony, into the lift for a ride up to Archie's bedside. Edith's biographer, Sylvia Jukes Morris, recalled, "The 350-pound animal was understandably nervous at first, but soon became interested in his own reflection in the elevator mirror, enabling the footman to press the second-floor button. The sight of Algonquin trotting into Archie's bedroom did wonders for the invalid, who immediately began to mend."[65] Quentin was, undoubtedly, exceedingly proud of his accomplishment, and the episode entered the annals of White House lore.

By the time Edith signed the final monthly report card of Quentin's first grade (all subjects "excellent"; behavior still just "good"), the children were being packed off to enjoy the cool Long Island breezes of the summer White House. "The children's delight at going to Sagamore Hill next week has completely swallowed up all regret at leaving Mother and me," Theodore told Kermit.[66]

The president was staying at the White House for the time being, preoccupied with organizing his campaign to gain election to the office he had inherited from McKinley almost three years earlier. In June, Republican delegates convened in steamy Chicago. And following a spirited July convention in St. Louis, Democrats selected a reluctant candidate, Chief Judge Alton B. Parker of the New York Court of Appeals, as T. R.'s opponent. It would be a hectic yet lackluster campaign between two New Yorkers who shared similar middle-of-the-road views.

At the start of the campaign frenzy, the president had a melancholy heart; he yearned for his children, his dear "bunnies." "Blessed Quenty-quee," he hand wrote on June 12, 1904 from the White House. "The little birds in the nest in the vines on the garden fence are nearly grown up. Their mother still feeds them."[67] The forlorn parent illustrated his text with a tender pen-and-ink sketch of a mother bird dangling a worm over the gaping beaks of her brood.

Ten days later, on the day his nominating convention opened, Roosevelt paused to send another message to Quenty-quee. He told of coming across a real B'rer Terrapin and B'rer Rabbit while out riding. "They were sitting solemnly beside one another and looked just as if they had come out of a book," he reported to his son. "But as my horse walked along, B'rer Rabbit went hippity, hippity, hippity off into the bushes, and B'rer Terrapin drew in his head and legs until I passed."[68]

If Father was experiencing separation anxiety, his family was reveling in the excitement of summer fun at their great Long Island estate: "Young voices chirped and called. A maid opened the front door. There was a rush of children across the porch, down the steps and out onto the sloping lawn. There were somersaults and impromptu wrestling matches on the dewy grass in the cool morning air; and shouts and howls and wails," Hermann Hagedorn recalled.[69]

To occupy everyone, there were tennis matches with young cousins in a hollow beside the sloping access road, hide-and-go-seek in the lofts of the barn, and pickup baseball games on the lawn. Children could select a mount and ride off toward the periphery of the acreage or find the family catboat for a leisurely sail along the near edges of the sound. When sunburn or exhaustion preempted the fun, there were plenty of shady, quiet corners in the big house where one could nestle on a rug with a fine book and a sweet snack until sleep conquered all.

One Saturday, toward the end of July, Quentin receded to his room behind a sign that read, DOOR LOCKED. He had privately scribbled a request to his mother who was temporarily away. The soon-to-be second grader wrote, ". . . Will you get me a game of 'Going to the North Pole'? I will send you the ten cents for it. . . . Go to the Boston store, for I will tell you how it looks." Quentin proceeded to describe the game and illustrate its large, egg-shaped appearance. "If you do not find the ten cents, wright [sic] to me, and I will send it to you, and if you pay for it yourself send the ten cents back to me. . . . Your loving QUENTIN. The End."[70]

Most Sunday mornings would witness Edith and the children on a buggy ride to the Episcopal church in the nearby village of Oyster Bay, armed Secret Servicemen at the reins. "The townspeople had a particularly warm spot in their hearts for the children," Hagedorn wrote. Despite their status as the nation's first family, "these were just plain American kids who dressed sensibly, played sensibly, got their hands and faces dirty a dozen times a day; and didn't put on airs when they came to town."[71] After church came time for worldly indulgence. Young Ted Roosevelt fondly remembered one occasion when an adult friend of the family found his brother, Quentin, in Snowder's, the corner drug store:

He was grasping a nickel in a grimy hand and looking longingly at the soda fountain. It so happened, that she [the family friend] had been lunching at Sagamore a few days before and had noticed that Quentin was being kept on a diet. Divining his thoughts she said, "Quentin, I would not take a soda. It will make you sick."

"How sick?" said Quentin, turning his eyes solemnly toward hers.

"Perhaps sick enough to be sent to bed."

In the space of a minute, Quentin resolved this in his mind, then deliberately walked forward, placed his nickel on the counter and said, "Chocolate sundae, please."' He had weighed the consequences and decided that the pleasure outbalanced them.[72]

As the last of the plump tomatoes and the white sweet corn ripened in the gardens at Sagamore Hill, the Roosevelt clan packed up for the return to the White House. Quentin surely was anticipating, with the usual combination of excitement and dread, the start of second grade at the Force School. The children's chief fixation, however, was the kick of being with their father again. Theodore had spent most of the searing and parched summer in Washington, acting as the statesman who needed his own full-fledged election to the presidency.

The fall campaign against Judge Parker would be humdrum. Parker's complacency reflected the widely-held view that he had a hopeless assignment to unseat the wildly-popular incumbent. Perhaps sensing his destiny, Theodore Roosevelt campaigned with assurance and resolve when he campaigned at all. He left the daily machinations of securing a full term to his allies who ran the Republican National Committee.

One day, the partisanship of a presidential campaign reached down to the school yard on Massachusetts Avenue. Some audacious schoolmates of Quentin's took to wearing Parker badges and buttons, inciting foreseeable rage in the president's young son. There were well-remembered scenes of Quentin pulling the buttons from garments in the cloakroom and stomping them to the floor. Soon, some of the fellows flaunted their Parker paraphernalia just to get Quentin's goat. He responded as they had hoped. During recess, Earle Looker remembered, "Q would charge all Parker buttons and Parker partisans with the fury of a small but thoroughly-roused young bull, seeing red in every corner of the meadow."[73]

Quentin's schoolyard "electioneering" did neither good nor harm. His schoolmates were, of course, too young to vote. And besides, the federal district had yet to win the right to ballot for president.

In November, Theodore Roosevelt's enormous popularity won out; voters awarded him the presidency in his own right in the greatest landslide victory in U.S. presidential history to that point.

As was prescribed in those days, Theodore had to wait until March to be inaugurated. Quentin had Inauguration Day off from school and joined his family in the rollicking procession from the Capitol to the White House, still under the careful eye of Mame, now nearing 80. Escorted by a band of government officials, rejoicing Rough Riders and Civil War vets "shaky on their poor old pins," Theodore hoisted his hat and waved at the ecstatic crowds with childlike enthusiasm. Later, as he stood on the inaugural platform in the sweet March sunshine presenting his inaugural remarks, two robed justices boosted Quentin, prepared with his tiny Brownie camera, onto the stage to record a keepsake of the historic scene.

The president in his own right could not constrain his eagerness to watch the inaugural parade that was to follow; some of his old Badlands rancher friends and Maine hunting guides would be marching. But first, there was the obligatory appearance at an exclusive luncheon for twenty on the east side of the Capitol. Also present, and excessively fashionable among all the Roosevelts, was Mrs. Cornelius Vanderbilt, young Flora Payne Whitney's aunt. If Theodore had any reaction to her unanticipated presence it was not recorded. But most of the other guests, who were there to mark the victory of the working man's friend, were intensely aware of his inherent aversion of the "merely rich."

Seven

The Spirit of Her Dream

Flora's upbringing was, in a word, untidy. She was her parents' first and favored child but grew up as an afterthought to their whirlwind life of activities and ambitions. When Harry, her father, was not capitalizing his riches on Wall Street, he was squandering them on polo ponies, thoroughbreds and, increasingly, drink. Gertrude, Flora's mother, was finding herself more and more unfulfilled in an unstable marriage. "I wanted to work. I was not very happy or satisfied with my life," she wrote at the time.[74] In consequence, during the early years of the century—Flora's toddler years—Gertrude asserted herself as an independent artist, a sculptor of creations both exquisite and inspiring. By the time Flora turned eleven in 1908, her mother was sculpting with success and enthusiasm. Gertrude was working steadily and had arranged small exhibitions of her work in New York and Paris. At the same time, she began to act on her ambition of becoming a patron of undiscovered American artists by arranging exhibitions of their works.

Often in the care of guardians, Flora emerged shy and uncertain—often solitary—because of her parents' habitual travels abroad. She began, however, to exhibit an innate intelligence, coupled with an evident natural grace. Yet, as her daughter, Flora Miller Biddle, later observed, young Flora lacked the energy and ambition of her mother. And there were the societal constraints imposed on young women of their generations. "We were supposed to suppress or overcome by willpower whatever inadequacies, puzzlements or depressions we felt . . . ," Biddle observed. Flora Payne Whitney found her principal fulfillment early on in poetry, with special appreciation for the works of Shelly, Keats, and Byron. Her exceptional memory would allow her to recite hours of verse, often completing poems that her brother, Sonny, had started to narrate, in their sibling game of cultured gamesmanship.

The record reveals little of Flora's elementary schooling, other than on-and-off attendance at her mother's alma mater, the posh Brearley School on West 44th Street in Manhattan. Because she sometimes accompanied her parents abroad, Flora missed many classes. But in time, the intrepid young girl caught up on her work with the help of a tutor here, a governess there, and through her own irrepressible curiosity about the matters of the world. And Flora's facility with languages was nurtured during the times that she traveled abroad. Concurrently, she began to show interest in her mother's artistic endeavors; briefly, she considered a career as an artist in her own right. Gertrude, of course, encouraged her daughter's interest and welcomed her companionship on occasional forays to the arty workshops of Paris.

In a family of Whitneys and Vanderbilts, rare was the consideration of the vast amounts of money required to keep up multiple estates, acquire clothing and jewelry, and take repeated overseas voyages. In fact within the family, discussion of finances was deemed to be in bad taste. "My mother had grown up with absolutely no idea of the value of money," Flora Miller Biddle remembered. "It must have seemed limitless to her . . ."[75] (Apparently it *was* limitless until about 1913, when the Sixteenth Amendment to the Constitution imposed the graduated federal income tax, and the family fortunes began to erode systematically.)

During the winter when Flora was 14, Gertrude introduced her to a new Paris studio and sculpture garden on the *rue Boileau*. While Mamma burnished her technique and hobnobbed with the elite at sidewalk cafés and restaurants, Flora sought diversion with daily training in ballet, clay modeling, and roller skating in the Tuileries Garden, always under the vigilant eye of her English governess, Miss Irene Givenwilson. One memorable afternoon, Gertrude took Flora on a Parisian shopping binge that a teenage girl of any era would envy. The bounty: twelve French designer dresses, a blue suit, three hats and four coats. "I love them all," Flora proclaimed as Gertrude scribbled her signature on a bill of exchange drawn on a New York bank.

Gertrude Vanderbilt Whitney in a 1916 work by Robert Henri.

(Courtesy Flora Miller Biddle)

Flora recalled the following summer of 1912 with far less delight. She had injured an ankle and was told she could not accompany her parents and brother on yet another trans-Atlantic excursion. Instead she was remanded to the care of her strict Vanderbilt grandparents at The Breakers. There, one rainy afternoon, a few days before her fifteenth birthday, Flora sat for an obligatory meal at a table of older relatives. "It was the 'horridest' lunch I was ever at," she irritably confided to her journal. "They gossiped and talked stupid things all the time. Oh, how I wish we were back in New York."

A few days later: "I had dinner alone with Grandma, and after we each took turns reading a book. It was a horrid evening. The book is nice."[76]

Grandmother Alice Gwynne Vanderbilt was a strict disciplinarian in contrast to the distracted Gertrude. It seems that most mornings in Newport, Alice would summon her granddaughter to the drawing room for the comportment lecture of the day. A bewildered Flora would often be reprimanded for breaking rules that she hadn't known existed.

Among the more egregious errors was her practice of allowing boys to visit her room unchaperoned. Earlier, Flora had encouraged a male cousin and some of her brother's friends to sneak into her bedroom through an open window. "Horrors! Boys in her room? Terrible! Shocking!" grandmother scolded.[77] Flora Miller Biddle later elaborated on the story: "Once, [the boys] hid under the bed and heard familiar footsteps outside. As the door opened, Alice noticed a boy's straw boater on the floor. 'And how did that get here?' she demanded. Flora's attempt at explanation was clumsy and far-fetched."[78] Later, she resorted to fleeing the mansion to meet up with boys elsewhere in Newport. Predictably, on one of those evenings, she lost track of time and found herself locked out of The Breakers for the night. According to the tale told by her daughter, Flora cautiously climbed a fire ladder attached to the masonry structure and crawled in through an open bedroom window. Grandmother Vanderbilt was snookered. Evidently, she never was the wiser.

Following that memorable summer, Flora resumed formal studies at the Brearley School. It apparently did not matter that she had missed every day of school, save one, since January 9 of that year. But there, in very small classes, beneath the school's seal that bore the stern motto, "By Truth and Toil," Flora caught up with most of her studies. Among all the blackboard drills and classroom lectures, and during off-time spent with close friends, she labored to discover herself, who she would become, and what she would accomplish as a promising young woman of talent and privilege.

Because Flora's parents had taken her out of school regularly, her academic fundamentals were ragged. "No wonder she had a lifelong struggle with spelling and math," her daughter would later admit.[79] But the young lady otherwise satisfied her natural curiosity, trained her extraordinary memory, and cultivated her love of the English poets.

Like most adolescents, Flora continued to assert her independence. She often complained to her journal that Gertrude wouldn't or couldn't understand her needs. "I admire and respect and, of course, adore Mamma but there is no companionship at all," she wrote.[80] That assertion would seem to contradict stories of the good times they spent abroad. Perhaps the problem at the time lay not exclusively with the teen, but also with her mother who was channeling her emotions in a new and unexpected direction. Gertrude had taken up with another man. Her beau, William Stackpole, a Harvard alumnus and successful stockbroker, was a close friend of her husband's. Harry, who had had an earlier dalliance of his own, was unaware of his wife's affair. Oblivious, he treated Stackpole as a virtual member of the family. Flora, who often accompanied Mamma and Stackpole to outings at the circus and opera while Harry was away, sensed that there was something unusual about her mother's relationship with Stackpole, but she was too naïve to realize that she was being exploited by Gertrude as cover to deceive Harry.

It would be several years before Harry caught up with his wife's infidelity. It happened when he came upon a cluster of Gertrude's letters to her lover that she had laid out indiscreetly—and perhaps intentionally—on her desk. In reaction, Harry sent a letter to his wife. It was around the time of their 23rd anniversary. "Dearest, I am nearly crazy. I have not slept a wink all night. . . . I believed in you and trusted you because you are true and big. . . . Now the bottom is kicked out of life. It's all lies. . . . I have got to know how many men—but I don't want names—I want you."[81]

About the same time, in a journal entry, Flora reacted, ". . . [A] change came o'er the spirit of my dream. . . . I felt to wishing I were the daughter of a different kind of people and in an entirely different environment."[82]

A few weeks before Christmas 1913, Flora had a jarring experience of her own. She was nearly killed when the chauffeur of her motor car took a too-sharp turn near Old Westbury, propelling Flora from the car seat onto the road. She landed on her head, according to a news account in *The New York Times*,[83] and appeared stunned to passers-by who lifted her off the pavement. In the absence of any nearby hospital, Flora was driven to a local church where the rector and a nurse attended to her. An hour later, she returned to Old Westbury, about five miles away, apparently not seriously hurt but undeniably sore and greatly embarrassed.

In part to overcome her daughter's detachment, Gertrude took Flora to Italy in the summer of 1914 to contemplate the artistic masterworks in Florence and Rome. Returning after the guns of August had heralded the forthcoming war in Europe, Gertrude immediately enrolled Flora in boarding school 300 miles from their New York home.

The elite Foxcroft School of Middleburg, Virginia eagerly welcomed its first class, including 17-year-old Flora Payne Whitney. Sited on 500 unspoiled, rolling acres in "horse country," 50 miles west of Washington, D.C., the institution gave restless young women—some students were as young as 10—an opportunity to study the classics, build character, and perfect their riding skills. Miss Charlotte Noland, the founder, recalled, "No one will ever know the excitement I felt that October day in 1914 when 24 girls came to me."[84]

Flora's mandatory uniform included two pairs of tan bloomers and one green corduroy coat. Her school wardrobe was expected to further include four hats, one each for uniform, sport, riding, and traveling.

A roommate and friend, Nancy Perkins, recalled the Flora of Foxcroft as a charming girl with "lovely eyes and fluted mouth" who loved to don formal riding clothes and a banded hat for jaunts through the fields. And she spoke of her vivid recollection of a shivering Flora, standing determinedly on a chair in winter in one of the school's outdoor classrooms. It seems that she had dressed in ballet slippers and golf stockings (the latter to repel the cold) to practice toe standing. "She had the loveliest disposition," Nancy observed wryly.

Another childhood friend, fashion editor Diana Vreeland, recalled Flora as ". . . beautiful, bewildering, and magnetic with an enchanting laugh. . . . Flora was flirtatious and gave away charm beguilingly. She was naughty, very naughty. She loved fun and laughter as children do." Vreeland's telling words were written in loving tribute to Flora in the 1980s but could easily have characterized the adolescent Flora in her boarding school years.

Like most youngsters separated from family, Flora had her blue days. During the depths of winter in January 1915, Flora required bolstering from Miss Givenwilson. "Just face this term courageously," she wrote, "and say to yourself, 'it is a discipline and test for your powers of endurance.' Go through it manfully and cheerfully. In that spirit, things will become lighter and easier." In the same letter, Miss Givenwilson scolded Flora for her careless misuse of the word "whether." "Please spell it correctly the next time you use the word," she demanded. "You spelt it 'weather' three times in one letter. Anyway, you are consistent, aren't you?"[85]

Seventeen-year-old Flora at the Foxcroft
School in 1914.

(Courtesy Flora Miller Biddle)

At school, Flora befriended Katherine Linn Sage, a sweet girl from a moneyed family in Albany, New York, who shared her love of poetry. As Kay Sage, she would become a renowned surrealist painter before suddenly taking her own life. Flora and Kay sustained a long and vital friendship over the years via dozens of letters and exchange visits. It was Kay who, four years from their meeting, would comfort Flora with original verse at the most heart-wrenching moment of her young life.

Notwithstanding their erratic relationship, or perhaps because of it, Gertrude took an opportunity in July of 1915 to counsel her maturing daughter on a sensitive matter. "Be very careful with the boys," Mamma warned in a letter from New York City to the Adirondacks where Flora was staying. "You are older now and must not be the least immodest or familiar. They will like you all the better for it. Don't let them touch you, even jokingly."[86]

Gertrude's timing was auspicious. That summer, at age 18, Flora confided to her diary, "IT has happened . . . took Mamma out in a motor [car] and told her. Oh! Ooh!! Oooh!!!" Flora had fallen in love with Quentin Roosevelt.

Eight

Seven Bad Pennies

As Flora Payne Whitney was swooning over Quentin, she was probably only vaguely aware that much of the nation had already fallen for the "roly-poly, happy-go-lucky personage, the brightest of any of the [Roosevelt] children." From the time the family occupied the White House in 1901 through Quentin's adolescent days at Groton, the antics of that strong-willed and fearless kid had enthralled newspaper and magazine readers everywhere. Hardboiled White House newsmen were charmed by Quentin, and they gushed to their readers accordingly. For them and the nation, there had been little delight in the White House during the stodgy McKinley days or in the terms of their immediate predecessors. In fact, not since Willie and Tad Lincoln had youngsters brought such delight to observers of goings-on inside the president's house.

About the time President Roosevelt was overseeing the construction of a transoceanic canal in Panama and mediating between the warring Japanese and Russians, Quentin was forming a tight circle of friends at the Force School. They were early-grade boys who, like himself, enjoyed skating around the rules and challenging those with authority over them.

Dressed alike in jackets and ties, britches, and knee socks, the group would congregate in a corner of the schoolyard during recess, well out of earshot of teachers, to plot their next escapade. There was Charlie Taft, "Taffy," the son of Roosevelt's secretary of war William Howard Taft; the enthusiastic Bromley "Brom" Seeley, whose pale eyebrows gave him the appearance of the tallest of foreheads; freckled Dick Chew, whom they called "Sailor" because, the boys thought, they could envision him chewing tobacco on deck; undersized Walker White; skinny Edward "Slats" Stead who could squeeze into any tight place; Earle Looker, who would later chronicle their adventures; and, of course, Quentin, with his ruffled hair and a forceful air, the designated leader of the pack.

By now, Quentin had begun to resemble his father physically. Edith dramatically illustrated the parallel: "He has the blood," she said.

Indeed, Earle Looker recalled that Quentin had his father's "same qualities of enthusiasm, swift anger, quick forgiveness, explosive speech, frankness, aggressive leadership [and] imagination."[87] Under his management, the White House Gang would become legendary.

The gang often gravitated to the White House after school and on Saturdays under the watchful eyes of security men. They were often greeted by Quentin's father who rarely passed up an opportunity for a romp with the boys when his schedule allowed, and sometimes when it shouldn't have. "For the last three days there has been snow . . . ," the president wrote to his childhood nurse Dolly Watkins around Christmas 1905. "I have agreed to have a great play of hide-and-go-seek in the White House itself."[88]

Ever astute, the gang recognized that the mansion's attic was a singular place: cavernous and musty-smelling, inhabited by crawling creatures and cobwebs. There were ancient cedar chests, stuffed with forgotten treasures going back to John Adams. Above all, the old attic was dark and spooky—the ideal place for play.

One late winter afternoon, the gang assembled there to roughhouse. Suddenly, someone threw a light switch. T. R. appeared from the shadows, in shirtsleeves, his frock coat over an arm. As Earle Looker remembered, "It was our signal for fight."

He threw the coat away and chased us, growling ferociously. I was hiding behind a post and beheld Sailor Chew being closely pursued by T. R. I saw that he was going to be caught, and at the same time saw the switch. I pulled it; there was immediate darkness followed by wild shrieks of delight from the gang. Just then, we heard a loud smack. It was that irresistible president striking an immovable post. "By George!" T. R. bellowed from the center of the attic. "Lights! Turn on the lights! This is worse—worse—than anything I've heard of in darkest Africa![89]

As the brightness came up, there was the president leaning on the post, his hand cradling his face. He had collided with an upright and just missed a protruding nail. As Roosevelt descended from the attic to nurse himself he muttered, "I'm quite all right. But never again turn off a light when anybody is near a post." With that the gang set out to punish Looker for injuring the president, stuffing the boy into one of the cedar chests and sitting on the lid. In time, T. R. heard Looker's calls for help and returned to the attic, freeing him. "Shutting up boys in cedar chests for more than 60 seconds is strictly forbidden," he lectured.

"Henceforth!" the gang responded in unison.

Quentin, who at all times had to have the last word, added, "For evermore!"[90] It is no wonder Roosevelt thought of his son as "a cheerful pagan philosopher."[91]

Then there was the sad fate of poor Old Hickory. Andrew Jackson, his stately portrait hung reverentially on an upstairs wall, had been splattered with spitballs. The globs of wet paper had been rearranged deftly on his forehead, earlobes and the tip of his nose. Four of the gang, gratified with their accomplishment, had turned in for the night, having been invited by Quentin to the White House for a sleepover. One by one, sluggish eyelids lifted to focus on Quentin being dragged from his bed by his father. When the lad returned to the bedroom, he sheepishly admitted to his pals that the president of the United States had ordered him to remove the spitballs, one by one.

In the morning, Roosevelt convened a mock court of justice, assembling the gang beneath the cleansed portrait. "Just imagine how I would feel if you rowdies, gangsters and villains threw spitballs at my portrait."

"You wouldn't mind a bit," a knowing Quentin replied on behalf of the accused. "Besides, Andrew Jackson doesn't know—he's dead."

"Guilty," proclaimed Judge Roosevelt. "Quentin may not see any of his friends for one week." As for the gang, "You can't come to the White House for seven whole days."

". . . They had acted like boors," T. R. explained in a follow-up letter to Archie at Groton. "They were four very sheepish small boys when I got through with them."[92]

Jackson's successor as president, the balding Martin Van Buren, also had a run-in with the gang. It seems that one day the boys were chasing about the basement hallway of the White House. As the president hurried into view, one by one they pretended to swoon in awe, collapsing theatrically to the floor. As he fell, Looker inadvertently bumped a pedestal holding a 350-pound marble bust of Van Buren and set it wobbling, threatening to crash to the floor. "Look out!" shouted Theodore as he pulled Looker and another boy out of the way before the bust stabilized. "Nobody hurt, least of all Van Buren," he sighed with relief. Then he wondered aloud what had caused the boys' "fainting spells."

"We were pretending," Quentin explained, "to be alarmed by your coming, Father."

"Is there anything so very alarming about me?" T. R. questioned. When he got no answer from the intimidated lads, he continued, "Not denying it, it must be so. Now what do you suppose I can do about it?"

"Take a bath," Quentin quickly responded. "That's what everybody keeps telling me is best for everything!"

Sometimes, the president himself was the target of a stunt, such as the day Quentin and three other members went into hiding, waiting for him to emerge from his office. Striding with a full head of Roosevelt steam, the president came into view and bypassed them unaware. Looker recalled that "we jumped up and followed behind him in single file, mimicking his strenuous pace, arms pumping up and down, our short legs striding as far as we would go." Eventually, the president looked over his shoulder and grinned. Quentin did the same, and the grin was passed from boy to boy as the procession paraded through the ceremonial rooms.

"Wasn't that simply breathless?" Quentin asked his mates. "Like a king walking through his palace as fast as he pleases . . ."[93]

Shortly thereafter, Theodore coined a moniker for the gang; henceforth, they would be known as the "Seven Bad Pennies."

Acting out on his own, Quentin sometimes took his impudence to the edge, such as the time when the 10-year-old roller skated home from the pet shop with a king snake and two other serpents coiled about his arms. Without taking off his skates, Quentin careened into a White House suite where the president was deep in conference with the attorney general of the United States. Quentin proclaimed to a shocked presidential aide, "Going to show my father my new snakes. . . . My father likes snakes."

With the president now startled and the attorney general about to climb up the back of his chair, Roosevelt gently advised his son, "Suppose you go into the next room? [Congressmen] Pete Hepburn and [John] Lacey are in there, and they are very fond of snakes."

When Theodore later peered into the outer office, Lacey was standing, terrified, on the top of a table and an agitated Hepburn was wrestling with Quentin, attempting to rescue a terrified snake that had wiggled inside Quentin's shirtsleeve.

There was a final act to the story. Later, a concerned Quentin brought the snakes, now in distress, to his father for close inspection. The president swiftly determined that the king snake was devouring one of the others. With manly determination Theodore rescued the victim, patted a relieved Quentin on the head and returned unshaken to matters of statecraft.

Quentin enjoyed most of the perks of being a presidential child, including the opportunity to travel with his father's entourage from time to time and to experience the attendant pomp and circumstance. "Almost with the dawn of the morning sun, Provincetown, [Massachusetts] was astir, and out to watch for the [presidential yacht] *Mayflower* with the president on board," a town newspaper reported August 20, 1907. "And there she was. It was just nine o'clock when a little tinge of black smoke far off on the horizon proclaimed her coming. It was a glorious sight."

Quentin surely watched in awe from the deck as the *Mayflower* passed through a ceremonial lane in Provincetown Harbor, flanked by no less than eight battleships decked out with colorful flags raised in tribute to the commander-in-chief. As a 21-gun salute boomed, the president, first lady, daughter Ethel, and Quentin walked the pier and boarded open carriages for the ride through town. They drove past 1,500 Marines standing at attention to the top of Town Hill where T. R. would preside at the groundbreaking for a tower marking the Pilgrims' first landing in America. There were cheers aplenty for the popular president and more than a few shout-outs for Quentin. At nine, going on ten, he had achieved a celebrity status of his own, even on the remote outer tip of Cape Cod.

Part of a young upstart's role requires classroom unruliness. Often Quentin's parents had to step in, especially when prompted by a bedeviled instructor. When Edith was away or retired to her sick bed, it fell to the president to exert parental discipline—or the threat of it. In fourth grade Quentin was a particular hellion, and teacher Virginia Arnold pleaded for help in a note to the president. On official White House stationery, Theodore responded tersely: "I do not think I ought to be called in merely for such offenses as dancing when coming into the classroom, or singing higher than the other boys, or failure to work as he should at his examples, or for drawing pictures instead of doing his sums. . . . If you find him defying your authority or committing any serious misdeeds, let me know, and I will whip him. . . ."[94]

There's no record of Quentin ever being disciplined with a whip or paddle; like other upstart kids, he was deprived of privileges at times, sometimes scolded, or ordered to his room. His father often used punishment time as an opportunity to acquaint Quentin with a work of Kipling or Jack London, who later became his favorite writer. And yes, a book report—written or verbal—often was part of the sentence but never posited as a penalty.

There were times when Quentin took up hell-raising solely with his older brother, Archie. White House old-timers told the tale of the two boys sneaking from the White House at dusk to covertly follow the lamplighter on his rounds. ". . . As soon as he was out of sight, [they climbed] like monkeys up the posts and turned off the lights," historian Hermann Hagedorn related.[95] The escapade ended prematurely when an alert watchman intervened and escorted the boys back into the White House.

Quentin's audaciousness may have been, in part, a defense against his brothers. He was regularly put upon by Archie, Ted, and Kermit to run faster, ride better, and row stronger. "The brothers were constantly challenging him, the youngest, to brave each and every rite of passage they had braved," explained author Edward J. Renehan, Jr. "They sensed that, as the baby, he had had it somewhat easier than they [had had it]."[96]

In almost every instance, Quentin met his siblings' test and did so good-naturedly. At the same time, perhaps because he was the runt of the Roosevelt litter, he showed a veiled, softer side. He sometimes demonstrated vulnerability and a tendency to isolate himself. His demanding father noticed this but did not routinely discourage it. Neither did Quentin's sister, Ethel, who would play the critical role of confidante and counselor in the years immediately ahead.

Once in a while, Quentin would use his solitary time to write poetry. It was the beginning of a lifelong affinity for verse, one he would cultivate and share with Flora in the years ahead. As a child, he would show his work to his father or mother, seeking their approval and, when needed, asking forgiveness for a mischievous deed. Here is an early example, authored when he was not yet nine:

> When I went to sleep at night
> In my little bed, I dreamt
> I saw a goblin
> Standing near my head
> His pants they were in tatters
> His coat was out of style
> His hat was nowhere to be seen
> But you could see his smile
>
> But when I looked around me
> Everything seemed strange to me
> For I saw my bed a hanging
> From the top limb of a tree

I turned to look behind me
And I saw my little chair
A chasing what appeared to be
A tiny paste board hare

I saw a pair of foxes
Which belonged in Noah's Ark
And then the ark came floating
Down a stream in Cleveland Park

Then out of a small mouse hole
There came a wooden mouse
Who took the chairs and put them back
Within her tiny house

But then I saw a cottage
And on it was my name
The goblin then did tell me
That it was the house of fame

I went into the cottage
And there I bumped my head
The goblin gave an awful cry
And I woke up in my bed[97]

Like his father, Quentin was an absorptive reader. At the least expected moment, he would reference a work that had impressed him. One summer at Oyster Bay, Edith was tending to her son's sunburned legs. "They look like a Turner sunset, don't they," young Quentin deadpanned. Pausing, he added, "'I won't be caught again this way! quoth the raven. Never more!'"

When Edith shared the comment with her husband, Theodore was astonished. "I was not surprised at his quoting Poe," he told his daughter, Alice, "but I would like to know where the ten-year-old [sic] picked up any knowledge of Turner's sunsets."[98]

Quentin's fifth grade teacher once alerted the Roosevelts that his school work was often smudgy and ink-splashed—a demerit on the report card to be sure. But in the next breath, she gushed about "his ability to use his imagination to a remarkable degree at ten years." That skill was illustrated by his short composition, "A Trip on an Airship." In it, Quentin expressed both an attraction to the new-fangled phenomenon of manned flight and the mechanics that made it possible. He skillfully described his own imaginary invention:

> It's a balloon which holds hydrogen gas [and] is 25 feet long. The boat below the balloon is 15 feet long and, at its widest, two feet. It has a 24-horsepower, six-cylinder Packard engine and has a tank which has a cubic capacity of two cu. yds. It has a rudder capable of steering it up or down, and is propelled by a screw. . . . My opinion is that airships will sometime be a success.

The paper was one of the earliest examples of Quentin's fascination with flying, an interest that would be reinforced the next year when his mother took him to the international air meet in France. Man's ability to soar into the heavens would consume Quentin's fantasies. Coupled with a mechanical bent that would emerge later in his life, it would manifest itself in his decision to take up pilot training for the U.S. Air Service as the Great War raged in Europe.

But all that lay ahead. Now, Quentin faced the upsetting expectation of finishing his days at the Force School, moving on to prep school, and watching the Seven Bad Pennies drift apart. Referencing a military frieze on downtown Washington's notable Pension Building, Quentin philosophized to his gang, "The best thing for all of us to do is just try to keep . . . marching on forever and ever."[99]

Recalling this period with the White House Gang, Earle Looker mused, "Somehow, the old days of joyously riotous behavior had gone forever. For one thing, we were growing older and, in some very important aspects, the gang just naturally died when the small boy in each of us gave place to one of a larger, less spontaneous age and mold."[100]

Theodore Roosevelt's days as president were coming to a close as well; he had impulsively declined to seek a third term on Election Night in 1904. Now, nearly four years hence, he was campaigning hard for Charlie Taft's father whom he believed would carry on his progressive policies. The Roosevelt family was imagining the prospect of life in the year ahead. "There is a little hole in my stomach," Quentin confessed to his father, "when I think of leaving the White House."[101]

Nine

Holy Hill

Edith Kermit Roosevelt was determined, in the fall of 1908, to separate Quentin from some of the vulgar, ill-bred types she had encountered at the Force School. And so, with about six months left in the White House, she enrolled her almost-11-year-old at the Episcopal High School, a reputable and private boys' boarding school in Alexandria, Virginia, just across the Potomac River from Washington, D.C. While Quentin certainly had benefited from mixing with children of working class families at Force, his parents felt that he now required a higher level of academic and social challenge. He needed to prep for the entrance exams at the Groton School. And then, of course, there would be Harvard—in the family tradition.

The Episcopal High School of Virginia stood smugly on Holy Hill, 80 sweeping acres once owned by Elizabeth Parke Custis Law, George and Martha Washington's eldest granddaughter. It had been founded almost seventy years earlier as Virginia's first high school. In Quentin's time it was affectionately nicknamed "The High School" even though it also accommodated grades for early adolescents of Quentin's age.

During the Civil War, almost the entire student body of 75 left to fight in the Confederate Army, and more than 80 percent of them reportedly died.[102] Union soldiers from the other side of the Potomac pressed the vacant school into service as a troop hospital.

The austere headmaster, Launcelot Minor Blackford, had presided over The High School for the previous four decades, ensuring robust academics, pioneering interscholastic sports, and enforcing a strict honor code that required students to turn in classmates who were caught lying, cheating, or stealing.

Quentin made respectable grades at Holy Hill for a single school year before transitioning to Groton. Those who studied alongside him remember him endearingly for his out-of-class antics. "Quentin Roosevelt was very young . . . when he was here," recalled author John White. "He was modest, hated publicity, was impulsive but full of magnetism."[103]

He was a "rat" like the other new boys and hazed further by upperclassmen. "I am G. G. White's squid," Quentin disclosed to his mother in a letter written on White House stationery in the first weeks of school. "It isn't bad. All I have to do is call him at quarter past seven, and carry water for him."

At first, Quentin was a boarder, and he reported that it was "awfully nice here." Yet he allowed to his mother that some of "the big new boys" in his form "are very homesick and have written to go back." He was putting on a brave face for his family. But there was a clue in his longing P.S., "Are you coming to chapel? Please do."[104]

The next day's communiqué home from the newly-nicknamed "Rooster" was decidedly less upbeat. Referring to himself in the third person, Quentin told his mother, "The cat is sad. . . . His joy has had a reaction. Yesterday he had a terrible attack of homesickness." Perhaps that was due in part to the constant hazing he was undergoing: "I had to stand on a gym horse and speak on Prohibition," he wrote. "Then four of us had to sing, 'I never smoke, I never chew that nasty dirty weed' to the tune of *Auld Lang Sine*."[105]

One of Quentin's essays from this rickety period has survived. In "My Favorite Sport," he showcased further literary promise that foretold the Hemingway style:

> My favorite sport is fishing, not the sort that you go out with a party of girls in a launch and eat ginger-pop while the fish runs away with your line, but real true fishing starting out early in the morning and tramping with a friend to a good place and fishing all day depending on your catch for your meals, taking no refreshments except water in your canteen and coming back after sunset tired, hungry and dirty, having had a fine time.[106]

There was capriciousness bubbling in the lad, left over from the days of the White House Gang. One time, Quentin went AWOL from school and rode back on his own to the White House. Surprised by his presence at the dinner table, his father asked why he was not with his classmates. Quentin did not reply truthfully, prompting Theodore to give him "a whipping" and angrily order him back to school. "Mother and I are worried about him," Theodore informed Kermit.[107]

Edith's mood surely turned apprehensive a month or so later when Launcelot Blackford called to suggest that Quentin might do better as a day boy. The hazing aftermath, including his getting "deathly sick" from forced cigarette smoking, had gotten to him. The Roosevelts agreed, and Quentin was welcomed back to his White House room.

Change worked its magic. A few days after William Howard Taft was elected on November 3, 1908, as Roosevelt's successor, Theodore reported to Archie that "Quentin is getting along very well; he plays centre on his football eleven and, in a match for juniors in tennis, he got into the semi-finals. What is more important," he wrote, "he seems to be doing very well with his studies, and to get on well with the boys."[108]

A typical November weekday morn would find Quentin aboard Achilles, a family mount, making his way from home to school. His pace along the 7.5-mile route was usually deliberate, distracted from time to time by events along the way that caught his fancy. An observant Secret Service agent on horseback followed at a discreet distance.

Quentin typically would follow the route of the Washington, Alexandria and Mount Vernon Street Railway, beginning at 12th and D Streets, N.W., a few blocks from the White House. Crossing the Potomac on the new highway bridge, he would pause to gaze at a hoot owl in a tree or an occasional barge making its way to Old Town in the swift current below. From there, he traipsed on to Alexandria via a busy riverside path that would someday host a runway for a busy airport. When it was cold or snowy, Edith would instead give Quentin carfare to ride the creaky electric streetcar which stopped near the school.

The continuing challenge that Quentin presented to his parents was illustrated by another tale, whether fact or fable. "Big Tuie" Kinsolving, a fellow "rat" at Holy Hill, remembered young Roosevelt in the spring of 1909 as "wild as mountain scenery," deserving of five punishing whacks. When the headmaster called to ask T. R. whether he should discipline Quentin, Roosevelt reportedly replied, "Beat him good! Bully!"[109]

Quentin competes in an "egg race."

(570 R67q—013, Theodore Roosevelt Collection, Houghton Library, Harvard University.)

At precisely 11:35 on the morning of November 14, 1908, a big automobile ferrying President and Mrs. Roosevelt pulled up to Dr. Blackford's residence on the school's campus. In cold, driving rain and sleet, Quentin's parents had crossed the river to celebrate the annual Athletic Day, a significant event at Episcopal High School. Edith shunned the weather by watching events from the back seat, but Theodore stepped from the rumbling car, hatless in the downpour, to give a vigorous speech to the assembled students on the virtues of sportsmanship. "I am so glad to be here because my boy is here," he began. Long, lusty yells rose up from the shivering crowd. "If there is anything I believe in it is sports," he declared. "Play fair, and try to win. Do your best . . . and get all you can out of it. When you are in business, do the same thing."

Tailed by two Secret Service men, the president walked over to the track where the high hurdles race was about to begin. "Bully for you, my boy," he shouted as the panting young winner crossed the finish line. Later, after prizes were handed out, Roosevelt summoned Quentin into the limousine and, as three cheers from the school kids rang out, sped away to the White House as mud flew from the tires.

By Thanksgiving Quentin was "thoroughly devoted to school" and, come early December, had become "sincerely attached to the school," in his father's words. Theodore told Archie, "Very shortly, he will begin to spend his nights [again] at the school."[110] In fact, Quentin resumed boarding after Christmas.

Inauguration Day, March 4, 1909, brought the most ferocious winter weather to Washington in years. Heavy, wind-swept snow forced Taft's swearing-in ceremony into the Senate chamber. As soon as the new president's inaugural address had ended, Roosevelt slid out through a back door to join Edith and a few family members at Union Station for a private lunch and the symbolic train ride to Sagamore Hill. Only one Roosevelt stayed behind for the inaugural parade. That was Quentin. He had planned to play hooky from school so he could share the festivities with Charlie Taft, his buddy from the White House Gang. William Seale remembered the poignant scene: "The son of the president and the son of the ex-president, both 11, shared a single chair [on the reviewing stand] huddled against the wind. . . . They remained with all the others until the last band had played its last note and night had fallen."[111]

Within three weeks of relinquishing office, Theodore was off to fulfill a lifelong yearning to go on a big game safari in Africa. Edith stayed behind at Sagamore Hill, leaving Quentin for a few months under the oversight of Theodore's sister, Bamie, who had a home in Georgetown.

A month or so later, an unexpected letter arrived at school, directed to Quentin. "Blessed Quenty-quee," Theodore addressed his son as he often had when Quentin was a tyke. Writing from Aden at the foot of the Arabian Peninsula, en route to Africa, Roosevelt described a peculiar place, "very hot, without a blade of grass or a bush." He went on, apparently hoping to evoke wide-eyed wonder in his young reader. "The population was composed of all kinds of wild Arabs, and wilder Somalis from Africa—with

Hindus and Jews. We passed two boys, each of whom had lost an arm, and a man who had lost a leg. I made inquiries and found that the sharks were very bold and fierce in the [Gulf of Aden] harbor and carried off a good many people."[112]

A walk through the buildings and grounds of today's Episcopal High School would reveal scant evidence of Quentin Roosevelt's time there except for the Hoxton House, the original school edifice, now the central administration building. But if you were to visit Pendleton Hall where the arts are performed today, your eyes might chance to notice an aged marble tablet with incised block letters in the vestibule. It is more than half a century old now, greeting all who come to be entertained, with sobering remembrances. It was erected to honor "in perpetual memory" 461 alumni and faculty who fought during America's time in the Great War of 1914-1918 and, notably, the 22 who died in the service of their country. There, in the spare, reflected light, you would notice the name of Quentin Roosevelt who spent eight brief, unbridled months on Holy Hill. Of the remembered heroes enshrined on the tablet, author Arthur Barksdale Kinsolving wrote that ". . . their willingness to die for freedom, humanity and right in their glorious youth might, in the hushed hour of prayer, help the fellows coming after them the more nobly to live."[113] Indeed. *Dulce et decorum est pro patria mori.*

When Quentin finished school in June—and with Theodore away on safari—Edith hustled him, his brother, Archie, and sister, Ethel, aboard the *S. S. Crete* for a four-month tour of Europe. Edith believed that the children were mature enough at 11, 14, and 17 to absorb the sights and cultures of the Old World and still have some summer fun. Arriving in Genoa in mid-July, the family settled in with Edith's sister, Emily, who lived there. The children studied Italian, Latin, and French from "an old Corsican monk" and rode rented bicycles around the ancient city for recreation. Later, in France, the group paired off, with Ethel and Archie wandering *en Provence* with an American diplomat, and Edith and Quentin visiting sites in Paris, Lyons, and Reims.

With the help of a French chauffeur "with a real French temper," Quentin soaked up the sights of Paris. Notre Dame Cathedral was "wonderful," he told a pen pal, the son of his school's headmaster, but "it would take at least a year to see the Louvre." As for trains in France, the young visitor thought "they are the rottenest I ever saw."[114]

It was during their stop in Reims, in mid-summer's scorching heat, that mother and son took in *La Grande Semaine de l'Aviation de la Champagne*, the Reims international air meet. Quentin's fascination with airplanes had been imaginatively demonstrated in his prep school essay, "A Trip on an Airship." Now, at the edge of the airfield, he gazed at the young pioneer pilots, the illustrious sportsmen of their age, as they propelled their flying machines high into a windy, azure sky, then dove suddenly at heart-stopping speed to the squeals of the crowds below. Quentin and thousands of other cheering fans gasped excitedly as the young daredevils chased new world records for speed and altitude.

Reprise: "You don't know how pretty it was to see all the aéroplanes sailing at a time," Quentin relayed to a school chum. "At one time there were four in the air. It was the prettiest thing I ever saw." Of his favorite, a monoplane called the *Antoinette*, Quentin likened it to "a big bird in the air." He observed, "It does not wiggle at all, and goes very fast."[115]

By mid-September, with the colors of fall erupting across Europe, Edith and Ethel carried on their explorations of Italy. But vacation time had run out for the boys. Quentin, Archie, and an adult escort sailed home to the States where the classroom beckoned. Quentin was expected to check in with Archie at the Groton School in Massachusetts, where he would spend six eventful years in budding manhood. Growing into his teens, Quentin would learn to apply his increasing attraction to flying through an innate aptitude for mechanics. Later on, his personal library of "explosive motor" volumes included Francis John Kean's *Aeronautical Engines* and Gardner Hiscox's *Gas, Gasoline and Oil-Engines*. There seemed always to be a motorcycle to fix or an auto engine to tune or, later, a propeller to adjust or a fleet of military vehicles to manage.

Ten

As Lively as a Young Bear Cub

12-year-old Quentin at the
Groton School

(570-R67q – 014, Theodore Roosevelt Collection,

Houghton Library, Harvard University)

Rigorous academics, a Spartan regimen, and weeks of "muscular Christianity" awaited Quentin Roosevelt in his First Form (comparable to seventh grade) at the Groton School. He would turn 12 in the late fall of 1909.

Nestled on a winding country road adjacent to tall pine woodlands and farms, 44 miles northwest of Boston, the school was a Colonial outpost for privileged families. Several brick classrooms and dormitories, trimmed in brilliant white, ringed a broad circular green. Young men, dressed in jackets, ties and caps, walked alone or in groups around the circle—never through it—since tradition forbade it.

A surveying eye wandered from the wavy stained glass above the doorways to the pointy pinnacles of the Gothic Revival student chapel. If you imagined Harvard or Yale for your student, and you could afford the $850 annual tuition and board (about $21,000 in today's dollars) at Groton, you had him prep there. You likely had reserved his place hours after his birth, as Theodore Roosevelt had done wisely for Quentin.

The Groton School was the quintessence of one man on a Christian mission. The Reverend Endicott Peabody was a plain-faced Episcopal priest whose "arms were big, his shoulders broad, his chest thick, his hair very blond, his eyes very blue."[116] Frank D. Ashburn, his biographer, said Rector Peabody was "the last of the Puritans," a man who "believed in old fashioned things, quality, smallness, personal integrity, the family . . ."[117] A cousin of Theodore's first wife, Alice Lee, Peabody founded the school in 1884 following his graduation from Trinity College at Cambridge. At the time, he approached Theodore to gauge his interest in co-founding the school. Roosevelt declined politely, saying he was unable to picture himself as a career academic. Instead, Roosevelt had climbed aboard a train and headed west.

Peabody aimed to train young men for leadership roles in the public arena rather than in private enterprise. His goal was reflected in the school motto, *Cui Servire est Regnare*—To Serve is to Rule—taken from the Anglican Book of Common Prayer. Now, with the arrival of Quentin Roosevelt, Peabody would commence his 26th year as rector. He already had educated Theodore's three older sons (only Kermit graduated; Ted left to study with a tutor, while Archie departed under duress for a more healthful climate in Arizona) and a cousin named Franklin Delano Roosevelt.

FDR once characterized the Groton experience as a "survival course."[118] Peabody and his masters enforced rules with an authoritarian hand to keep their charges focused on the tasks at hand and to help them avoid "distractions." Worse still, the boys' mail was censored, packages from home were searched, and the only available girls were family members and friends who happened to visit. In fact, the rector's wife, Fannie Peabody, was usually the only female that students encountered for long stretches of the school year. For many, she acted as a comforting mother figure.

Quentin Roosevelt and each of his classmates dwelled in tight dormitory cubicles, about six by nine, thinly furnished, with only a cloth curtain to imply privacy. After a mandatory daily shower—cold water only—the boys sat down for breakfast at 7:30, attended chapel at 8:15 then proceeded to their classes. The routine rarely varied.

Quentin's form at Groton consisted of just 25 students. Small classes and one-on-one tutoring were the norm. From the start he excelled in math, French, and sacred studies; he struggled in Latin, English composition, and history. "There are far too many black marks," Rector Peabody complained on Quentin's first report card home. "He is getting an idea of what is expected of him . . ."[119] The headmaster did not specify the cause of the demerits, but it does not take much to imagine the continuing high jinks of the boy who led the uproarious White House Gang. Black marks and scholastic weaknesses aside, Quentin ranked 14th in his class, an acceptable, if disappointing, start for a first former.

From surviving accounts, it seems that Quentin adapted to the exacting life of a Groton boarder, relying on the support of his schoolmate brother, Archie, and his own brief experience at the Episcopal High School. His oldest brother, Ted, a Groton veteran, offered some advice on how to fend off the jollying that sons of President Roosevelt inevitably experienced. ". . . All one has to do is to keep up a brave front, behave like a man, and it will pretty soon pass, and people will take you at your true worth. . . . After all, it is all in a day's work, and we must accept the bitter with the sweet."[120] But a boy as young as Quentin, coming from the heady and robust experience in the Roosevelt White House, was entitled to some initial homesickness. Writing early on to his sister, Ethel, Quentin admitted that he missed his family. "I am scratching off each day until Thanksgiving," he wrote.[121]

In another early letter to Ethel, Quentin observed, "My, but Groton is different from The High School." He reported that on his third night there, Rector Peabody called some of the new boys to his study to learn a Bible lesson from Matthew 5:8: "Blessed are the pure of heart for they shall see God."

Rector Endicott Peabody

(Courtesy St. Andrew's Episcopal Church, Ayer, Mass.)

"I thought it was such a good one that I copied it in *my* Bible," Quentin allowed.

Ethel, six years older than Quentin, emerged during this period as his primary family communicant and confidante. It was a natural extension of her self-designated role as the overseer of the younger Roosevelt children and as her mother's helper. From birth, Ethel's golden blonde hair and gentle blue eyes softened her plump figure and a bold, interventionist manner. During Quentin's years at school and later in France during the war, Ethel was a faithful intimate to her kid brother, a role that his parents could not hope to play. She was, above all, an unabashed Quentin devotee, a loving sister, and a protective ally, especially in times of emotional trial.

With Theodore on the hunt for big game in Africa in the fall of 1909, it was Edith who journeyed to Groton to spend Thanksgiving weekend with Quentin. Whatever the nature of her motherly admonition might have been, it was enough to diminish the number of black marks on ensuing report cards. But she failed to immediately improve his scholastic achievement. Quentin's weakness in Latin and underachievement in English prompted Rector Peabody to observe on a March 1910 report card, "He has not yet learned how to study." Part of the problem, Peabody observed, was that Quentin had not been well physically since the Christmas holidays. In a letter to Edith, he prescribed "a great deal of rest and a careful diet" during spring vacation.

May 1910 brought "more interest in his work" and "decidedly better" conduct, according to reports. Still, at the end of term in June, Peabody was warning Edith that poor class work would prevent Quentin's promotion to second form. He ordered summer homework in Latin and English and the opportunity to retake qualifying examinations in the fall.

The threat of being held back worked. And so, apparently, did Theodore's return to the states in June for the wedding of his son, Ted, to Eleanor Alexander, the daughter of prominent New Yorkers. There's no confirmation to support the claim, but it is more than likely that Theodore laid down his expectations to Quentin in the most exacting Rooseveltian manner. By October, the boy's class work in the second form was "excellent indeed," and Latin had become his strongest subject. It was a remarkable academic rebound. In fact, Quentin earned a coveted place on the "Honor List of the School," a distinction he would maintain well into the next academic year. By the end of 1910, the youngest Roosevelt son and protégé was top ranked in his class of 32. "Heavens!" wrote Quentin's father to his son when he heard the news. "To think of one of our family standing as high as that, it's almost paralyzing."[122]

Outside of the classroom, Quentin was competing in team tennis and playing on the third Wachusett football team. He was also maintaining his passion for baseball, encouraged by his father who passed along his Major League season pass. At Groton, sports were not an elective but a requirement: to Rector Peabody, competitive athletics ranked in importance right alongside academic achievement.

Quentin's interest in aviation mechanics had not waned despite the demands of the classroom and athletic fields. "Dear Sirs," he wrote on Groton School stationery to the Held Promoting Company of Oakland, California. "Please send me your Held handmade biplane and literature as described in *Popular Mechanics*. I am much interested in aéroplanes and am making an experimental glider."[123]

"I am very nearly kicked out of school for smoking," a contrite Quentin confessed to Ethel in 1911. "Gabby Hodges had some tobacco and was smoking up in the wireless room. I had some grains of caution left and refused to smoke tobacco, but I smoked some willow leaves to disprove the assertion that I was a . . . spoil sport." It seems that the ill-fated Gabby was turned in by a school janitor, prompting Rector Peabody to impose a punishment of three weeks' "black death." Quentin explained that a black-death victim "comes down for chapel and recitations, takes a one-hour exercise and stands the rest of his time in solitary confinement in the infirmary." As for his own fate, Quentin believed he had escaped the wrath of the rector's tongue. "His speech . . . when exploding in anger, had in it the feel of heavy artillery," biographer Ashburn wrote. But Gabby, Quentin predicted, would face withdrawal by his parents or, worse, expulsion.

At age 13, and now allowed to take excursions into the village of Groton to shop for supplies and playthings, Quentin was content and excelling at his studies. At the time, a *Boston Post* profile illustrated a "wholesome boyish boy . . . enjoying a breezy, happy preparatory school life, getting a handsome coat of tan on the athletic field."[124]

Spring brought his best report card ever and a continued presence on the honor list. But black marks for misbehavior climbed to ten in May and 11 in June. Nonetheless, the rector wrote Edith, "Quentin had a very good year."[125] And Quentin pleaded with his father, "Please don't tell Mother if you see her before me [sic] as I want to tell her myself."[126]

Spring found Theodore Roosevelt increasingly "living in a state of anti-climax" as an ex-president, confiding to friends his growing disillusionment with Taft, his chosen successor. It began while Theodore, on safari, received word that Taft had dismissed Gifford Pinchot, Roosevelt's pioneering conservationist and close friend. To Roosevelt it signaled a sharp, right turn in Taft's policies, away from his own progressive agenda. In part, to voice his displeasure Roosevelt embarked on a 34-day, 15-state speaking tour. It included a stop in Mesa, Arizona where Archie—recently departed from Groton—was toughening up at a ranch school. True believers were encouraging Theodore to make a run at Taft and the presidency in 1912.

Summer laid an unusual cast on Sagamore Hill. No longer were there gobs of young children in restless motion on land or in water. You could not watch Theodore playing "bear" with the boys or engaging the girls in hide-and-go-seek in the back barn. The offspring had grown and scattered, pursuing their own lives. "This summer has marked the end of the old Oyster Bay life that all of you children used to lead," Theodore wrote ruefully to his son, Ted.[127]

Quentin was at home and often alone during the sweltering summer of 1911, spending solitary hours at the piano and on horseback in the fields. Occasionally he would feed his hunger for baseball by playing catch with James Amos, his father's longtime valet. Quentin's proximity afforded Theodore a rare opportunity to closely observe his youngest. "Quentin is a very thoughtful, considerate boy," he noted in a letter to his sister, Bamie. "He has become a good ride." Moreover, Theodore recognized "an affectionate, soft-hearted, overgrown puppy kind of boy, absorbed in his wireless and anything mechanical."[128]

Quentin's return to Groton in the fall for his third form was shattered by frightful news from Oyster Bay. His mother had taken a life-threatening fall from her horse while riding with Theodore and Archie. Sylvia Jukes Morris illustrated the incident: ". . . For no apparent reason, [Edith's] horse, Pine Knot, suddenly swerved and shied. She was thrown onto the macadam road in front of Cove School and knocked senseless. Try as Theodore might to revive her, she showed no signs of coming to."[129] Once home, Edith lay in a coma for a worrisome day and a half. And for more than a week thereafter, she drifted in and out of consciousness, monitored around the clock by two nurses.

Theodore chose to keep Quentin updated through letters to Bamie, who happened to be visiting Groton, and to Rector Peabody. "She is, I think, now slowly getting better but in great pain," he wrote to the rector October 6.[130] Four days later—again to Peabody—"I have been driven nearly mad."[131]

By the 19th, Rector Peabody could reply, "Mrs. [Bamie] Cowles . . . tells me that there is a decided improvement now, and I trust that Mrs. Roosevelt will march forward rapidly to perfect recovery."[132] Edith's healing was, in actuality, agonizingly slow. She suffered from headaches for weeks thereafter and permanently lost her sense of smell.

His mother's injury may have traumatized Quentin but it did not adversely affect his classroom performance. October's report card was superior, and he remained at the top of his class. "Well done!" proclaimed the rector.[133]

Despite some academic slippage late in the year, Quentin approached the holidays in good spirits. Journalist friend Jacob Riis informed Theodore, "My wife and I were at Groton yesterday and saw Quentin. He is as happy and lively as a young bear cub."[134]

It was just after Thanksgiving that Theodore visited Groton to fulfill an invitation from Rector Peabody to address the students. According to a newspaper account, Quentin was a mere "interested spectator" as his father spoke to the school's civics club and, later, to the entire student body. Using stereopticon views, the former president excited the boys with exploits from his African safari. He lectured, surely with less audience enthusiasm, on "the wholesomeness of living." A school stenographer also recounted a faculty supper followed by "a delightful chat about the whole political situation."[135]

A few weeks later, Quentin pulled a surprise on the family, which now included the first grandchild, Grace Green, born in August to Ted and Eleanor. He showed up unexpectedly at Sagamore Hill three days before Christmas. His arrival delighted his mother and astonished Theodore. "He is half an inch taller than I am and is in great shape," Roosevelt exclaimed in a letter to Archie. "He is much less fat than he was and seems to be turning out right in every way."[136]

Quentin was old enough to travel home on his own, making connections by train from Groton through Worcester, Massachusetts and Providence, to New York City and, finally, Oyster Bay. Many years later, Edith learned of a heartwarming incident involving Quentin on a train that was making its way through New England.

It seems that a woman passenger was seated, contentedly knitting socks, when a young man approached to ask whether she would teach him to knit. "The knitting lessons began immediately," a correspondent informed Edith. "After the first few rows were completed, the young man with his knitting returned to his friends. By the time the train reached Boston, the boy was quite proficient with the needles. Of course, the young man was Quentin."[137] It seems that Quentin had made a wager with his mates that he could learn to knit before the train reached Boston. Determinedly, he did.

Eleven

Rough and Ready Adventures

"My hat is in the ring," Theodore Roosevelt off-handedly declared to a reporter February 21, 1912, while en route to a speech in Columbus, Ohio. "The fight is on, and I am stripped to the buff."[138] He had decided to challenge Taft by contesting him in state primaries leading up to the Republican convention in June. Disgruntled by "the mess" over the nomination and with Ethel in tow, Edith sailed for Panama.

Following the holidays, Quentin resumed his studies at Groton, again topping his class in February. He demonstrated proficiency in French, a language that would serve him well in the war years ahead. In a letter to Ethel, he expressed subtle skepticism about his father's bid to try again for the presidency. "What are father's chances in the primaries?" he wondered. "Will he stand any 'show' for the nomination?" In the same letter, mailed in April sometime after the 15th, Quentin referenced one of the great disasters of the era. "Isn't it too terrible about the Titanic? . . . Poor Archie Butt." His father's friend and White House military aide was among those lost in the sinking.

Nearing 15, Quentin was evolving into an able composer of both poetry and prose. He savored the works of the adventure novelist Jack London and allowed facsimiles of London's dark characters to creep into his writings. ". . . [Quentin] tended to churn out macabre tales of madness, desperation and suicide that he did not dare to show his parents," recalled author Edward J. Renehan, Jr. "Every hero was a tragic, thoughtful, existential intellectual: brave but doomed . . ."[139] These works were the forerunners of writings that would emerge later from Quentin's "blue periods" at Harvard and through his often eerie characterizations of premature death.

About this time, Archie, now in the last year of his teens, committed what he would later characterize as "a very foolish and thoughtless act."[140] He had mailed a letter from Arizona to a former classmate at Groton and, egged on by friends, appended a query to the outside of the envelope. "How are things at the old Christ factory?" Someone in the Groton mail room brought it to the attention of Rector Peabody who sent off an angry objection to Theodore. Declaring himself shocked at the "vulgar and profane inscription," Archie's father promised to confront him "with the seriousness it demands."[141] The upshot was Archie's two-page, handwritten letter of apology to the rector—"I plead guilty"—and the family's decision to have him finish prep school at Andover. Contrary to traditional understanding, Archie was not expelled from Groton because of the episode.

The springtime Republican presidential primaries brought victory after victory to Theodore, including one in Taft's home state of Ohio. But the party bosses, who controlled state delegations without "progressive" primaries, were amassing backroom convention votes for the incumbent president, setting up a head-on confrontation at the convention in the Chicago Coliseum.

Commencing an extraordinary series of back-and-forth letters early that month, Edith wrote to Rector Peabody, asking that Quentin be excused to attend the convention. "The battle itself is the victory," she declared. "I want Quentin to realize keenly this great fight for high ideals and to have planted firmly in his nature his father's deep love of his country and strict standard of purity and honor."[142]

The rector was not inclined to grant the request, declaring that "the course is not entirely clear." He told Edith that her son had missed some classes because of illness and reminded her that end-of-term examinations were looming. "It seems to me important that the youngest representative of the family should not be taken away at a time when his school duties are urgent."[143]

Although deferential in her comeback, Edith would not back down. "You are the best judge," she flattered the rector. "The days at Chicago would be a lifelong lesson." She promised to see that Quentin made up his schoolwork "to the fullest extent."[144]

Peabody knew when to retreat. "I am very glad indeed to be instrumental in having Quentin in touch with the rest of his family at a time which means so much to his father—which as you say, he might regret all his life if he were not allowed to take some part in it." Peabody reserved some bit of victory. "I have asked Quentin to write me an account of all he sees in Chicago, and he assures me he will do so."[145]

The goings-on of June 19-22, 1912 inside the teeming coliseum certainly provided the "lifelong lesson" that Edith anticipated. In the days leading up to the convention, Roosevelt's delegate total exceeded Taft's, but the outcome would turn on the votes of hundreds of challenged delegates, most of which were announced eventually for Taft by party bosses. As furious Roosevelt delegates walked out, Taft was nominated. Roosevelt countered by accepting the nomination of the third-party Progressives and running as the Bull Moose candidate in the fall campaign.

Ahead of what he was sure would be a tempestuous contest, Theodore took some time off to savor the environs of Sagamore Hill in the quiet company of his wife. In a remarkably candid letter to his 21-year-old daughter Ethel, he bared his devotion to Edith, "I have been taking Mother out to row instead of having her ride; she is as charming and pretty (in my eyes I think anyhow) as when she was the slender girl I made love to—and I can't help making love to her now."[146] It is one of the rare surviving letters in which Theodore Roosevelt allowed intimacies to flow from his pen.

In the end, despite months of vigorous stumping by Roosevelt, Democrat Woodrow Wilson defeated him and Taft. Quentin's father's quest to return to power was resoundingly denied.

Roosevelt's improbable pursuit of the presidency yielded a predictable backlash at Groton, and Quentin was the casualty. "His schoolmates' fathers tended to disapprove of Roosevelt's candidacy, sons parroted fathers, and Quentin had felt his isolation keenly," T. R. biographer Patricia O'Toole observed.[147] Ten days following the election, Quentin was feeling anxiety from the repudiation handed his family. "I'm awfully afraid I'm going to get a bum mark this month," he told his mother. "Somehow marks don't seem to go right, no matter how much I work. . . . Things up here are gloomy, gloomy, gloomy."[148]

Roosevelt almost did not live to see Election Day. On October 14, 1912, while campaigning in Milwaukee, he was shot in the chest by a crank who said he was acting on orders of President McKinley's ghost. Fortunately, the bullet was deflected by a thick folded speech and a metal eyeglass case in Roosevelt's breast pocket. With blood seeping through his shirt and clearly weakened by the blow, he soldiered on to deliver a long speech. Following a few days in the hospital, Roosevelt retreated to Sagamore Hill to rest and to mark his 54th birthday. "I loved the birthday gifts— the flowers and Quentin," he wrote in a note to Rector Peabody. "I appreciate Quentin's having been allowed to come home. I am all right now and feel as strong as, well, a bull moose!"[149]

Nineteen thirteen would be recalled as a calamitous period in Quentin's 15-year-old life. There were mishaps in his world, a disabling personal injury with long-term consequences, and a freak wintertime accident that cloaked him and the typically vibrant Groton campus in gloom. And the year would be capped by the start of his father's ambitious journey into the jungles of Brazil, a self-described adventurous last-call.

Philip Nichols was the unfortunate accident victim. He was a Sixth Former looking ahead to June graduation and entry into Harvard. While coasting swiftly downhill on a double runner "down in the woods" near the school, Nichols's sled flew over a gully and slammed into a large tree. The day's entry in the school log reported that "he was instantly killed—his skull fractured in front and the head forced over on the spine, probably breaking the neck at once. . . . Death had apparently come in a flash." [150]

"Poor Quentin has been much upset," Theodore alerted Kermit. "A poor young fellow . . . whose mother is a widow, was killed before [Quentin's] eyes . . . he had been taken back to the school on Quentin's sled."[151] It was a devastating jolt to the entire Groton community. Quentin and many of his school chums were forced to confront the horror and stunning unpredictably of death at an early age.

Not six weeks later, Quentin was released from school and returned to Sagamore Hill, "a very sad cat," according to his father.

The boy had broken his nose during a hockey game at school and had undergone a "painful chiseling out of his nose" by a local doctor. "Well he may be sad, poor Q," he father reported. "He was wishing to go with Archie and me next summer for a six-week trip in Arizona . . ."[152]

Perhaps to cheer him up, Theodore had arranged for Quentin to have a motorcycle. Models of that era typically were single speed with a drive-belt chain and a look that resembled a snazzy Schwinn bicycle. The motorcycle was less for driving (at age 15) but more for Quentin's insatiable need to disassemble, adjust, and reassemble anything mechanical.

"Well, you have had your troubles too, little bear," Theodore wrote to Quentin in a Valentine's Day note. "Nor has it all been pure comfort for me during the past few months. But, by George, I am pretty happy. I have come to the conclusion that I have mighty nice children, all of them!"[153]

Theodore was looking ahead with enthusiasm to the excursion to the Southwest with his "two little boys." "There will never be a chance for me to take, with either, any trip even remotely approaching our African trip," he wrote to Kermit. The journey was initiated by Archie, now 20; he had spent beneficial time in Mesa at the Evans School for Boys. It was an upscale ranch school with a program designed to make its students "physically robust, self-reliant, and inured to western outdoor life,"[154] while preparing them academically for university enrollment. Archie was sure his father would delight in the outdoors experience, and he predicted that the tenderfoot Quentin would benefit from "hardening up."

Theodore certainly required some saddle-and-sagebrush diversion at this point. He had been working at home with increasing discontent on his autobiography: "I fairly loathe it now."[155] Searching for his next act following defeat at the polls, he made an occasional speech in support of woman suffrage and raised money to help the Progressive Party stay afloat. But increasingly, Theodore found himself at the mercy of others, "forced onto a high wire above a crowd impossible to please."[156]

Theodore Roosevelt insisted, nearly right to the end, that he would not have undertaken the trip on his own account. At 54, he took on the taxing, six-week expedition to New Mexico and Arizona out of "a stern sense of duty" to Archie and Quentin. He believed they would benefit from days of rough and ready adventure, riding in hard saddles under the baking summer sun and sleeping in sandy bed rolls beneath the stars. Together, they would explore vast spaces and natural wonders, hunt for their meals, and engage with real-life cowpokes and native tribes. In Edith's view, the expedition would also bring Theodore closer to his adolescent son Quentin, an increasingly "complex sort of person."

In fact, Quentin was growing to resemble his father physically. At the time of the trip, family biographer Renehan observed, "He had the same chunky, muscular body. . . . His face, though not as jowly as his father's, nevertheless tended toward the same roundness."[157] Again like Theodore, Quentin was never far from a book.

The trio boarded a Santa Fe steam train in New York around the Fourth of July 1913 and arrived, hot and grubby, in Silver City, in western New Mexico, a week or so later. As long days unfolded, they would hunt and dine on wild cougar, probe the dark depths of the Grand Canyon, explore the Navajo reservation, and join, with the Hopi tribe, in an ancient ceremonial dance featuring more than a hundred slithering snakes.

Theodore proclaimed Archie and Quentin "good traveling companions." The older boy, he said, shared his love of the wilderness, the mountains, and the desert. On the other hand, he felt "Quentin's horizon is more limited by the motorcar and the motorcycle."[158] Nonetheless, the small family, with guides and pack animals, trudged determinedly into northwest Arizona to the North Rim of the Grand Canyon. The breathtaking vista of the steep, rocky gorge, carved over eons by the Colorado River, was a first for Quentin. But it was a nostalgic return for T. R. In the spring of 1903, he had visited as president. Awed and inspired then by what he saw, Roosevelt had said of the canyon, "Leave it as is. You cannot improve on it. The ages have been at work on it, and man can only mar it."[159] Five years later, he designated the Grand Canyon as a national monument, to be preserved forever.

Quentin, Archie, and their father descended to the gloomy depths of the canyon where sunlight could not penetrate. They camped in subfreezing cold, passed on stories, and shared confidences, warmed by campfires and their fraternal bond. Moving on, in late July, Theodore would tell Kermit in a letter, "This trip has been a great success, and I am exceedingly glad I came for it has . . . enabled me to take Quentin on a trip which he, on the whole, enjoys, and which has already done him much good."[160] But danger and misfortune lay ahead.

As the expedition headed east along a craggy trail on the ridge of a foothill, Quentin's pack horse lost its footing, sending Quentin over the side. As Theodore and Archie watched in horror, the horse rolled over Quentin. The boy lay stunned and bruised on the slope among sagebrush and rocks. His father and brother feared the worst but with their help, Quentin soon stood, clutching his back and a shoulder. ". . . [It was] an incident that nearly broke his back," wrote author Renehan years later. "It left him in recurring pain. . . . He might never have walked again."[161]

Quentin shook it off and vowed to continue—gingerly—on the rest of the journey, but the aftermath of his injuries always would trouble him. The following year at Groton, he failed to make the varsity football squad because of limitations from the injuries. And during the Great War that would follow, a nagging back would continually impair his movement in the confines of a body-hugging aircraft cockpit.

"Well, our trip came to an end in a blaze of glory at the Hopi snake dance," Theodore wrote Kermit in late August. "The boys had a very nice time, and were foolish enough really to enjoy my being with them. . . . I believe that the trip did everything for Quentin. He is so enthusiastic about it that he is planning to go back next year on his own account."[162]

As Theodore planned his expedition to South America, Quentin returned to Groton in September for his fifth—the second from last—form. Now an upperclassman, he was allowed to attend school dances on campus. The boys assembled beforehand to rehearse their steps and scrub up for girls that Rector Peabody had bused in from nearby private schools for the occasion. Peabody also saw to it that some of his five daughters were available to the young men of Groton for an occasional, well-chaperoned whirl around the dance floor. Quentin continued to achieve in the classroom, with the occasional aid of new reading spectacles, and on the gridiron where he played substitute left halfback on the intramural football team—when his aching body would allow.

His final two years at school would be marked by a standing near the top of his class, admissions testing for Harvard, and new achievement outside the classroom. He was coming into his own as a talented writer. In Rector Peabody's judgment, Quentin was "a boy of unusual ability" who was "gaining in many ways."[163]

A poem written by Quentin around this time opens a curtain on his ability—and his thematic fixation with the dark side:

> "Keep these to remember me by," she said,
> "In the years of long ago."
> And she gave me two roses, one was red,
> The other like drifting snow.
> She gave me two roses, white and red
> "Keep these to remember me by," she said.
> The petals are faded and scentless and dead
> Yet I guard and keep them still
> She, who gave me the flowers, lies in her bed
> On the lonely windswept hill
> White rose for memory, love for the red
> I remember yet, though they're scentless and dead.

In the fall of 1913, an editorial in *The Grotonian*, the school's monthly magazine, trumpeted Quentin's election to its editorial board. In that role, he would be expected to submit literary articles and opinion pieces for student readers. Launched in 1885, *The Grotonian* was a digest-sized publication, often with 20 or more pages of school news, team schedules, and literary pieces. Not only was the content authored by students, the newspaper was typeset by them and rolled out on an oversized, belt-driven press in the school print shop.

Later, Quentin would be promoted to press editor of the magazine and its sibling weekly newspaper, with responsibility for oversight of typesetting, printing, and proofing. "It was extraordinarily fussy work," explained Groton archivist Douglas Brown in 2012. But to Quentin, it was bliss. After all, it was mechanical.

At Edith's request, Quentin was excused from school in May 1914 to welcome his father and Kermit on their return to New York from Brazil. The excursion to chart the *Rio da Dúvida* (the River of Doubt), an unexplored tributary of the Amazon River, had not gone well. Roosevelt's scientific team encountered impassable rapids, unexpected waterfalls, torturous insects, and deadly creatures more hungry and desperate than the explorers themselves. The party suffered from death, severe illness, casualty, and real doubt that they would ever emerge from the rainforest. Roosevelt withstood an infected leg gash, contracted malaria, and endured delirium; he survived only through the courage and protective custody of his son.

The family almost did not recognize him as he hobbled down the gangplank at the New York pier, looking fragile and wasted. He had lost 57 pounds and was a fraction of the robust man he had been at the outset of the trip. Experiencing his "last chance to be a boy" transformed him into a sickened old man and nearly took his life. Yet, ultimately, he and his party had succeeded in charting the mysterious river, and the appreciative Brazilian government later designated it *Rio Teodoro*.

"I am 56 years old," he later acknowledged to Kermit's wife, Belle, "I have led a very active life; I am no longer fit, physically or in any other way. . . . I am really glad that it has become my duty to stay quietly at Sagamore Hill, and loaf and invite my soul."[164]

Long term, it was not in Theodore's nature to "stay quietly" and "loaf." Nor was it in the genes of his favored son. With the surge in nationalism about to explode into violence in Europe, both Theodore and Quentin would be hurled into the maelstrom with unforeseen and tragic consequences.

Twelve

No Longer a Boy

Flora Payne Whitney's mother scribbled "Gertrude Vanderbilt Whitney" on a check to the French volunteer ambulance corps for its relief work in the war zone. It was for $250,000, more than $5.6 million today. "For every joy [France] has given me, I want to repay her," she told Flora in explaining her decision to support what would become the legendary American Field Service during The Great War in Europe.[165]

During the year that 17-year-old Flora was practicing her studies and perfecting her riding skills at the Foxcroft School in Virginia, Gertrude was experiencing an epiphany. While organizing an exhibit at the new Whitney Studio in Greenwich Village and entering a design competition for a memorial to the Titanic's victims, she was overtaken unexpectedly by a greater calling. Now nearly 40, with her fame assured and possessing all the money she could ever hope for, Gertrude was struck by reports of the horror in Europe and the German march through Belgium toward France. "I wanted to be over there," she later recalled. "I wanted to stand beside my friends. . . . I do not know many French people, but the working people I love."[166]

And so, on October 31, 1914 Gertrude sailed for England, with typical resolve, on the British liner *Lusitania*, the first leg of a journey to the war front. "If I find I am no use over there, I shall come right back . . . for the holidays," she assured Flora.[167]

With the help of influential friends in New York, Gertrude had recruited a cadre of medical aides: four surgeons, 15 trained nurses, and a half dozen hospital interns. They journeyed with her to establish a field hospital at the commune of Juilly in north-central France, about 100 kilometers from Paris. There, in 1638, *le Collège de Juilly* had been established. Although in 1914, the unused school buildings were without heat and water, Gertrude's party took them over and turned classrooms and dorms into wards and operating theaters. B. H. Friedman, her biographer, reported that within weeks of Gertrude's arrival, the heat was on and the water was running. Moreover, 150 hospital beds had been set up, and a fleet of ambulances made ready.

This scion of Cornelius Vanderbilt, once America's wealthiest man, now could be found organizing and sorting "boxes of warm things sent from America" and delivering them by truck through the stark Belgian flatlands to the war front. "Stretching over the fields were what looked like gigantic serpents but, on close inspection, turned out to be trenches," Gertrude recorded in her journal. "Fields of barbed wire entanglements had been constructed, and I wondered if the wires were connected with electric current as I had heard many were."[168]

In the middle of December, she returned home to reflect on her life-altering experience: "It has made me see more clearly the line of usefulness in life and cast behind me more ruthlessly those people who will acknowledge no duties or responsibilities. God, grant me the clear vision."[169]

Gertrude would return to the front in the spring of 1915 to serve the wounded that were "lying on stretchers on the floor of the receiving rooms."

"Send a check—that's the best way," she was told.

"But checks could not still my desire," she conceded.[170] In November, Gertrude was awarded the French Foreign Office gold medal for her work at Juilly.

Of this turning point in Gertrude's life, author Friedman would observe, "She is to the public more than just a famous society figure, more than a sculptor of talent—she has been *there* at the front; the world cares about *that*."[171]

Indeed, America and much of the world were preoccupied with the tumultuous events on the Continent. During a span of four and a half years, from the summer of 1914 through the Armistice on November 11, 1918, some 60 million Europeans were mobilized to fight—70 million people overall—and more than nine million combatants perished. At least two million others died from disease, and six million more were lost and presumed dead. Much of the European landscape was burnt or scarred, disease ran rampant, and the economy lay shattered. The Great War would be one of the costliest and deadliest conflicts in history.[172]

The war's genesis could be traced to the clashing imperialist policies of the European powers, complicated by a mad arms race and multiple Byzantine alliances. On June 28, 1914, a sudden explosion of violence sparked the conflagration. Archduke Franz Ferdinand of Austria, the heir presumptive to the throne of Austria-Hungary, was assassinated in Sarajevo by a Serbian nationalist. The murder ignited public outrage and martial passions that had simmered for decades. Almost immediately, it precipitated a declaration of war by Austria-Hungary against Serbia. Soon the Central Powers, spearheaded by Germany, and the Allies, led by England and France, declared war on each other. German ground forces invaded Belgium and France and, over time, ghastly battles of attrition raged in trench lines along the Western Front in eastern France. Additional fronts opened farther east, drawing in Italy, Russia, and the Ottoman Empire.

At first the American people took an isolationist view of the war, and President Wilson mirrored their mood. He stood back to watch events unfold, determined to keep the U.S. out of the line of fire. But as the war stretched into the spring of 1915, a German U-boat torpedoed the British ocean liner *Lusitania* 11 miles off the coast of Ireland, killing 1,198 souls, 128 of them American men, women, and children.[173] That incident triggered an intense debate inside the U.S. on whether the nation should become involved.

Theodore Roosevelt was among the most vocal participants, breaking publicly with Wilson's neutrality policy and urging U.S. intervention. He said he was appalled at the atrocities committed by German troops in Belgium and the "act of piracy" perpetrated on the *Lusitania*. The immediate need, he believed, was for "preparedness," the training of young civilians—students, businessmen, and others—by the U.S. military for the inevitable.

At Groton, Quentin Roosevelt, now 17 and in his graduation year, trained militarily on campus and exercised the influence of his editorial post at *The Grotonian*. Inspired by a campus visit from General Leonard Wood, his father's superior during the Spanish American War, Quentin authored an editorial criticizing the country's "woeful state of unpreparedness to meet an enemy." Echoing his father's forceful views, Quentin claimed it was "criminal negligence" for the government not to build up an efficient, fully-equipped army. He had a good word, however, for General Wood and other military leaders who were organizing summer camps for men in college "that turn out volunteer officers in ten weeks—two summer's work."[174] Quentin was looking ahead, with some trepidation, to just such an experience—if his injured back would allow it.

There was now professional disagreement over the cause of Quentin's persistent back pain, a consequence of his having tumbled down an Arizona mountainside two years earlier. During the Easter break of 1915, Theodore had an Oyster Bay physician, a Dr. Helmar, examine him. The diagnosis confirmed two partially dislocated ribs at the juncture of the spine. Dr. Helmar recommended that Quentin absent himself from Groton for ten days to rest. "Dr. Helmar won't let me come back," Quentin explained to Rector Peabody in a note. "I think I will escape his clutches soon. . . . The osteopathic treatment can be very tiring."[175]

Reporting time for military camp approached, and when his back didn't improve, Quentin consulted Dr. Robert Lovett in Boston, a famed surgeon at Children's Hospital. Dr. Lovett's X-rays showed "no fracture, no displacement and nothing out of the way. . . . To my mind, it comes down to a severe contusion and wrench of the upper part of the back which he has not given a chance to get well," the doctor advised.[176] Quentin was cleared to put on a uniform.

Groton's graduation, however, came first. Rector Peabody was displeased with Quentin's academic performance in the months leading up to June. His report cards showed a steady decline in grades and class ranking, prompted by the distraction of his work with *The Grotonian* and a flirtation with a farcical class play in which he played the part of "Captain Swiss Cheese."

Quentin's last Groton report card, issued a week before graduation, was his worst ever—"a poor performance" in the mind of Rector Peabody. His class standing had slipped from second to seventh (of 17), and he finished with a low "C" average. Nonetheless, the rector acknowledged to Quentin's parents, "There has been growth in a good many ways this year."[177]

During class ceremonies on June 13, 1915, Quentin Roosevelt received his Groton diploma for having "attained the required standard of scholarship." His father pronounced himself pleased. "Quentin has matured much and is really good looking," Theodore told Kermit in a glowing note.[178]

One can infer from Theodore's observations at the time that he had come to realize that Quentin was the special child of his brood—that his youngest gradually had achieved favored status in his own eyes and heart. Quentin had overcome his bottom raking in the family birth order to surpass his brothers and sisters in ability and promise. Unlike his brothers Ted, Kermit, and Archie, he was sensitive and affectionate, yet he bore an elfin playfulness that instantly won over his contemporaries and older adults. Quentin had an effortless smile and charm that overcame any sense of family entitlement. Moreover, he was a good and decent fellow. He had an expressive talent for poetry and prose born out of a voracious appetite for reading and conversation. In short, Theodore Roosevelt had recognized that Quentin was a natural, self-motivated leader with admirable qualities and even greater potential for the future, especially if he should follow his father's path of public service. Theodore Roosevelt at last recognized his political heir.

Hamilton Coolidge, captain of the Groton senior football team and the school's star baseball pitcher, shared the graduation stage with Quentin and received a diploma of his own. Beyond being an especially well-regarded classmate, he was one of Quentin's best friends. A direct descendent of Thomas Jefferson, Coolidge would be recalled in later years as ". . . nearly a perfect physical specimen, tall, strong and straight, ruddy and of a fair countenance—a born leader." He and Quentin had connected during their six years at Groton, sharing experiences in the classroom, on stage, and on the gridiron. For the rest of their lives, they would maintain a fast friendship.

Quentin and Hamilton would enter the Harvard Class of 1915 together and subsequently leave school to join the fledgling U.S. Air Service when America entered the war. They labored, side by side, in the cold and mud at the Issoudun training center in France and in the dangerous skies over Germany. As Quentin nurtured his relationship with Flora during the war, Hamilton would grow close to her as well. In fact, it would fall to him, in just a few years, to console her in her desperate hours of grief.

In the weeks between graduation and the start of military camp, Theodore and Edith opened their home to Quentin's friends. Freed from the rigidity of Rector Peabody's rules, they danced the Cincinnati Two Step to the tinny sounds of the gramophone. "Quentin has developed strong social tastes," his father observed to Kermit. "And we like the girls and boys he has out to stay at Sagamore."[179]

For the Fourth of July, Quentin and Archie invited five of their Groton friends to spend the night at Sagamore Hill in advance of their departure for military camp the next day. The visit coincided with Theodore and Edith's annual Fourth of July costume party, adding welcomed gaiety to the boys' hours of apprehension. In a letter to Kermit and Belle, Theodore reported that "the dancing ended with the Virginia Reel as usual. . . . Mother and I [wore] fancy dress costumes. . . . Mother as a Puritan—and a very pretty and sweet Puritan—and I, with my cap and gown, as a college professor."[180]

Plattsburgh, New York, above the Adirondacks and with a lovely view of Lake Champlain, was the center of what became known as the Plattsburgh Movement. A band of its patriotic citizens, believing passionately in preparedness, had organized a military training program at a local Army base for non-enlisted, upper class students and young professionals who paid their own way. Its goal was to produce a fresh cadre of smart and enthusiastic officers who would help lead American forces in the event that the U.S. joined the war. Theodore Roosevelt and General Wood, now commander of the Army's Eastern Department, were understood to be its principal backers.

At Sagamore Hill, as Edith put away the costumes from the fancy dress dance, the young Roosevelts headed off to Plattsburgh for five weeks of vigorous training. By the tenth of July, Theodore would note with pride, "Archie and Quentin are now in camp. They are under a regular officer and are being trained in regular army work." He assured Kermit and Belle that "it is real work, without the slightest touch of the tin soldier business about it. It will do them both an immense amount of good."[181] Historian Edmund Morris would later confirm the camp's exacting profile: "The training program as laid out by Wood was intense, compressing four years of regular army education into four weeks of dawn-to-dusk discipline."[182]

Archie and Quentin at readiness camp.

(Courtesy The Groton School archives)

There is a surviving camp photo of the Roosevelt brothers posing side by side in a grassy field. They gamely sport military garb, long-sleeved blouses and flared trousers, high leather boots, waist gear, and flop caps. Their rifles are looped securely about their shoulders. Quentin's hands are set firmly on his hips in a mock show of readiness. Characteristic Roosevelt teeth erupt prominently from their beaming faces. One has the unmistakable impression that the photo was staged so it could be dispatched for their father's edification.

On August 8, muscled up and sun baked, Quentin received a certificate for successfully completing camp. He was certified as a first-year private and marksman. Of more significance, his superiors recommended him for promotion to non-commissioned officer in next summer's camp. "With more age and experience, [he] would make an excellent second lieutenant of volunteers," wrote the commandant on the diploma.[183]

After visiting the Plattsburgh camp once his sons had departed, and emboldened by the impressive array of patriotic young men paraded before him, Theodore couldn't help but unload on President Wilson. After all, Wilson opposed preparedness as contradictory to his policy of neutrality toward the European combatants. "Wilson is at heart an abject coward," Theodore declared in a letter to Kermit, "or else he has a heart so cold and selfish that he is entirely willing to sacrifice the honor and interest of the country to his own political advancement. . . . [W]e ought to have universal military service."[184]

In contrast to Quentin's summer of exertion and discipline, Flora Payne Whitney enjoyed an idyllic few months at her parents' retreat in the Adirondacks. Long sleepy days saw her swimming in lakes, fishing for dinner, and harvesting abundant, fat raspberries. Most evenings, family members gathered around a crackling campfire to ward off the chill. Gertrude stayed away to mourn the death of her 37-year-old brother, Alfred Gwynne Vanderbilt. In May, he was lost in the torpedo attack on the *Lusitania*. She took comfort, however, from survivors' tales of Alfred's on-board heroism. As the doomed liner took on water, he was spotted helping children into lifeboats and, in one noteworthy instance, surrendering his life jacket to an older woman. In Gertrude's view, Alfred had had "a splendid death."

It was during July, in that summer of 1915, that Gertrude cautioned her daughter in a letter to "be very careful with the boys." Flora had turned 18 and was spending more and more time away from the family, socializing with groups of boys and other girls. One fellow in particular, a 17-year-old Groton boy with a warmhearted nature, had begun to consume her thoughts. He was not from great money; his father did not hail from industrial nobility or Wall Street. He was an unpretentious gentleman from Long Island who just happened to be a president's son.

Quentin surely relished the special attention he was drawing from Flora, but as summer waned, his focus shifted to the start of college. On September 25, in league with his pal, Hamilton Coolidge, he strode through the gates of Harvard Yard. Fresh off the train from Oyster Bay and burdened with heavy cases of clothing and necessities that his mother had dotingly packed, Quentin settled into Gore Hall. A freshman dormitory built only a few years previously, it was a U-shaped, brick building of four stories that enveloped a courtyard. Its open side, facing the Charles River, bore a façade modeled on Sir Christopher Wren's 17th century garden way at London's Hampton Court. In years to come, Gore Hall would earn notoriety as John F. Kennedy's senior dorm.

Theodore stopped off to visit Quentin ten days later and reported to Belle that Quentin "is already absorbed in the Harvard Library and has taken to his room three books: the *Anti-Jacobin*, Layard's *Nineveh* and the translation of a Chinese life of Genghis Khan."[185] A few weeks later, Theodore updated Kermit with news that Quentin was trying out for manager of the freshman football team. "He has taken the utmost interest in Groton still," Theodore reported with an air of surprise, "and often goes back to supervise the printing press."[186] The schools were fewer than 50 miles apart, an easy weekend train ride.

Around the same time, during elaborate ceremonies in a Philadelphia shipyard, Flora was enlisted to shatter a bottle of expensive champagne over the bow of *Whileaway*, her father's luxurious new, quarter-million-dollar steam yacht. While stretching 175 feet in length, the vessel required only 13 feet of draught, enabling it to "easily cruise in shallow bays and estuaries." *The New York Times* explained that "Mr. Whitney is very fond of sailing in obscure waters, exploring any gulf, bay or river mouth that looks interesting."[187]

It was during the early fall of 1915 that Quentin and Flora began to exchange the first of a long series of private letters. Continuing to the summer of 1918, the letters would document the evolution of their relationship from awkward adolescent acquaintance to impassioned love, frustrated by separation and the uncertainty of war. Most of the one hundred-fifty or so surviving letters, typically handwritten, are from Quentin to Flora. She carefully preserved them as young women of the era did. There are considerably fewer from Flora to Quentin since in the midst of their correspondence, he went off to fight in Europe. The originals, with their tattered, stamped, and postmarked envelopes, are conserved at Harvard's Houghton Library—gifts of their families—and incorporated into the university's treasured Theodore Roosevelt Collection.

From Gore Hall on October 25, Quentin wrote mockingly to Flora, "Apparently you have an obnoxious habit of reading the letters you get from boys to the assembled family. If you read this to them, I promise faithfully to shoot you on site." He went on. "If you must read something to them, I enclose a copy of one of the rector's sermons which you can tell them I sent for the good of your soul." He signed off, "Ever thine."[188]

Just when and how Quentin and Flora met is lost to time. Neither recorded the moment in a letter or diary. Descendants claim not to know. But in the view of Flora's daughter, Flora Miller Biddle, it was likely that the teens came upon each other by happenstance within the "small world of people" that inhabited the upper crust of New York society. Their families were acquainted socially, she noted, so Quentin and Flora probably met at a house gathering or theater party. In any case, the letters make clear that they were soul mates from the start. He was always to be her sweetheart, Quentin. She was, forever, his dearest Foufie.

Thirteen

Ready for Love and War

On Valentine's Day 1916, a smallish envelope arrived in Flora's mailbox in New York. It was postmarked, "Cambridge, Mass." There was a bright red heart on the cover of a card inside but the verse was constrained:

VALENTINE GREETINGS

NOT AS A SWEETHEART,
BUT A FRIEND,
A QUITE PLATONIC HEART
I SEND!

In this card to Flora, Quentin stressed the companionable
nature of their relationship.

(MS Am 2923 (61), Theodore Roosevelt Collection, Houghton Library, Harvard University)

Now in their late teens, Quentin and Flora were carrying out an exploratory relationship by mail, on the telephone, and occasionally in person. She was one of a handful of girls he knew. There were, notably, Leslie and Lucy. All were chums either from Cambridge, back home in New York, or friends made mutually with Flora. But only with Flora did Quentin make overnight and weekend visits, superficially chaperoned.

In one letter to Flora, whom he now addressed affectionately as "Foufie,"—her family's nickname—he may have hinted intentionally that she occupied special status. Quentin shared details of a day he had spent with Lucy (no last name given) at the former Newgate Prison, then a tourist destination not far from his Aunt

Bamie's home in Connecticut. "We had supper over there and sat on a wooden porch at the back and watched the moon rise," he revealed. "I wish you could have been there." Quentin's descriptive phrasing again showed off his literary talent: "There was a long view out across the valley, black as the pit and as empty as the desert, with a little cluster of lights from a village just showing off in the distance. Just opposite us, over the outline of the hills, rose the newest of new moons." He concluded his tale revealingly. "I sat off and had a very nice time by myself."[189]

By the start of the year, Quentin had settled in at Harvard with classes and a full roster of activities. "[He] has enjoyed his Harvard experience so far as much as any Roosevelt freshman I have ever known," his father observed.[190] In two semesters, Quentin tackled math, comparative literature, and government and economics, supplementing the required courses with electives that satisfied his mechanical interest: engineering sciences, physics, and chemistry. He was excused from taking classroom French; he had already aced the college's oral entrance exam.

There is no record of Quentin making manager of the freshman football team. Certainly, his bad back would not have tolerated competitive sports. But he was welcomed into Hasty Pudding and the Groton School Club. An entry in the 1919 Harvard class yearbook observed that he "inherited his father's pluck and determination and, before his election to Delta Kappa Epsilon (DKE), he was put through a particularly severe initiation ceremony." By today's standards, the induction seems tame. "The public part of the ordeal included shining shoes, selling newspapers and the delivery of a long lecture on 'Why I am a pacifist.'"[191] Quentin shared DKE, Hasty Pudding, and most classes with Hamilton, who had been elected vice president of the freshman class and played on the first-year football and baseball squads.

Quentin somehow found time for Army R.O.T.C. training on campus in a program sanctioned by General Wood in defiance of the White House's opposition to readiness activities on campuses. "Military and naval activities . . . were the most important single element in the college career of the Class of 1919," the yearbook later asserted. And when his brother, Archie, helped to re-activate the Harvard Regiment—the legendary contingent that had distinguished itself during the Civil War—Quentin signed on. By the summer of 1916, he and Archie had joined their brothers, Ted and Kermit, and 622 other Harvard men for their second year of training at the Plattsburgh camp.

Whether it was the extracurricular activities, the heavy course load, or his attention to Flora, Quentin's first-year academic results at Harvard were sub-par. Theodore and Edith learned, in a report sent home, that their youngest managed mostly C's. One can only wonder about his father's reaction to the D that Quentin had earned in his government course. If the ex-president chose to admonish his son, there is no evidence extant. Roosevelt may have taken small comfort from the realization that Quentin's marks were typical for many Harvard freshmen and consistent with Archie's and Kermit's in earlier years.

Nineteen sixteen was a presidential election year and, predictably, there were calls for Theodore Roosevelt to challenge his adversary, President Woodrow Wilson. The losing Bull Moose candidate of 1912 had stayed in the limelight with his increasingly strident criticism of Wilson's "war weaseling" and his call for recruitment of a volunteer infantry division. "I despise Wilson," Roosevelt told his sister, Bamie, in July. "But I despise still more our foolish, foolish people who, partly from ignorance and partly from sheer timidity, and partly from lack of imagination and sensitive national feeling, support him." [192]

As tempted as he was to take on Wilson, Roosevelt resisted, ultimately declaring in March, "I do not wish the nomination."[193] Neither did he accept the nomination offered by the Progressive Party in June. Instead he focused on his nationwide call for readiness. "The deluge of mail about the highly problematical [infantry] division has swamped me," he confessed to Bamie in July. "At present I can do nothing but have the [applications] filed."[194]

Quentin reprised his "platonic" feelings for a vacationing Flora in March, using the language of romance. "*Tout à vous de mon coeur,*" he wrote from wintry Gore Hall. "I am feeling rather low. . . . Your letter, instead of cheering me up, made me feel even lower. There you are, down in a houseboat with warm air, green things growing, blue skies ever showing. And then, here I sit up in Cambridge, the ground six inches deep in sloshing snow, a dismal sleet storm going on outside. . . . If you are in Paradise, I am in hell. No, on second thought, I don't think it's like hell, for hell is at least warm, sociable and amusing. . . . "[195]

A few days after having a heart-to-heart talk with Flora during a house party at Old Westbury, Quentin began to openly question his feelings for her. "I am trying to make up my mind about you," he allowed. "I don't know exactly how much to say to you for the simple reason that I've not quite decided how 'safe' you are."[196]

When Flora expressed her affection for him in a reply, Quentin admitted that he had been "thinking a lot over it." He wrote, "Here is Flora, whom I care for a lot and consider a good friend. The only question is: does she merely look at me as an amusing character to study or is she really a friend. . . . I still think you are cold at bottom, but that does not necessarily mean, as you say, that you may 'never experience the greatest joys or the deepest sorrows of life.' Love—I speak with the certainty of ignorance—is the greatest joy and deepest sorrow of life, and love is a thing that comes to one and all, regardless of 'coldness' or not. . . . I think we are miles too young to have any right to be in love."[197]

Quentin felt that he had to see her again—and soon. He asked if they could talk over lunch at Old Westbury during the Decoration Day school break. He was going to Sagamore Hill, he said, to pick up his car and drive it back to school. "I hear from a reliable source that you have been warned against me which, I suppose, explains why I am 'perfectly horrid.' Well, you're not the only one! I've been seriously warned against you, and by two people!"[198]

Summer found Quentin back at Plattsburgh for another season of preparedness training alongside Archie, now top sergeant of H Company, 4th Training Regiment. "I am a corporal with a remote prospect of being a sergeant, which is nice," Quentin wrote to Flora, who was then in Newport. "The only drawback to my being under Arch is that I always have to work twice as hard as I would ordinarily, thanks to Arch's horror of being accused of favoritism."[199]

In a July 20th dispatch from the camp, *The New York Times* offered its readers an account of the goings-on between the two youngest Roosevelt brothers. During a ceremonial assembly on the parade grounds, the drop of a rifle suddenly shattered the quiet. "Top Sergeant Archie Roosevelt turned quickly, but the guilty one had adroitly recovered the weapon. 'Who dropped that piece?' he demanded to know. 'The soldier who did that ought to be sent to the guardhouse.'

'I did,' a meek voice admitted.

"Top Sergeant Roosevelt looked in the direction of the voice and discovered that Corporal Quentin Roosevelt . . . was the offender. This sort of work must be stopped. You will be placed on the blacklist for three days.'"[200] Quentin indeed was confined to camp and ordered to pick up all the trash from the streets.

Three days later, Theodore Roosevelt arrived in camp for an inspection. "Archie is working like a demon at Plattsburgh," he reported to Bamie. "Quentin, who does not enjoy it, is going thither dutifully this week."[201]

At Plattsburgh, war was played out in marches and drills and on the shooting range. In central Europe, the actual hostilities had turned intensely gruesome. Britain and France had introduced tanks to the trench-strewn battlefields of eastern France. The Germans responded with fearsome poison gas. On July 1, at the Somme River, a British expeditionary force and French army troops opened an offensive against the Germans. By the time fighting slowed in the fall, the *Bataille de la Somme* had become one of the war's bloodiest. On the first day of fighting alone, the British suffered more than 57,000 casualties including nearly 20,000 dead. In all, a million casualties were recorded.[202]

Back at the Groton School, Rector Peabody was perplexed about America's role in the war. "I cannot quite make out where our duty lies in regard to our own country," he wrote. "To increase our armament and raise a large army and navy would arouse the fighting spirit which we all deplore, and yet it is perfectly certain, I suppose, that we should be trodden under foot by Germany or Japan if we fall out with either of them."[203] His quandary mirrored much of the country's as well.

About this time, the Whitney family was finalizing arrangements for Flora's debut at their Newport cottage. The new ballroom was ready, and hundreds of invitations were out to the colony's fashionable society. Within days, the event was in bloom, and guests would observe that Flora was radiant, and Quentin was dashing. As they fox-trotted around the ballroom among the exploding corks and overflowing glasses, the young couple surely savored the moment—and wondered about their uncertain futures. Partiers nattered about the captivating pair as they danced nearly until dawn and, later, swam to the sunrise.

President Wilson notwithstanding, America was drawing closer to its fate in Europe. To Theodore's applause, there was movement in Washington to inaugurate a new air service branch within the Army. Young men who wanted to fly in service to their country would have an opportunity to do so and prove their stuff. Quentin, though, pondered his scheduled return to Harvard in a few weeks; hundreds of other boys would come back too with their reserve uniforms; they had worn them well in the previous spring as they marched all about Boston and Cambridge in flag-waving preparedness parades.

Making her way busily about the Whitney estate during the ball, a petite British woman with an air of competence and steel drew scant attention from the partygoers except for Flora and her mother, Gertrude. Miss Irene M. Givenwilson had tenure with the Whitney women. She was remembered as having been the ideal, multilingual governess for young Flora in Paris while Gertrude had gone about her hectic pace, managing artists and her studio. Miss Givenwilson supervised her charge's lessons and saw to it that she got to dance class on time. When the family summered in the Adirondacks, it was Miss Givenwilson who kept an eye on the budding young woman "with scarlet nails on long tapered fingers and black curls tumbling over pretty flowered shirts."[204]

Now, Miss Givenwilson earned the same appreciation as Gertrude's private secretary in her Old Westbury home and lavish "marble studio" on property. In the near future, in an extraordinary coincidence, she would come to Quentin's aid and comfort during a critical hour of need as a Red Cross supervisor in France.

In the early fall of 1916, Quentin Roosevelt returned to Harvard with a vague plan to graduate in two more years. Simultaneously, Flora stayed close by her mother and Miss Givenwilson at Old Westbury, helping with homeland duties for the Red Cross. Out of duty to his political party, Theodore Roosevelt began stumping for the Republican nominee for president, Supreme Court Justice Charles Evans Hughes, a progressive. Now considered an elder statesman, Roosevelt was unencumbered by party or platform. He was free to say what he thought about Hughes (not very much complimentary) and what he suffered viscerally about the incumbent, Wilson. Throughout the campaign, the president's supporters chanted, "He kept us out of war." Roosevelt countered that the slogan was "utterly misleading, the phrase of a coward."[205] In November Wilson triumphed narrowly, and Roosevelt retreated to Sagamore Hill to work on his papers and express his opinions in magazines and newspaper columns.

Before he was re-admitted to class, Quentin had to square up with the Harvard administration. "You have neglected to settle an account of fifty cents for damage done to the freshman halls," an official admonished. "In consequence, you are not entitled to the privileges of the university."[206] Apparently, Quentin hastened to settle his obligation since he soon reclaimed his seat in Comparative Literature class and five other courses.

By October, Quentin was in a sophomore slump, academically and personally. His marks sagged to between C and E. He was fighting repeated bouts of sickness and loneliness, often secluding himself in Room 15 at his new dorm, Claverly Hall. One time, his illness found expression in a stanza he intentionally turned in with a math exam:

> Still I plod on in a dull desperation,
> Head aching dismally, ready to sip
> Goblets of strychnine or morphine or vitriol
> How can I work when I've got the grippe?[207]

More than anything else, Quentin was missing the companionship of his brother Archie who had left in June. Only a continual stream of letters from Flora seemed to lift him out of the blues. "I'm all at odds with everyone and everything," he confessed to Flora. "Nothing seems friendly, and yet I'm naturally a gregarious animal, Lord knows. I suppose, as a matter of fact, it's all that I'm working pretty hard, and summer is over. . . . Cambridge is ghastly. It's either cold and damp or hot and muggy, and nothing but work, work, work." He practically begged her to write back right away. "I haven't a soul to cheer me up." [208]

Although Flora's letters from this period have not survived, we know from Quentin's other references to them that they were a rousing tonic for him. "I wish there were some more effective method of appreciation than saying thanks. [Your letter] rescued me from a bad fit of the blues." His P.S. hinted at more than friendship: "I wonder if you know what I wished on the full moon Wednesday night at 9:30?"[209]

Then, two weeks later: "I have been pretty lonely at times without Arch to see. . . . Last Saturday, I just decided to hike down [to Sagamore Hill] to see Arch, even if it was only for Sunday. I had hardly finished packing when the telephone rang, and I heard, 'Hello, Q' from the other end. It was Arch who had come up over Sunday. My, but I was glad to see him again. He certainly is a great person."[210] One suspects that Flora might have had something to do with arranging the surprise.

"It was the first time since 1908 that we got the entire family together at Christmas," Quentin reported to Flora early in January 1917. "It was real excitement even if I did sleep on a sofa in Father's dressing room." The Roosevelt "family" for the holiday totaled 17, brothers and sisters, their spouses, and Theodore and Edith's grandchildren. "Being unmarried, I was rather a footloose wanderer with no affiliations, so I could watch all the various campaigns carried on," Quentin remembered.[211]

Whether it was seeing his siblings and their caring spouses close up or experiencing the familial excitement of young children at Christmas, Quentin was feeling left out of love. Moreover, his letters to Flora that February suggest that he was falling in love. "After getting back to Boston, then traveling out to Cambridge, I found myself back in my room . . . and I began to feel low. . . . Each time I'd get started on a train of thought, I would revert back to those days I spent at the *Maison Whitney* and then it would shift to you, oh very distinctly."[212]

Referring to his studies, Quentin admitted that "this year has not been too smooth," and that with each return trip to Harvard, "I began to feel less and less like going back, even though I knew I had to."[213]

As he bettered his soldierly skills during R.O.T.C. drills, he had to be thinking of how he, who loved to tinker with machines and found aviation irresistible, would shine in a flier's uniform. The papers were full of news about the Army's budding Aeronautical Division and its need for pilots in the event the U.S. entered the war in Europe.

Quentin certainly appreciated the groundbreaking role his father had played in aviation history. Roosevelt had told his son—a thousand times it seemed—about the fall morning in 1910 when he became the first president to fly. He had left the White House by then but, nevertheless, what an unforgettable experience it had been! When he was invited to climb aboard a biplane at an air show in Kinloch, Missouri, Roosevelt did not waver. *The New York Tribune* reported the sight:

> The aeroplane sped quickly around the field at a height of less than one hundred feet. It made the first lap of a mile and a half before news percolated through the crowd that Mr. Roosevelt was [Pilot Alex] Hoxsey's passenger. When he swept past the grandstand, [Roosevelt] leaned forward a bit and waved his hands. . . . The pilot had been warning him to hold onto the rail less he interfere with the engine or fall out.

All in all, the plane remained airborne about four minutes. "It was the finest experience I have ever had," the ex-president beamed.[214]

Roosevelt's commitment to manned flight stretched back three years earlier when, as president, he had authorized $6,750 from his personal discretionary fund to build America's first military aircraft, a dirigible airship. Air Force historian Herbert Malloy Mason, Jr. observed that the president "thought that flying was just bully; he could not stand the idea that the United States should fall behind in anything especially in the field of powered flight which was, after all, an American invention."[215]

The big questions in Quentin's mind, as he seriously considered leaving school to train as a pilot, was whether his eyesight was good enough and whether his achy back would be an obstacle to passing a physical exam.

Overseas, the escalating naval war saw British and French ships falling increasingly to German U-boats in the Atlantic. Britain's naval blockade took its toll on Germany. The Kaiser's uniformed leaders retorted by raising the ante: announcing a policy of unrestricted submarine warfare. At home, President Wilson denounced the German move as he continued to cling to a hope for "peace without victory in Europe." Theodore Roosevelt stepped up the pressure on the administration for authority to raise a volunteer infantry division and cavalry brigade "in the event of war."

The tipping point for the U.S. was the discovery of a secret German telegram to Mexico proposing an alliance that, in the event of war with the U.S., would finance Mexico's recovery of Texas, New Mexico, and Arizona, American territory that Mexico had surrendered in the 1848 Treaty of Guadalupe-Hidalgo, following the Mexican-American war. Fueled further by the subsequent sinking of seven U.S. merchant ships, public opinion ignited in favor of joining the war.

On April 1, 1917, President Wilson sat in his private room at the White House, huddled over an old typewriter, laying out a message he would deliver to Congress the following day. Visiting *New York World* Editor Frank Cobb heard him wonder aloud, "What else can I do? Is there anything else I can do?"[216]

The next day, in the hushed chamber of the House of Representatives, Wilson, the discouraged peacemaker, asked for a declaration of war on Germany. "The world must be made safe for democracy," he intoned. Four days later, the House overwhelmingly agreed. And plans were laid for immediate conscription of a half-million men for service in Europe.

An applauding Theodore Roosevelt praised Wilson's "great state paper" and called on Secretary of War Newton Baker to grant his request immediately to lead tens of thousands of volunteers at the front. To those who remembered a young Rough Rider's courageous charge up San Juan Hill that helped to liberate Cuba a generation ago, it was flourishing trumpets and flapping flags all over again. But this time, Roosevelt declared, he would follow his four sons into battle.

Fourteen

Engagement and Departure

You cannot bring up boys as eagles
and expect them to turn out sparrows.

-Edith Kermit Roosevelt[217]

C ongress was hours away from agreeing to Woodrow Wilson's call for war with Germany when Quentin Roosevelt strode into the dean's office at Harvard. He was giving up college, he announced, to train as an aviator with the U.S. Air Service. Because of recurring illness, he had been unable to attend many of his classes, and he understood that his inferior marks reflected those absences. In a letter to Theodore—who now asked to be addressed as Colonel Roosevelt—a university official explained that Quentin could hardly expect to be given credit for his incomplete courses but could anticipate reinstatement later on if he wished to return.

Harvard granted Quentin a leave of absence, effective April 5, 1917. It became official May 29, the same day the college suspended intercollegiate baseball games; most of its players, including Hamilton Coolidge, had left for war.

His Harvard separation complete, Quentin returned to New York, and from there caught a midnight train to Washington, D.C. to take an Army physical. As the train rolled south through the tranquil blackness of the Northeast Corridor, he surely fretted over the prospect of an unfamiliar doctor denying him enlistment because of his damaged back and below-par eyesight. He was willing to sign on with the Royal Canadian Air Force if the U.S. rejected him. "I woke up the next A.M. in Washington with that evil-tempered, sandpaper-clothed feeling of filth which is the trademark of all midnight trains," he wrote.[218] After a refreshing bath, and breakfast at his sister Alice's home, Quentin reported to the War Department. It was, he said, a long day of obediently walking his papers through "various dens in the building."

"A hypochondriac with the darkest views of his fellow men" conducted Quentin's physical, he told Flora, stretching, measuring, and probing in a "twentieth century refinement of the Inquisition." To ensure that he passed the vision exam, Quentin memorized the eye chart, and he downplayed his back problems.

Following a second day of less arduous mental evaluation, Quentin was pronounced fit for military service. The outcome probably never was in doubt. It is hard to imagine any Army doctor taking the responsibility of telling Colonel Roosevelt that his son was defective for service.

In a 1921 remembrance, Quentin's brother Kermit assessed what his military evaluators evidently had concluded. "Quentin was gifted with that sixth sense that singles out the born aviator. Some men have an ability to call forth from machinery the best that is in it. . . . Quentin possessed this gift to a very marked degree."[219]

Quentin could not contain his exhilaration at the prospect of flying. He hastily scrawled a letter to Flora as he returned to New York: "Wild excitement! I have been put in the aviation school at Mineola [New York] instead of the one at Newport News. I haven't seen my family. I wonder if they will approve."

Quentin did not know then, and perhaps never knew, that his father had interceded to ensure that his son's flight training would take place near Sagamore Hill at Hempstead Plains Aerodrome— soon to be renamed Hazelhurst Field—a two-year-old National Guard base on Long Island. Described as the only natural prairie east of the Allegheny Mountains, it was an ideal setting for would-be aviators to test their skills in the tricky air currents between the Atlantic Ocean and Long Island Sound. Besides, Hazelhurst Field was just a brief aerial soar and dip from Old Westbury.

Perhaps understanding that his assignment to Hazelhurst was the start of a long-term commitment in uniform that would cut short his time with Flora, Quentin added a personal regret at the end of his letter from the train: "I do wish I hadn't seen so much of you, Fouf, then I probably shouldn't miss you so much."[220]

Quentin constantly worked to meet Flora's expectations. One time, in the spring of 1917, he fell short. "I am thoroughly ashamed of myself," he wrote apologetically. ""What a hypocrite you must think I am. I have preached disapproval and said that you shouldn't get drunk with girls around. . . . Father says that 'didn't mean-to' is no excuse. I am a very ordinary person I am afraid, but you have meant more to me than anyone else, far more than you can imagine."[221]

The spring of 1917 in America was a time of coming together for purpose, intense human drama, secret diary entries, and romantic poetry; of Kipling, Tom Swift adventures, and music hall diversions. As the war in Europe grew to occupy people's minds, life on the home front was defined by the ubiquitous recruitment poster, the allure of far-off lands, and soldierly honor. Amateur pianists played songs of patriotism, sacrifice, and separation in front parlors across the land. Newspaper and magazine photogravure imparted the horror of deadly trench warfare, steel helmets, raised bayonets, and clouds of yellow gas. The Great War twisted lives and dreams relentlessly and rushed decisions. America's young sat on the edge of resolve, wrapped in uncertainty and self-doubt.

For Quentin and Flora, his enforced absences at Mineola and the looming prospect of wartime separation infused urgency and passion into their relationship. They often stole away for private moments. By the time he reported to Hazelhurst Field April 25, Quentin's few letters to Foufie show a deepening dialogue about the meaning of love, even the possibility of their engagement and eventual marriage. Roosevelt biographer Edmund Morris observed that the young couple had plenty of opportunities during the period to "spoon" at Old Westbury. And, he added suggestively, "Sagamore Hill was available for weekend trysts." Edith, who understood the significance of Quentin's few remaining days with Flora, was ready to look the other way if necessary.

Quentin wrote to Foufie from the guardhouse at Mineola May 12: "It's funny how times have changed. A year ago, you could have gone to Japan and, barring a few letters, I shouldn't really have

cared. Now you go away for four days, and I am lost without [you].
. . . If two people really love each other, nothing else matters."[222]

Two weeks later: "Ah, Fouf, I don't yet see how you can love
me—still I feel as tho it was all a dream. . . . You see how very, very,
ordinary I am and how wonderful you are."[223]

The next day: "You are what I think of in the days, what I plan
for. You lighten and color my dreams."[224]

Quentin at Mineola, May 1917.

(Photo by Underwood & Underwood,
570 R67q, Theodore Roosevelt Collection,
Houghton Library, Harvard University)

The congressional signatures on the declaration of war were
barely blotted when Colonel Roosevelt decided to call on President
Wilson in person at the White House. He would pitch directly to
the commander in chief his plan for a division of volunteer soldiers
under his command. By all accounts, the 45-minute meeting was
cordial but officially inconclusive. A Wilson aide later quoted the

president as remarking condescendingly: "[Roosevelt] is a great big boy. I was, as formerly, charmed by his personality. There is a sweetness about him that is very compelling."[225]

Days later came the formal decision. Secretary of War Baker wrote to Roosevelt that his request was denied for "purely military reasons." Sylvia Jukes Morris, Edith's biographer, reported that "[Wilson] concurred with the opinion of General John Pershing, commander of the American Expeditionary Force [AEF] in Europe, that Roosevelt was not sufficiently trained, nor in sound enough heath, to withstand the rigors of modern trench warfare."[226] Edmund Morris put it more bluntly: "Baker could not have made it clearer that he and Wilson considered Roosevelt to be an amateur soldier from the last century."[227] But the astute colonel could read between the lines. The decision was barefaced political payback. Whatever the rationale, Roosevelt knew that he had to accept the end of his role as a national warrior-in-chief. He would never again raise a sword against an enemy. That obligation had passed to the next generation. It was time instead, he said, to ensure the appropriate posting of his sons to theaters of war.

Distraught at the thought that all four of her sons would be going abroad more or less simultaneously to serve their country, Edith Roosevelt busied herself with last-minute preparations for Archie's wedding. The date was moved up to April 14 so that he could wed dark-haired and slender Grace Lockwood of Boston well before he departed. There would not be time for a honeymoon, just a service in a Back Bay Episcopal church where Quentin would serve as best man. Not long after the ceremony and a reception for friends and relatives, Archie bid Grace *adieu* and returned to training camp at Plattsburgh where he and his brothers were awaiting orders.

Although the brothers probably could have wrangled cushy desk jobs in Paris, it was not in the Roosevelt character to do so. They wanted to be in the trenches, fighting alongside other Americans. Theodore expected no less of Ted and Archie but wanted to be sure that they received commissions at the ranks of major and second lieutenant, respectively, ones that they had earned at Plattsburgh. Putting his busy pen to paper on their behalf, he wrote, "My dear

General Pershing, I write to you now to request that my two sons . . . be allowed to enlist as privates under you, to go over with the first troops." The AEF commander, who surely must have understood Roosevelt's unstated objective, replied that he would endeavor to station them with his troops—*with no loss of rank* [italics added].[228]

Citing Kermit's facility with languages and his experience as a global traveler, Roosevelt arranged for him to serve in the war zone as a staff officer with British commanders in Mesopotamia.

His younger daughter, Ethel, would put her nursing skills to work at the American Hospital in Paris. She served valiantly alongside her husband, surgeon Richard Derby, before returning home in the spring to give birth to a daughter, Edith, in 1917.

Quentin's buddy, Hamilton Coolidge, followed a separate training track but one that would lead to their eventual reunion in France. Imbued since childhood with a zeal for flying that perhaps exceeded Quentin's, Ham trained at the Curtiss Flying School in Buffalo during the spring of 1916. Returning to Harvard that fall with a pilot's license from the Aero Club of America, he stayed on until February when he left for further aviator training in Miami Beach. Later, he took advanced ground training at the School of Military Aeronautics at the Massachusetts Institute of Technology.

The proximity of Sagamore Hill to the Mineola flight school enabled Quentin to live the life of a commuter student during some of his three months in training. He prepared with his fellow cadets during the day and returned to his childhood bedroom at night. There were, of course, many days when he lived on base and spent long days training. Like everyone else, he pulled overnight guard duty and strove to stay alert for the 5 a.m. camp reveille.

Hazelhurst Field was a work in progress, coming together hurriedly with odd bits of men and materiel. Following an inspection, Canadian Lt. Colonel Cuthbert Hoare described it as "backward in the last degree. They're as advanced, I should say, as we were in 1913. There is, in fact, no organization whatever."[229] Conditions could only get better.

We learn a lot about Quentin's time at Mineola from letters written home by two fellow cadets, the Hughes brothers—George and Jerry—South Texas natives who had moved to the Boston area early in the century to attend private schools. Like Quentin, the Hughes brothers left Harvard around the time the U.S. entered the war to sign up with the Air Service; they arrived at Mineola in mid-April 1917, concurrently with Quentin.

The shared class of about 50 was a mix of men, many from Ivy League schools: Princeton, Yale, Columbia, and of course, Harvard. "The business of training a group of young college boys in the art of flying was a new experience for the old Army," Jerry Hughes observed soon after unpacking his gear.[230]

Quentin and the others spent their first few weeks learning camp routine, drilling, and attending ground school classes on such disciplines as engine mechanics and Morse code. Flight training began intermittently around May 1 and was slow to progress because of persistent bad weather and a shortage of trainers. "When things began, there were so few military pilots that [six] civilian instructors were hired to provide training," Jerry Hughes told his family.

The men learned to fly in the open-cockpit Curtiss Jenny JN-4 biplanes, some taken over from the New York National Guard. Jerry Hughes remembers other planes as "some old [ones] that had been kicking around the Signal Corps at various posts." He added, "The repair shops and ground crews were hard pressed to keep enough of the craft in flying condition so that we could get the necessary time in the air."[231] The shortage of planes was blamed on the virtual absence of a developed aircraft production infrastructure in America. The scarcity of pilots was laid to the virtual absence of flight schools.

Quentin's typical day began with reveille at 5:15 a.m. and breakfast at 6:10, followed by guard duty at the flying field and time spent in hangars with men and machines. Afternoons brought classes, drill instruction, and machine shop training on aircraft motors. "After supper, we are supposed to work until dark on wireless, semaphore and all methods of signaling," George Hughes informed his mother.[232]

Jerry Hughes got to know Quentin quite well, since their bunks were next to one another's in the barracks. "Roosevelt is not particularly interesting looking," he recalled. "He is big and heavy and looks very young."

Jerry told his mother of a time when Quentin complained about his nagging back. "His bunk, at first, was one of those old canvas cots. He soon came to me and said, 'Last summer, I was out in Wyoming [*sic*] and was thrown by a horse. It gave me a bad back, and this old cot is killing me. Would you swap beds with me?'"

Acknowledging that his bunk was a sturdier iron bed, Jerry felt sorry for Quentin and said okay. "I always believed he was telling the truth and not just pulling my leg," he concluded.[233]

Flora, probably at Mineola, about age 20.

(Courtesy Alan D. Toelle)

When flight training began in earnest, Quentin learned to take off and land in the Jenny. He mastered the plane's dual controls, wheels that powered the ailerons on the wings' trailing edges, and a foot bar that worked the tail rudder. Author Edward J. Renehan, Jr. later wrote that Quentin's "takeoffs were cockeyed . . . and his landings brutish. . . . He just liked to fly."[234]

The next test was flying the plane solo in the landing pattern and performing other critical maneuvers. Finally, Quentin and the other cadets were required to solo "cross-country" to a distant airfield in 30-mile legs and, of course, return safely to Mineola.

"Flying is something that everybody cannot do," Jerry Hughes believed, "and something comparatively few people have indulged in to date. Add to the prestige, the pleasure of flying—the thrill and excitement which is possible to get—and you can easily see that the average young animal (like ourselves) will not soon tire of it at all."[235]

When Quentin got the hang of solo flying, he would sometimes set out for familiar skies. He would playfully fly circles over Flora's Old Westbury home, hoping to catch a glimpse of her on the grounds. According to Renehan, "He would [also] buzz Sagamore, flying low, tipping his wings and waving to his father who stood on the porch in a white suit, shielding his eyes from the sun with one hand and waving back enthusiastically with the other."

There was no question that Quentin was one of the most popular fliers in his outfit. Some thought that he may have lacked discipline in the cockpit but his gregarious personality and fun-loving demeanor, as well as his heritage, won over a host of admirers. Quentin may also have been one of the most accomplished aviators in training camp, judging from his record—or perhaps he had been placed on a fast track. Historian Alan Toelle determined that Quentin passed his Reserve Military Aviator skills test earlier than many others and was commissioned ahead of expectations as well.

One of those in his inner circle was Roderick Tower, an enlisted Harvard man. In a group photograph from the time, Quentin is seen standing behind and leaning in toward a seated Tower with a fraternal hand on his shoulder. What Quentin could not know at the time was that his buddy, Tower, would someday fall in love with and marry Flora Payne Whitney.

Advanced flight training would occur not in the States, but at European flying schools because there were few planes in the U.S. suitable for advanced training and no pilots qualified to give such instruction. About that time, senior officers were making plans for a completely new American flight instruction center at Issoudun, France, about 150 miles south of Paris. In Washington, Congress was appropriating more than $600 million for wartime aircraft that would "darken the skies over Germany."[236] Quentin and his buddies undoubtedly heard the excited talk of Issoudun and, concurrently, worrisome reports that for every 18 flying officers fully trained in Europe, one died in an air accident.

Quentin, top left, and Rod Tower, front left, at Mineola, probably May 1917.

(Photo by Paul Thompson, (570-R67q – 018,

Theodore Roosevelt Collection, Houghton Library, Harvard University)

Although we do not know the date, Quentin Roosevelt proposed marriage to Flora in late May 1917. A note to Flora on May 31 hinted at a significant rendezvous in New York City: "Friday's coming, and I'll see you there. Very much love. Q. R."[237] If he had written of his love with a vapor trail in the sky or sent Flora on a romantic treasure hunt through the Old Westbury estate, either surely would have given away the secret. The engagement was hush-hush. There was no ring since Quentin could not have afforded one on his cadet's wage. Besides, a diamond would have been too demonstrative. The engagement would have to be kept secret from both sets of parents; after all, the couple was only nineteen.

Quentin and Flora's letters from the period yield only a single announcement of sorts. On a Tuesday in June, they were together at Old Westbury. From the tone of a letter Quentin was scratching out to Kermit and his wife, Belle, the couple was relaxed and giddy, perhaps enjoying a celebratory drink or two. "The Scripture moveth us in sundry places to confess our manifold sins & wickedness and, that being the case, we—Flora and Quentin—announce that we have decided, for our sins, to become engaged." Since both would sign the letter—the only one of theirs known to contain both signatures—you can envision them huddled together over pen and paper cautiously choosing the words. "Seriously, we are reasonably happy," he wrote. (She objects on the grounds that I will probably be abroad within two months, Quentin inserts). We are telling nobody [underlined three times] except the family [immediate family, she remarks] so breathe not a word."[238]

There were familial complications. The Vanderbilt/Whitneys were not likely to condone their daughter's marriage into a highly-charged political family, even one nominally Republican, that identified with progressivism and disdained the über wealthy. Given the circumstances, Gertrude and Harry would not have been willing to send out a formal announcement or host an engagement party. Flora's father simply did not approve of young Roosevelt, mostly because he was not a man of means.

Edith was hesitant at the outset about uniting the Roosevelt family with those she considered the self-absorbed, moneyed nobility of Fifth Avenue and Newport. There had been a history of conflict between the families on public policy issues that mattered deeply to Theodore. How would a union of families with little in common be received by their friends and the press?

Quentin and Flora conceded that their families "inhabited different planets," and were a clear mismatch. But the youngsters loved each other deeply and wanted urgently to bind their commitment against the perils that lurked ahead during months or years of separation. Flora agonized, too, over whether Quentin would come home wounded or disfigured by battle, only to be utterly dependent on her, or whether he would return at all.

Nonetheless, with each of Flora's increasingly frequent visits to Sagamore Hill on Quentin's arm, for dinner and overnight stays, Theodore and Edith warmed to her. Flora showed them intelligence, graciousness, and an obvious affection for Quentin. She was down to earth, they came to realize, striving to establish a place for herself apart from her family. Theodore's attitude brightened considerably when he learned that Flora's younger brother, Sonny, was training in Texas as an aviator.

By the 1st of July, Theodore would write to Kermit, "After some hesitation and misgiving, Mother and I have become much pleased with Quentin's engagement. He and Flora seem very happy. She is a dear."[239] But the secret would continue to be kept from the Whitneys and Vanderbilts.

Five days later, Quentin earned his commission as a 1st Lieutenant in the Aviation Section of the Army's Signal Officers' Reserve Corps. The certificate was signed by Newton Baker, the same secretary of war who had denied Colonel Roosevelt's wish to lead volunteers into France. Within a week, Quentin received orders to report to active duty at Fort Wood, New York. In another ten days, he would be heading overseas with a detachment of fliers, many of whom would become part of the 95th Aero Squadron.

About that time, Flora sent him a longing letter to take with him abroad: "With every breath I draw, there will be a thought of you and a wish for your safety, success and good luck. Also, I will cling to my foolish habit of wishing on falling stars, new moons, wish bones, etc., and the wish will always, always be for you." She added with prescient wistfulness, "And if things are so to be that you don't come back, why then the slim consolation I will have will be that your influence has made me what I am . . ."[240]

The air temperature at the 14th Street wharf on the east side of Manhattan was climbing to the oppressive upper 80s in the late morning of Monday, July 23rd when a car carrying Quentin Roosevelt and his parents pulled up dockside. Nearby, the Whitney steam yacht, *Whileaway,* tied up with Flora, Gertrude, and Harry on board. This was to be a private family gathering to see Quentin off to war. Flora had somehow convinced her reluctant parents to bid safe travel to the person who meant the most in the world to her.

The days leading up to Quentin's scheduled departure on the *RMS Orduna* had produced cherished memories that he could hold close to his heart on the long journey across the hazardous North Atlantic. On Saturday, Quentin's last night at Sagamore Hill, Edith had supervised the packing, secretly tucking bread and chocolate deep into his bags for hungry days at sea. More evocatively, she had climbed the stairs to Quentin's room, silently and alone, to tuck him in one last time. No matter that he was a U.S. Air Service flier and engaged to be married. Quentin would forever be her baby.

Flora wanted to spend the eve of Quentin's departure alone with her fiancé. According to what Quentin later told his mother, Flora had arranged for them to spend the night secluded on the *Whileaway*. Perhaps in a private moment in a darkened place, she repeated a sentiment from her earlier letter: "There is nothing in me that could make you care for me as much as I care for you . . . it is absolute worship on my part."[241]

The *Orduna*, a three-year-old 550-foot ocean liner, was being readied for departure. It had been requisitioned earlier from the Cunard Line by the British admiralty to transport troops between New York and Liverpool via Halifax, Nova Scotia.

When the ship's departure was delayed, the Roosevelts and Whitneys opted wisely to leave the young couple to themselves. It was about then, according to author Renehan, that Flora sprinkled a small amount of salt water on Quentin's uniform in a good luck wish.

Quentin later recalled his final few hours with Flora in a letter to his mother:

> Monday after I left you, Fouf and I had lunch, then [we] trotted down to the boat. Of course, it didn't go at two, not till nearly three, so she and I sat on a bale of hides and waited until it was almost time for the boat to go. Then I packed her off, for I don't think she could have stood watching the

boat pull out. She was wonderfully brave and kept herself in. I don't see how she did for I don't mind confessing I felt pretty down myself when I saw the Statue of Liberty and the New York skyline dropping below the horizon. Still, I'll be back sometime within a year, I've a hunch, and anyway, I'm gone now and there's no use objecting.[242]

Flora remembered their parting in much the same way. She confided to Ethel the next day: "The accumulated sea of tears had gradually mounted and had now lodged itself in my throat, and I thought . . . ah, I will go down to my room [in the yacht] and have it out, and I'll feel better—but that didn't happen. . . . I read last night until I was so tired that I knew that I would fall right asleep, which I did."[243]

On his sixth day at sea, Quentin vowed to Flora in writing, "If I am not killed, there will be a time when I shall draw into New York again, and you will be there on the pier, just as you were when I left, and there will be no parting for us for a long time to come."[244]

Fifteen

Adventures at Issoudun

The Orduna lumbered northeastward, its lone, great stack disgorging coal-colored exhaust into the humid air. The big ship hugged the New England coastline, its twin masts trimmed of their colors as a precaution. The Orduna was bound for the Nova Scotian port of Halifax with its prized cargo of apprehensive but keyed-up young warriors. "Ah, sweet, war is a cruel master to us all," Quentin wrote to Flora in the early hours of his journey. "I love you, dearest, and always shall—far more than you know or believe."[245]

The gregarious son of Theodore Roosevelt sought to stave off the blues by reacquainting himself with eight other Air Service officers sailing with him. Some he knew well from Mineola, others were strangers, but all were eager to get to Europe to fly for their country.

Bunking in the ship's bowels, well-segregated from those who wore wings, was a detachment of about 50 cadets. Quentin went below in search of his buddy, Hamilton Coolidge. Although he was fully trained and deserving of a commission, Ham's paperwork had not come through, and he was consigned to steerage with the lightly-trained privates. During the trip, however, his seniority would be acknowledged, and Ham would be designated acting first sergeant in charge of the unit. For now, he pronounced himself upbeat, informing his mother by letter, "I am as cheerful as can be . . ."[246]

It would be the better part of a week before the Orduna made it to Halifax, and there it berthed for what seemed to Quentin like an endless wait for the naval convoy that would escort it across the North Atlantic. He complained to his mother of the dull life aboard ship, its main activities confined to "shuffleboard, interminable bridge games [at a quarter of a cent a point], and reading."[247]

"All of us are heartily sick of it," he confessed to Flora. But abruptly, in the next line of his letter, his emotions warmed. "Wake or sleep, you are always in my thoughts. . . . Sometimes I wonder whether I shall ever see you again and feel your sweet lips on mine."[248]

It was apparently a coincidence that Flora's family was on a fishing getaway along the Restigouche River, deep in the New Brunswick woods, just a few hundred miles from Halifax when Quentin was cooling his heels. Secluding herself with pen and paper in an anglers' club in rural Kedgwick, she anxiously fretted, "Oh, Quentin, why does it have to be? It isn't possible that it can be for any ultimate good that all the best people in the world have to be killed. It isn't possible that you will be [killed]—no I don't honestly believe that you will be. . . . Quentin, be careful, please."[249]

"We are still stuck here [in Halifax], and goodness knows when we will get away and get over to the other side," Quentin replied to Flora. "Still, even though things are dull and stupid, I'm managing to have a pretty good time getting to know the outfit. They really are a corking bunch." It seems that 19-year-old Quentin, as the youngest officer, had been kindheartedly nicknamed "Babe" and "the Kid" by his shipmates. "I am to give my baptismal party [buy drinks] when we get to Paris," he predicted.[250]

Events began to move swiftly in the Nova Scotia port. The convoy was approaching. "It was great to see our escort come out of nowhere," Hamilton wrote to his mother. "First, all we could see were brilliant flashes of light on the horizon and, hardly two minutes later, we [made] out the forms of the tiny destroyers tearing through the sea toward us. We all felt quite relieved."[251]

Soon thereafter, Quentin excitedly announced in a postcard home, "Goodbye Mother dear—we're off at last. You'll hear from me from London."[252]

The Royal Navy gets the credit for promoting the use of armed convoys to protect merchant vessels and troopships during the Great War. In fact, in the view of historian Paul E. Fontenoy, it was the effective use of convoys that blunted Germany's submarine warfare campaign.[253] Long term that may have been true but in the summer of 1917, it fell to Quentin to take on-board responsibility for protecting his ship from marauding U-boats. He was given oversight of submarine surveillance as the *Orduna* resolutely plowed toward England. "I'm officer in charge of the men who are watching for submarines," he told Flora, "so I have been up all night seeing that the men were on their jobs."

In carrying out his duty, Quentin had plenty of time to ponder his future. From time to time, at night on deck, he would while away the hours by gazing upward into the warm, starlit blackness. Hamilton Coolidge later remembered that while Quentin was "thoroughly enthusiastic about the job ahead," he would occasionally express "fatalistic thoughts" and surrender to "black gloom." "Often we walked together in the evenings on the unlighted decks," Hamilton recalled. "He was completely absorbed in his love for Flora. . . . Never was he sorry for himself. Almost never did he speak of the dangers ahead of him, and then only in a most casual way. Once in a great while he wondered, 'Shall I ever come back?' But far more often it was, 'I wonder how long it will be before we come back.'"[254]

To Flora, Quentin wrote of his dream: "Oftentimes . . . I have pictured to myself the carrier being towed into New York and, in all the crowd, your face stands out before me. Somehow, when I think of that, I feel sure that I shall not be killed—fate could not take away so great a joy from me."[255]

The "appalling dullness" and "total atrophy of the brain" that Quentin experienced during the transatlantic journey ended temporarily on August 5 when he took part in an onboard boxing match. "I succeeded in getting [a punch] on the nose which the doctor thinks may have broken it," he reported to his mother. "It doesn't look crooked, tho, so I think he may be wrong." Son tried to relieve mother's certain anxiety when he added, "The bread and chocolate [are] just finished and were a howling success."[256]

As summer waned and Flora returned to Long Island, she received scant emotional support at home. She told Quentin, "Strange as it may seem, I never talk about you or mention your name to my family. I suppose I will—sometime."[257]

On the other hand, the Roosevelts showered her with increasing attention and affection. Sagamore Hill became her refuge. One time, while Quentin was at sea, Flora was welcomed to dinner by Theodore and Edith. "I cannot overstate how fond I have grown of her, and how much I respect and admire her," Theodore told his son afterward. "[Flora is] so pretty and young and yet so good and really wise."[258]

Between visits, Flora received admiring letters signed, "Quentin's Father." "If things go well, dear Flora, I believe that you and he will know the greatest of all kinds of happiness—that of married lovers who, all their lives, [will] remain lovers. In any event, you and he have had some golden months, whatever comes hereafter."[259]

In a personal note to Flora that same day, Edith candidly observed, "His love for you has made a man of Quentin. Before it came to him, he was just a dear boy."[260]

Flora's frequent presence in Oyster Bay filled a huge void in the Roosevelt nest. In addition to Quentin's leaving, Ted and Archie also had gone overseas. As arranged, they reported directly to General Pershing at his Paris headquarters where they asked for immediate "service with the troops." Pershing's deputies assigned 2nd Lieutenant Archie Roosevelt to the 16th Infantry, and soon saw to it that Major Ted Roosevelt was appointed battalion commander with the 26th Infantry. Eventually, Archie was placed in his older brother's unit. As expected, Kermit and his wife, Belle, sailed for the Middle East to work with the Royal Engineers in Mesopotamia in the fight against Ottoman Empire forces allied with Germany.

Surveying the weighty events of the past month or so, Theodore voiced a sense of isolation but, at the same time, paternal fulfillment: "It is dreadful to have had you all go, and it would have been far worse not to have you go," he confessed in a letter to Quentin. "My veins thrill with pride when I think of you."[261]

In gentle defiance of Theodore's dictate that Roosevelt women would not follow their husbands to the front, Eleanor Alexander Roosevelt, Ted's 29-year-old wife of seven years, sailed July 24, 1917 for Paris. In the end, she left hastily, with her father-in-law's reluctant blessing, because of an imminent government rule that was to forbid soldiers' wives from going to France.

Eleanor left three young children (the oldest was six) in the care of her mother to serve as a full-time volunteer with the Y.M.C.A in Paris. At the time, the Y.M.C.A. was responsible for managing recreational diversions for U.S. forces abroad, and Eleanor assumed the obligation of canteen manager and teacher of beginner's French to American soldiers. Most of all, being in Paris satisfied her yearning to be near Ted.

For the duration, Eleanor would stay in a large Parisian house owned by her aunt, Alice Hoffman. It was at the edge of the city, just west of the *Arc de Triomphe*, on what is now Avenue Foch, one of the most fashionable boulevards in the city. That residence, and Eleanor's fulsome presence in it, would become home away from home for the young Roosevelts abroad. It also would serve as an essential refuge for Quentin in his months to come at Issoudun.

The *Orduna* navigated the Irish Sea, steamed up the Mersey River, and docked uneventfully in Liverpool on Sunday, August 12. Shouldering their weapons and loads of other gear, Quentin, Hamilton, and the rest of the detachment packed into a "filthy little troop train" and shot off for Folkstone along the Strait of Dover. Window views along the way prompted Hamilton to remark to his mother how impressed he was with "the neatness of everything and the charm of the little country farmhouses, always of brick and good repair."[262]

Additionally, Quentin observed, "The hedgerows are green, and the little canals mirror the sky, and all about, there is a feel of 'lots-of-time' quiet as tho the war were an idle speculation and not hideous reality."[263]

Life outside the window changed dramatically once the troops steamed across the English Channel to Boulogne and boarded another train for Paris. "The signs of war were everywhere," Quentin told Flora. "Every little while there would come a concentrating [sic] camp of some sort—a food depot or a gang of Chinese or German prisoners that worked along the railroad tracks."[264]

The street scenes in Paris were even more disturbing to Quentin's eyes: "It is not the Paris that we used to tour, the Paris of five years past," he relayed to Flora. He wrote:

The streets are there but the crowds are different. There are no more young men in the crowds unless in uniform. Everywhere you see women in black, and there is no more cheerful shouting and laughing. Many, many of the women have a haunted look in their eyes as if they had seen something too terrible for forgetfulness. There is a sobering like no other feeling I have known. The sight of a boy my age helped across the street by someone who takes pity on his poor blind eyes. It all makes me feel older.[265]

While Quentin refreshed himself at Eleanor's home—"a delightful place at the edge of the *bois*"—Flora was back home aboard the *Whileaway* alerting him to an unforeseen conversation that had occurred out of her earshot after dinner at Sagamore Hill. "Apparently your father said that if you got off at any time, for a certain length of time, and were home, he would very much wish us to be married. In fact, he said he would do everything in his power to fix it. (Don't quote me as having said that)," she cautioned.[266]

Following a breakfast of "war bread and eggs" with Eleanor, Quentin hurried off to American headquarters to receive his assignment. There would be no immediate flying at the front for him. He was ordered to report to the American training school that was under construction at Issoudun, a city dating to the Middle Ages, a three- or four-hour drive south of Paris. "I don't fancy that I shall care very much for it, tho," he told Flora. "I confess I'm sorry, for I wanted to get started flying and have it over with. I know my back wouldn't last very long."[267]

The new 3rd Aviation Instruction Center was budding from the soil in the flat farmers' fields of central France. According to military aviation historian Alan Toelle, an American construction team of 200 carpenters and machinists had arrived at Issoudun three weeks earlier, and three ships' worth of materiel and supplies had made their way to the site from a French port on the backs of 47 Packard trucks. The first task was to complete a railroad to access the site of the new aviation camp, Toelle reported.[268]

Lieutenant Cord Meyer was prominent among the crew at Issoudun. Born in New York City and crew captain at Yale, he was, at 22, solidly-built and broad-shouldered, and a friend of Quentin's. Cord had trained at Mineola and been a member of the Army's first reserve flying squadron. Now, in the temporary absence of Hamilton Coolidge, who had been ordered to stay behind in Paris, Cord had assumed the role of Quentin's best buddy.

Quentin was hardly unpacked at Issoudun when he was given "more responsibility than I had ever had." Appointed the camp's supply officer and acting transportation officer, he would initially be responsible for keeping a fleet of 52 motor trucks in running order. His years of tinkering with engines and all things mechanical had paid off but ironically, they frustrated his broader hopes. "I also have to look after endless supplies of gasoline and parts. . . . In between times I act as buffer between irate [French] railroad officials full of jabbering complaints and American construction officers who would like to consign the entire French railroad system," he told Flora.[269] He was one of only two officers there who spoke fluent French.

Quentin took advantage of his first Sunday off to scrub up. "There isn't a bath tub within less than 25 miles," he pointed out with seeming disgust. "Cord and I became so desperate that we took to our motorcycles—as supply officer and quartermaster officer we have them—and went off 20 miles to the nearest river to swim. . . . Issoudun is a forsaken hole." To Foufie, he bid, "Goodbye, dearest sweetheart, and think of me and write often—as I always think of you. All my heart is yours and given without recall."[270] The next day, Quentin was nearly killed. "I have been in two motorcycle mishaps," he reported to Flora.

> I was on my way over to Nevers [70 miles away] to arrange some supplies, and Cord, who is mess sergeant, had gone with me on his machine. [About half way there], we were passing a truck with him in the lead when, for some unknown reason, he slowed up. I was coming on him so I slammed on my brake, which jammed, and so I started on down the road skidding side[ways] and every which way. Cord put on power to get out of the way, but as [my] brake was locked I could do nothing, so I saw a bully spill coming

my way and tried my best to get clear of the truck. The next thing I remember is lying on the bank with Cord and the truck driver pouring water on me and trying to put first aid compresses on my face. I was pretty well banged up—a couple of deep cuts on my face, some loose teeth and two hands with not much palm left. By luck, we happened to be near the aviation school. . . . We had intended to stop there, and I was bundled into the truck and sent over there to the hospital and bandaged up. Then, after about an hour, I went over to the barracks. . . . This morning, stiff all over and about an inch deep in bandage, I had to go into town to see about loading some cars. As there was no auto, I went by motorcycle side car, and on the way in, the man who was driving ran into the wall of a house and shot me out onto my ear. That time I re-opened both hands and laid out one hip with a bad cut and bone bruise so that at this moment, tho in excellent form, I am somewhat dilapidated.[271]

Back in New York, autumn was approaching and the breeze off Long Island Sound was picking up by the day—enough to vigorously whip the four-star service flag that the Roosevelts had hoisted at Sagamore Hill. It silently and honorably proclaimed that the family inside had four of its own in uniform.

Edith Roosevelt was going about her days, but she was unable to shake the worry of having a quartet of sons in harm's way overseas. "It is like becoming blind or deaf—one just lives on, only in a different way," she wrote to a friend.[272]

Edith spent a good deal of time looking after Theodore who was now alarmingly portly and increasingly housebound due to a swollen, reddened leg that he had injured in the River of Doubt in Brazil. In the absence of effective antibiotics, it had not healed. Worse, the ex-president was fighting off another bout of the debilitating Cuban fever, a variety of malaria, that he had contracted 20 years earlier during the Spanish-American War. With too much time on his hands, Theodore continued to fulminate against his absence from the action in Europe. He told Quentin, "My disappointment at not going myself was, down at bottom, chiefly reluctance to see you four, in whom my heart was wrapped, exposed to danger while I stayed at home in do-nothing ease and safety. But," he added with some brightening, "the feeling has now been completely swallowed in my immense pride in all of you."[273]

To occupy his hours and bring in some money, Theodore took on two editorial assignments that would give voice to his increasingly strident opinions. For $25,000 a year, he would write critically about the war for the widely respected *Kansas City Star*, and pen a monthly editorial for *Metropolitan* magazine, owned by Flora's father, for a similarly lucrative fee. The compensation, he said, would be used to launch Archie and Quentin on their careers once they came home.

In many of his war writings, Theodore conceded that President Wilson deserved to be backed up for "whatever good he does," but Roosevelt was reluctant to give his outright approval to Wilson's war policies. T. R. simply could not get beyond his personal distaste for the man. A blunt letter Theodore sent to the legendary Midwest newspaper editor William Allen White encapsulated his views: "Fundamentally, our whole trouble in this country is due more to Wilson than any other man. . . . He not only appeals to base and foolish men, he appeals also to Mr. Hyde who, in many good and honorable men, lurks behind the Dr. Jekyll in their souls."[274]

Quentin and Flora's 3,500-mile separation was causing temptations to build up on both ends. But to their credit, the young couple was forthcoming about them to each other. For example, in September, there was a dinner party at The Breakers in Newport attended by Flora, some relatives, and "six sailor boys." "Gould [Jennings] is beginning to say 'nice' things to me," she reported to Quentin, "but I am not a bit encouraging, and Joe says he is falling in love with me, but I'm sure it's not true. . . . After the others had left Joe turned and said, 'I think it's perfectly rotten of you not to tell if you are engaged to Quentin or not.'"[275]

From France, Quentin relayed to Flora word of a father-son type of conversation that he had had with Hamilton about the enticements that awaited American soldiers on the streets of Paris. "He was worried about me in Paris with our crowd," Quentin allowed. "He said—which is quite true—that none of them have any morals, and the only way to allow for that was to make up your mind beforehand [about the temptations]. He was evidently afraid that I'd just said to myself, 'I'll see when the time comes.' I told him—which was the truth—that I didn't see how anyone who was in love with a girl could think of going on a party with 'chickens,' and that I had no intentions of doing anything like that or even speaking to one." Quentin further reassured Flora, "I promise you, dearest, that you not think that of me."[276]

"I never for an instant worried," Flora replied. "I trust you too implicitly dear. . . . I wouldn't think of suspecting you did anything that I know *you* disapprove of or that you know *I* objected to. I love you always and live for the time when you will be back, and we will be 'us' again."[277]

As the Issoudun base took form, Quentin was working productively and winning plaudits from his men. Unambiguous testimony came from a colleague in a letter that has survived: "We have a real man commanding us now," Sgt. Orrin A. Gardiner, Jr., wrote to his parents around this time. "Just like his father I guess—one of Colonel Roosevelt's sons. We have only had him a short while but would do more for him than all the time we knew the other man."[278]

Despite his successes, Quentin was intensely frustrated. At the end of August, there were no planes yet at camp and thus no opportunities for the airmen to fly. The most promising news was word that parts of an airplane hangar were being shipped to Issoudun. "I want to start flying. I am very anxious to get up to the front as soon as possible," Quentin told Flora.[279]

Predictably, he and Cord Meyer took matters into their own hands. "[Cord] has arranged for [us] to go over to the French school [at Chateauroux] and fly," Quentin announced. "He flew twice with an instructor then went alone." He and Cord likely flew two-seat Nieuports that were in extensive use by the French at the time. "As except for the controls, the machines aren't much different from the Curtiss," Quentin reported. "They are as safe as an auto and as safe, really, as the old [Jenny]."[280]

His officer's rank and fluency in French opened the way to one of the most pleasurable episodes of Quentin's 10-month stay in central France. On his Saturday afternoons and Sundays off, he would fly from Issoudun to visit a French family that had taken a shine to him by happenstance. One time, Benjamin Normant, a well-to-do businessman with a woolen textile factory and home in the commune of Romorantin, northwest of Issoudun, had broken down on the road. Quentin came along, tinkered under the car's hood, and soon set Normant on his way. When Normant learned that Quentin was Theodore Roosevelt's son and that he was conversant in French, he invited Quentin to spend off-time with him, his wife Edithe, and their family at their riverside chateau.

"They are nice people," Quentin informed Flora. "I went over there last Sunday . . . and they treated me like family. They said the next time I was to bring clothes over, and they would have a hot bath waiting for me—and also to bring a friend if I wished. Consequently, Cord and I are going over again next Sunday to relive our approach to civilization again."[281] The Normant family would endure as a valued source of companionship and support for Quentin as the long months in France wore on.

Quentin's loneliest hours came when he returned from excursions, whether to Romorantin or Paris, or from remote destinations to retrieve truck parts. Alone in his bunk, his young heart ached as he picked up a pen in the evening stillness: "I'm very lonely, and I want you so," he confessed to Flora. "Come what may, war cannot take from us the thing that has made life sweet and wonderful, cannot deprive me of the thrill and glory of that moment when, loving you as I did, I knew that you felt it too."[282]

Following a visit to Paris by Quentin, Eleanor advised Flora, "I have never seen anyone quite as homesick as Quentin. While he was here, the thing he wanted most was to sit quietly at home with me, talk about you and what you had done together this spring." Eleanor assured his fiancée, "I will keep a constant eye on him and shall report to you from time to time on how everything is going."[283]

A probable transfer to the war zone and the prospect of marriage "before anything happened," were relentlessly bearing down on Quentin's psyche. Flora's parents had learned of their engagement and, now, talk of marriage had intensified within both families. Perhaps, they wondered, Flora could sail to France to wed there before Quentin was sent to battle. But unexpectedly, at the time, Quentin was having second thoughts.

In a rambling letter to Foufie on September 9, Quentin tried to explain himself: "Of course, the thing that I want most in the world . . . is to marry you and go out into the hurry and struggle of life. . . . And suppose we were married, and I came back here in a month to be killed or, worse still, wounded in some hasty fashion as I have seen, so that for the rest of my life I could be but a cripple, a helpless, useless chain to which you are tied. For that I am doubtful of father's suggestion. . . . For that, I would not give you sorrow more than this war brings to everyone."[284]

Aware of his muddled thinking, Eleanor scolded Quentin for being "selfish" and "for seeing only the man's side of it." She explained, "Even if you don't come back, [Flora] will be much happier for having been married."[285]

Apparently chastened by Eleanor's admonition, Quentin righted himself four days later, asking Foufie, "If I'm in the spring offensive, I ought to have [a long leave] at the end of next summer. If I do, will you marry me then? There's the first real proposal I've made to you, and please don't say no."[286]

Unexpectedly, though, Quentin received his orders. "Just last Monday, the word came thru that Cord and I were assigned to the 1st Aero Squadron, and to report there at once for flying," he alerted Flora.[287] Talk of marriage ceased; he had been called to war.

Sixteen

An *Embusqué?*

Quentin's assignment to the 1st Aero Squadron on September 10, 1917 set up a noteworthy string of events that later would become the most contentious and divisive of his military career. In the months ahead, those events would pit brother against brother, sons against their father, and even Quentin against himself. At its core were disturbing allegations that the youngest Roosevelt son, sworn to defend his country, was less than courageous, a shirker or, as the French would say, un embusqué.

When the call to serve in the squadron came, Quentin's response produced some unexpected reactions. Alan D. Toelle, the U.S. historian who, in 2012, published an exceptional study of Quentin's military career, concluded, "Heeding the worst of advice, and with the lamest of excuses, he refused [the] call. He would spend many months contemplating the word *embusqué* before another such call would be directed his way."[288]

Was Quentin naïve or was his choice a straightforward accession to the practical but self-serving reasoning of his superior officers? At the time, he was forthcoming about what took place, notably in letters to Flora and his mother. In fact his recall of the events, including the repeated use of indirect quotes by the participants, enables us to understand what happened, using reconstructed dialogue:

Quentin (Sept. 13): I am very sorry to leave the supply department just at this moment; I had expected to leave it about three months later. As it is, I leave just as I was beginning to get things running well and had really become attached to the men who were under me.

Unidentified supply sergeant: Oh hell, sir, can't you take me with you to that outfit?

Quentin: That made me feel a lump in my throat, if you know the feeling. That was pretty nice of him, but I have to do it [obey orders]. If I had wanted to, I could have stayed with the job—but it wasn't worth it. If I had stuck [as supply officer] this time, it meant that I was running the risk of being stuck with it permanently, a sort of *embusqué* occupation. And so, I am changed, and become the juniorest of junior lieutenants in an outfit composed mostly of regular Army flyers. Still, I get back to planes again—and it means that I'll probably see service [at the front] fairly soon. I was beginning to feel rather like an *embusqué* but this changes it all. I don't mind so much an out and out slacker who says he is afraid or unwilling to go, but I hate the one who gets a bullet-proof job in the Red Cross or Y.M.C.A. and then proceeds to talk of 'doing his bit.'

Quentin (Sept. 17): I was all prepared to leave at once for the 1st Squadron. Major [Lawrence] Churchill, our base commanding officer, met me at the station and on the way out in the car, began talking to me about Lt. Colonel [Raynal] Bolling's visit to camp.

Major Churchill: I gave you a darned good recommendation to him, but why are you changing to that other outfit? You don't gain much for you're getting some flying over here, and the experience you've gained in supply work is worth twice what you can get of the job of plain, flying lieutenant.

Quentin: It was a big surprise to me, but the upshot was that I agreed to put it [the decision] before the colonel who is second in command of the American Air Service in France. To my surprise, he agreed with the major.

Colonel Bolling: The only reason I was transferring you was for the flying. If you are getting your flying here, stay by all means. You apparently have made a good job of this one. The reason I sent you [to Issoudun] was to give you experience. If I were you, I should stay, for it will count a good deal more in a man's favor if he has made a good job of something like this supply position of yours than if he has merely flown as a junior lieutenant in a squadron.

Quentin (Sept. 20): After that, of course, I stayed, especially as [the colonel] promised to put me in a squadron at the front as soon as they got started sending them up there. I am glad in a way, for now I know for certain that I shall not be "*embusquéd*" here.

The key to understanding Quentin's decision to decline a flight assignment is knowing that Colonel Bolling was the top training and supply officer in France at the time of his intervention. Ten days before his crucial conversation with Quentin, Bolling had been appointed Director of Air Service Supply for the AEF. Undoubtedly he was inclined to ensure that critical supply and infrastructure positions in France were staffed with capable men such as Quentin Roosevelt, and that people of his caliber were not lost to rival officers in the flying squadrons.

In his study, historian Toelle speculates that Quentin's orders to fly "must have originated close to Pershing . . . since the 1st Aero Squadron was being sent to the [combat] Zone of Advance."[289] Could Colonel Bolling have wanted to inoculate Theodore Roosevelt's son from the dangers of aerial combat in its early and uncertain days? Toelle says no, but whatever the rationale for the senior officers' intervention, the colonel did not make good on his promise to send Quentin to an air squadron at the front. Soon after giving his advice to young Roosevelt, Colonel Bolling was transferred out of supply command. And six months later, on March 26, 1918, he became the first high-ranking American officer to lose his life in the Great War. Colonel Bolling's vehicle was ambushed by a nest of German machine gunners while on an inspection tour of the front lines at Estrées with Britain's Royal Flying Corps.

"News," Quentin announced to Flora. "I think you'll probably be pleased. My orders have been changed, and I am not to be placed on active flying service at once." He marked the change by enjoying "a delightful Sunday in Paris with Eleanor, Mass at Notre Dame and time in the café scene."[290]

Flora responded without comment on his decision: "Dearest, I love you and want you home so terribly and if you don't come home ever, I honestly don't want to live. It couldn't be worthwhile."[291]

Quentin reported the chain of recent events to his mother (notably, *not* to his father who may not have understood as readily). "I am going to be here [at Issoudun] probably for a couple of months before I get sent up to the front. . . . I am, as Arch would say, 'busy as a one-armed paper hanger with an itch' trying to keep about four different jobs straight." The camp, he said, is growing "like a mushroom out of nothing."[292]

On September 22, the first airplane for cadet use reached base. It was a French-made Nieuport 15-meter type, a diminutive open-cockpit pursuit biplane equipped with a 120 horsepower rotary engine. It was, said Quentin, "an object of considerable curiosity." About a week later, eight more Nieuports flew in, setting up plenty of opportunities for flight training.

Quentin could not wait to get airborne; he saw his chance and took it. A French flyer, piloting an antique Caudron aircraft, landed unexpectedly at the base late one day. "I told him I'd put [the plane] inside for him," Quentin relayed to Flora. "When I got there, I found his goggles, clothes and everything else in the machine. The temptation was too big. . . . So I swore the mechanics to secrecy and took it up. It's easy—as easy as the Curtiss. However, my back is bad—I think it slows me a little."[293]

As the weeks wore on, the young supply chief had no time to second-guess his decision to stay at Issoudun. He had to inspect the vehicle fleet weekly, oversee the delivery of carloads of "things, ranging from stoves to monkey wrenches" and ensure an adequate supply of gasoline from French railway officials "with an early Neolithic range of intelligence." Additionally, he had been asked to shape up "a disorganized squadron" to see what he could make of it. "It was," he said, "a very big step toward getting my own squadron to take out in the spring when we start sending air squadrons to the front."[294]

Quentin offered his mother some unexpected news. "Guess who has been put in charge of the Red Cross canteen here? Miss Givenwilson! I nearly fell over, first backwards and then into her arms, for she seemed like a real message from home."[295] Irene Givenwilson, Flora's one-time governess and Gertrude Vanderbilt Whitney's recent secretary, had arrived unanticipated for a six-month tour.

Along the front in eastern France, there was a lingering stalemate. Earlier in the year, a major French ground offensive had failed, producing little else but tens of thousands of casualties. Some desperate French soldiers resorted to mutiny and were court-martialed. Into that torrid cauldron hurried elements of America's 1st Infantry Division, many of whom were not fully trained for hand-to-hand and artillery combat. General Pershing ordered them to the less-dangerous easternmost edge of the front to be schooled and phased into combat. In *When Trumpets Call*, a splendid retrospective of Theodore Roosevelt's post-White House years, Patricia O'Toole observed: "The story of the [AEF] mobilization was a story of indecision, delay, mistaken assumptions and epic failures of coordination." Secretary of War Baker later confirmed that view in testimony before Congress: "Accustomed to peace, we were not ready," he admitted.[296] By the war's end, the U.S. placed some two million men into Europe.

Irene Givenwilson with Secretary of War
Newton D. Baker and General John J. Pershing.
(Courtesy National Archives and Records Administration
111-SC-7842)

Archie and Ted, at the front with the 26th Infantry, confirmed the deficiency of readiness in letters home to their father. They complained regularly of shortages of good food, warm clothing, and boots. Although troubled by the situation, Theodore was not surprised. His unwavering public criticism of the Wilson Administration's war conduct had extended down to conditions experienced by fighting men at the front. His overriding worry was more parochial: two sons fighting within the same division, Archie as company commander and Ted as battalion leader. "I emphatically disbelieve in two boys being together, where one has anything to say about the duty of the other," he told his sons in separate letters.[297]

The slow American buildup was affecting the Air Service as well. General Pershing originally had wanted 260 air combat squadrons operational by the end of 1918 but was forced to settle for 20 percent fewer because of shortages and delays. Observation squadrons were his priority, followed by those that would engage in pursuit, and night and day bombing.[298] Because the U.S. aircraft industry could not commence production fast enough, Pershing turned to the French to supply American flyers with 5,000 war planes, a collection of fighters, bombers, pursuit, and reconnaissance aircraft. It would be February 1918 before any U.S. squadron entered aerial combat.[299]

As Quentin's days at Issoudun ground on, it seemed that Air Service brass didn't know what to do with him. From week to month, he received random assignments—"stupid little jobs" he called them—that made him feel as if he were pigeonholed and "lost in some backwater branch of the game."[300] In late October it was a "beastly job" in Paris of overseeing 50 men en route to England to study technical and mechanical supply work. He protested the assignment and was able to avoid the duty. A few weeks later, he was directed temporarily to a debarkation port to supervise the unloading of supplies from arriving ships—"I am not going to have anything to do half the time. . . . [T]here will be two weeks with no boats in."[301] And then, in early December, there was the duty command of a headquarters detachment: "It is really no job for a flying lieutenant."[302] In frustration, he turned his attention skyward.

With plenty of Nieuports finally available at the airfield in the fall of 1917, Quentin resumed aerial training, often under the tutelage of a French monitor. He described formation flying, what his instructors termed *vol de groupe*, as "the prettiest" kind. "They send about seven machines up at the time," he explained. "It looks fairly easy too, but when you get up in the air, trying to keep a 120-horsepower kite in its position in a V formation, with planes on either side of you, you begin to hold different ideas as to its easiness."[303]

Quentin was thrilled with the Nieuports. "These little fast machines are delightful. You feel so at home in them, for there is just room in the cockpit for you and your controls, and not an inch more. And then they're so quick to act. . . . You could do two loops in a Nieuport in the time it takes a Curtiss to do one."[304]

Old friend Hamilton Coolidge had arrived at Issoudun in time to watch the camp reinvent itself, in response to the crowds of men that were swarming in. In October, he and his mates were "flying to our heart's content from 6 till 10 a.m. and from 2:30 till 5 p.m." By mid-December, he had completed training in acrobatics, tactics that could be used by pilots to escape the enemy in close confrontation. Hamilton confessed, "I had moments of doubt beforehand whether my mind would continue to function normally when I was upside down in midair and dropping like a stone. . . . If you forgot and did the wrong thing at the wrong time, the strain would probably be too great for the wings, which would promptly collapse."[305]

Flyers sometimes would stray intentionally from their routines to have a little fun barnstorming the countryside. Hamilton acknowledged that at times he would "get in a good, reliable plane and fly all over the country, just five or ten feet above the ground. You chase autos, and the farmers are scared stiff sometimes, but you always go up before you get to them."[306]

In spite of the derring-do in the skies, the safety record at Issoudun was considered acceptable. "We have had a good many pretty nasty smashes," Quentin observed. "No one has been killed yet or even permanently injured." But Quentin had a close call in late November. He told Flora of a time when his plane had just left the ground. A chunk of airfield mud rose up, struck his propeller and shattered it. Parts of the propeller sliced into the gas tank, and the plane burst into flames. "I made a wild snatch at my safety belt and got it undone, and slid out of the plane . . . before the wheels were really down on the ground again. It can't have taken me more than 30 seconds and yet when I got out, my boots and pant legs were on fire."[307] From his telling, it seemed an uneventful incident– all in a day's work. Incredibly, he was not seriously injured and wrote nothing more of the incident.

Back home, the October 12th *The New York Times* headlined, "Colonel at Health Farm." With Edith's steely encouragement, Theodore Roosevelt indeed had signed up at a fat farm to get some excess poundage off his waist to help reduce his blood pressure. The Stanford, Connecticut camp was run by former prize fighter Jack Cooper and featured diet regimens, daily massage, and vigorous exercise. At check in, Cooper was said to have found Theodore at least 35 pounds too heavy. *The Times'* report explained that the ex-president was overworked and needed rest. In fact, the opposite was true. "I lead a life of irksome monotony," he had admitted to Archie.

The reluctant colonel was ordered by Cooper to hike three miles each day before breakfast, submit to a lengthy massage, and engage in several hours of strenuous training. "The exercises bore until I feel as if I should scream," he confessed to Archie, "but I am losing weight a little, and the people of the house amuse and interest me."[308]

After nearly two weeks at camp, Theodore was back at Sagamore Hill looking more exhausted than anything else. His middle may have receded a few inches but his gargantuan appetite persisted. Edith observed, "I fear it was too much of a strain on his nerves."[309]

About a month later, Theodore was off on a campaign swing to Canada to pitch war bonds, with Edith, Ethel, and hoped-for future daughter-in-law Flora in tow. "My dearest, look where I am," Flora exclaimed in a note to Quentin from Toronto. "Aren't you perfectly astounded?" The ex-presidential party had arrived by train at the city's opulent Government House where Theodore planned a fist-pounding plea to Canadians to buy bonds for the nation's Victory

Loan Campaign. The whole thing resembled an old-fashioned, high profile political event, and it was almost too much for the novice Flora. "I am severely terrified," she wrote, but "having the most thrilling time."

While the men backslapped each other and smoked malodorous cigars, the Roosevelt women were consigned to a "ladies' luncheon." "The whole thing is so new and interesting to me that I remained open-mouthed the entire time," Flora reported. "My tongue becomes paralyzed . . . and I am perfectly incapable of articulating. My stock phrase is, 'What wonderful air up here—how invigorating' or something equally prosaic." In closing, she begged Quentin, "Please do not go into politics."[310]

This author is not alone among Roosevelt historians who have speculated about Theodore's intention in exposing Flora to the high energy scene in Toronto. He was known to believe that among his four sons, it was Quentin who had the aptitude and personal magnetism to succeed in politics later on. Was he shrewdly rehearsing Flora for the role of candidate's wife which, someday, she might have been asked to play? The speculation is delicious.

The approaching year-end holidays at Issoudun brought homesickness and serious illness to Quentin. He turned 20 on November 19. "It wasn't a very cheerful birthday," he acknowledged, notwithstanding a congratulatory cable from Flora and a miniature soldier's prayer book—with photos enclosed— from his parents. Quentin marked his birthday by shopping for his fiancée's Christmas present at Tiffany's in Paris. He couldn't keep the surprise so he told Flora about the gift. It was a 28-piece amber necklace from "a little antique shop on the other side of the Seine." He paid the equivalent of $620 in today's dollars.

"I thought there was a chance you might like it as two bracelets," he wrote. He had it adapted by the jeweler and supplemented with engraved gold snaps. It was hand-delivered to the States by a friend of Eleanor's. Quentin said he envisioned Flora wearing the bracelets with "one of those nice smocks to which I used to object so strongly long ago."[311] Upon receiving the gift in early December,

Flora judged the bracelets "too perfect." Her holiday present to him was a cigarette case—"so offensively unoriginal" she admitted—and two boxes of Benson & Hedges, the English brand of smokes.

In her thank-you letter to Quentin, Flora revealed that she had enrolled in business school to learn typewriting and shorthand. She wanted to help the war effort by working with the Y.M.C.A. or the Red Cross at home and eventually abroad, if she were given the opportunity. "You have no idea how hard [the shorthand] is, and I don't expect that I shall ever get through it," she seemed to sigh.[312]

In the week before Christmas, Quentin came down with pneumonia. In the early 20th century, when antibiotics were not in use, pneumonia was often fatal. Bedridden in the officers' barracks with a debilitating cough, chest pain, and a 104-degree fever, Quentin blamed his condition on the "beastly hole of the camp of ours." He explained that he had been "trailing around here thru mud and cold and draughty unheated barracks."[313]

He had also been complaining to Flora of the "frightful cold" he had experienced while flying high in his open cockpit. "Even in my teddy bear—that's what they call those aviator suits—I freeze pretty generally. . . . Aviation has considerably altered my views on religion," he added. "I don't see how the angels stand it."[314] (One wonders whether Quentin's mates knew that the phrase "teddy bear" originated from publicity after his father declined to shoot a helpless bear while on a presidential hunting trip in Mississippi in 1902.)

Irene Givenwilson stepped in. She refused to send Quentin and other sick men to the base hospital, telling Flora, "You can guess what such places are like." Instead, she said, "I just nursed them in their own bunks"[315] and supplied warm food and comfort. Since her arrival at Issoudun, Miss Givenwilson had adopted Quentin as her special charge. During his convalescence, she did what no other nurse could credibly do: read and reread excerpts of Flora's letters to him to help improve his morale and restore his strength.

"Fouf, you should give him the dickens . . . for not taking care of himself," Hamilton told Flora in a letter around this time. He reassured her, however, that "Miss Givenwilson is taking care of us."[316]

In a letter to his father, Quentin downplayed the severity of the pneumonia. He described it as "mild," and assuaged Theodore with the development that he had just been given permission to read and write again. "It's funny, isn't it, that the *embusqué* member of the family should be the first to be hit by a trench sickness?"[317]

In Paris, Eleanor learned of Quentin's illness and hurried to Issoudun. "[I] found him in bed in a long, narrow barracks inadequately heated by a stove at one end. It was bitterly cold and damp," she recalled in her memoir.[318] The doctor prescribed three weeks of rest and urged Quentin to return to Paris with Eleanor, regain his strength and head to the Riviera for some warm sun. It was an unexpected and probably unwelcome assignment for an airman already feeling like the slacker of a heroic family.

Christmas 1917 within the City of Light, in the comfort of his sister-in-law's warmhearted care, was nonetheless "ghastly" and "rather awful" in Quentin's judgment. "It was my first Christmas away from home, and I hadn't realized what it would mean," he lamented to his mother. The one holiday bright spot, apart from Flora's gift cigarette box, was a framed photo of Theodore and Edith that Eleanor had presented him. "I haven't had any picture of you or Father before," he allowed wistfully to his mother.[319]

During his enforced recuperation, Quentin surely had time to ponder the emerging family backlash to his decision to remain at Issoudun. Already, it was beginning to course from his uniformed siblings. It seems that Arch had sent him a letter "trying to jog up the slacker brother." Later, from Issoudun, Quentin was especially forthright about his tight spot in a long letter to his father:

I'm not over-pleased with my status at present. I know both Ted and Arch feel that I am the *embusqué* member of the family, and the trouble is they're right. The only thing is that *I* [emphasis original] am certainly not responsible for it. I am going ahead with my advanced flying down here as fast as I can, and trying by every means possible to get up in a French or British squadron. . . . What Arch and Ted don't see is that I have really done everything in my powers to get out. . . . I don't stay behind the lines [by] choice, and I'm not hunting for a non-flying occupation.[320]

Quentin had had the unusual option to decline a military assignment, and he had done so. He apparently felt that his superior officers had left him with little real choice but to stay in supply work. Or at least, that was how he seemed to rationalize his situation and a corresponding sense of being ineffectual and vulnerable: "For all I have done to help the war, I might have stayed at home," he told Flora.[321]

In hindsight, an observer is left to wonder whether Quentin felt that he was failing to live up to his father's high expectations. In discussions with the author, historian Toelle brought to mind ex-President Theodore Roosevelt's most well-remembered speech, "Citizenship in a Republic," delivered, ironically, in Paris seven and half years earlier. Here is the key excerpt:

> It is not the critic who counts; not the man who points out how the strong man stumbles, or where the doer of deeds could have done them better. The credit belongs to the man who is actually in the arena, whose face in marred by dust and sweat and blood; who strives valiantly; who errs; who comes up short again and again, because there is no effort without error and shortcoming; but who does actually strive to do the deeds; who knows great enthusiasms, the great devotions; who spends himself in a worthy cause; who at the best knows in the end the triumph of high achievement, and who at the worst, if he fails, at least fails while daring greatly, so that his place shall never be with those cold and timid souls who neither know victory nor defeat.[322]

By December 28, Quentin was obeying doctors' orders and traveling by train to Marseille on the Mediterranean coast. But on arrival, he found nothing more than chill and wet. "I cannot see much reason for calling this the *Côte d'Azur*," he explained to Edith. "The sky is a dull leaden color, and [the air] is very cold. In fact, we have had a snow storm."[323]

Quentin fought off the wintry weather and the solitude of his Marseille hotel room by writing affectionate letters to Foufie. "All my hopes and ambitions are for you, and I plan and plan again for that time when we can stand side by side with our life before us, and the war [is] a black cloud of the past. I wonder what you are going to think of me when I come back. I know you have changed—grown older—and also I know that I have not, and it worries me. So love me as I love you."[324]

He had hoped to journey along the Riviera to Nice but decided in light of the cold to return at once to Paris, "Where at least you can have a good time."

Quentin Roosevelt faced an uncertain future and an ominous New Year. Initially, 1918 would see his family bitterly divided over his circumstance. Later in the year, his parents and siblings would rapidly come together during days of shock and unspeakable grief.

Seventeen

"Very good pilot . . . very good shot"

A mid the snow, cold rain and mud that troubled Issoudun in January 1918, Quentin Roosevelt was weighed down by two lingering worries: Flora's growing emotional distance from her parents, and his brother Archie's accusation that he was intentionally dodging combat. Edith had amplified Quentin's anxiety about his fiancée when she wrote, "I think little Flora is having a hard time; she does not seem to have a family to fall back on."[325]

The blues besetting Quentin deepened during the long winter nights at base, and he withdrew into himself. He stopped writing home, believing that his day-to-day work paled in contrast to his brothers' valor at the front line. Why brag to loved ones about derisory trials of a self-designated *embusqué*?

It was Ethel who recognized his state of mind. "Father and Mother and I swell with pride over all you have done," she wrote from Sagamore Hill. "Even *we* do not have your contempt of ground jobs!" She derided Archie as "an old pod" whose ideas were "too absurd." And she reported that Flora, too, was "frightfully blue, not having heard from you in ages and rather feeling that you were consoling yourself abroad."

Ethel sought to brighten Quentin's mood with wishful talk of Flora's going to France to marry him. "Flora was insisting that I break the idea to her mother. . . . The strain is very great, and you know her surroundings are not conducive to comfort. Her family are cuckoos."[326]

It was Theodore who evidently broke his son out of his funk with a blunt scolding. He chided Quentin for doing everything in his power to lose Flora by halting communications, and he wondered aloud about whether that was his intention.

By the first of February, letters began to pour forth from

Issoudun, addressed to Old Westbury and Sagamore Hill. Still, Quentin was down on himself. "I'm afraid that you will think I am very stupid and dull for I can't write interesting letters like Archie's," he told Flora. "If you want them I shall write them. . . . Oh, dearest, please write and tell me that ever more you will love me."[327] Just the day before, Quentin had bared his soul to Ethel:

> When I first got over here, I wrote often and told all about what I was doing. Time went on and I didn't do much flying, and most of my work was *embusqué* and things went all wrong. About that time, I got a long letter from Arch written on the theory that I was a slacker, that I had better buck up and try again to get into active service and get to the front as he was. Then just a week later, Ted and Arch came to Paris and told Eleanor that if I had really tried, I could have been out in a French squadron already. . . . You'll probably think that I am all kinds of a fool but when your own brother thinks you are a quitter, and you have been fighting tooth and nail to get to the front and know it's not physically possible, it's different. . . . I know what a fool I've been.[328]

It wasn't long before Quentin seemed to right himself emotionally, buoyed by several days of excited flying. "I wonder if you will come over here this summer dear," he asked of Flora. "Do you think you will, and we could get married here? Just think."[329] In his own mind, he had doubts, confiding to Ethel of Flora, "She's awfully young to be dropped entirely on her own, as she would be over here. She has been all the time under her family's wing, such as it was, and has never been off on her own . . ."[330]

At Sagamore Hill, the Roosevelt family's attention suddenly and fearfully shifted to Theodore who was rushed to a Manhattan hospital in severe pain from acute rectal bleeding, a scorching fever and multiple abscesses, all traced to his momentous days in Brazil. He underwent surgery on the abscesses—one was in his left ear—and rebounded after a day or two of touch-and-go recovery. In consequence of the surgery, Theodore suffered a debilitating loss of equilibrium and permanent deafness in the abscessed ear. From his hospital bed he dictated to Quentin: "I have been perfectly happy and comfortable but heartily ashamed of myself for being sick at such a time."[331]

The family patriarch was cheered during his month-long confinement by sacks of jovial cards and letters from admirers and, in particular, a visit from Flora. She wrote about it to Quentin: "If you knew how frightful it has been about your father. Thank heavens he is out of danger now. . . . You can't imagine how marvelous he was, so cheerful . . . and infinitely sorry for the worry he had caused his family."[332]

Early on, Flora had cabled Quentin about his father's illness but the message arrived late. "I picked up the paper, and the first thing I saw was [a report that] the condition of Roosevelt is serious and that the doctors are considering a new operation," Quentin bristled to Flora. "It was the first I had heard of Father's illness, and you can imagine that it was not pleasant to hear of it that way."[333]

The *embusqué* squabble seemingly would not recede. At home, it was topical in many of the Roosevelts' writings and burning deeply within Flora's breast.

Ethel to Quentin on February 26: "I am furious with Ted and Archie. I can't help thinking Ted must have put Archie up to it. . . . I think you have been too wonderful throughout it all, Quentin."[334]

Theodore—still in hospital—to Quentin on February 28: "I am exceedingly indignant at Ted and Archie; I am more proud of you and satisfied with you than I can say."[335] Edith, too, was said to be "very angry" with her older sons.

Flora to Ethel Roosevelt Derby: "I did not know I could be so mad. . . . I am boiling with rage! It's too much—I shall never, *never* forgive Archie and Ted!"[336]

Theodore sought to put an end to the strife by rushing a cable to Quentin in early March. Its contents were transcribed before sending by Edith, apparently for posterity: "Am shocked by attitude of Ted and Archie. If you have erred at all, it is in trying too hard to get to the front. You must take care of your health. We are exceedingly proud of you. Roosevelt."[337]

His father's declaration seemed to have achieved its purpose and soothed Quentin's soul: "Of course, it makes the most tremendous difference to me knowing that the family understands and doesn't think I'm quitting," he told Flora.[338]

The tumult was a rare divergence from a long-established Roosevelt family practice to avoid being mean-spirited and treat one another as comrades. A family member told this author in 2013 that they traditionally outdo each other to protect themselves without "eating the weak." What they say "in the huddle," he said, the rest of us will never know.

Flora and her mother, Gertrude, decided to peel themselves away from Old Westbury to visit their brother and son, Sonny, who was training with the Air Service in Fort Worth, Texas. A sought-after private railroad car was "not allowed," according to Flora, so they made the journey in coach and sleeper with everyone else. Cornelius Vanderbilt Whitney, 18 months younger than Flora, had signed on with the Signal Corps and completed his ground training at Princeton. Now, he was receiving instruction with the Royal Flying Corps. The visit, prompted by Gertrude's growing concern that Sonny would be sent "prematurely" overseas, was a not-so-subtle attempt to prevent that. Gertrude's biographer, B. H. Friedman, wrote, "They feel that by establishing ties with [Sonny's] commanding officers that they may be able to assure the extension of his training, perhaps in Mineola."[339] The fact of Sonny's service would have a significant bearing for Quentin's and Flora's plans in the coming months when the U.S. military sought to restrict overseas travel by siblings of soldiers.

During their stay, Flora chanced to encounter Roderick Tower, Quentin's Air Service pal from Mineola, who was directing cadet training at Ft. Worth. According to Friedman, Flora knew Tower from "Wednesday afternoon dancing class in New York." She could not possibly foresee then how dramatically their lives would intersect a year hence.

On a Friday afternoon in February, after a tiring week of reconnaissance training and mapmaking, Quentin caught word that an 18-man squadron of Issoudun flyers was preparing to go to the front. He relayed to Flora, "I went hot foot over to the main camp to see the colonel [Walter G. Kilner, base commander] to get permission to go out with that squadron. He refused absolutely, and I put up a tremendous fuss."

According to details in Quentin's letter, Col. Kilner explained that the squadron's shift merely was a "political move" so the people in charge and "the loud-mouthed fools back in Washington" could say that we have a squadron at the front. "They haven't even got machines for them yet or any sort of organization to allow for breakages or spare parts," Quentin quoted Kilner as saying. Further downplaying the significance of the move, the colonel predicted that the squadron "will sit there [in the Zone of Advance] for about a month until our organization can take care of them."

What the colonel said next gave Quentin renewed hope. "I am going to keep you back here for that reason but I will do this: I will send you out to the front as soon as it gets back . . . in a real squadron, either English or French."

"You can imagine how cheerful I am," Quentin bubbled to Flora, "a real squadron, in real machines and men who know something about the game. I rather think it will be a French squadron. At all events, cheers! In about two weeks, I will have stopped being *embusqué* Quentin."[340]

Within days, Quentin turned down an opportunity to spend three months in Paris, ferrying newly-built French planes from factories near Orly Airport to depots scattered throughout the country. "It would be wonderful fun," he told Flora. "Of course I'd be flying all over France, out to the front and to the various schools." But in the end, he reasoned, "It's no occupation for one who has never been to the front. . . . It's a job for a man back from the front for a rest, or one who's had a bad crash and lost his nerve. . . . I am hanging on like grim death until I get sent out to the front."[341]

There was a rare pinch of humor in Quentin's next letter to his fiancée. "Miss Givenwilson had organized a dance, under the auspices of the colonel, on Washington's Birthday," he reported. "It was rather amusing, for the female element was 'all Y.M.C.A. and Red Cross,' and most were old enough to be my mother!"[342]

He may have dismissed the festivities in part because he had recently "jumped at" a new assignment from Col. Kilner. "Guess where I am?" he trumpeted to Flora. "Cazaux." Located along the southwest coast, Cazaux was the site of a major French aerial gunnery school, and Quentin was headed there in charge of a 20-student detachment to learn airborne gunfire. It was valuable pilot training, the colonel had advised, and the diversion would not delay his designation to the front. "I've got a big room in a good hotel looking across the ocean, presumably toward New York," Quentin wistfully told Flora.[343]

Instruction began with machine gun training, and advanced to shooting at unmanned boats and at toy balloons aloft. "Then you have to go up a couple of thousand meters, drop over a paper parachute, then chase it over and over," Quentin explained. The next phase involved firing at fixed balloons and at sleeves towed by other planes. "The training is interesting and very valuable," Quentin thought. "From what I can gather, about half the game is good machine gun work."[344]

Quentin's main complaint was about "the most awful old crocks,"—French planes "that have been in service for ages and have old motors and fuselages and wings that are all warped and bent out of shape."[345] Notwithstanding the antiquated aircraft, Quentin and his men were expected to achieve top shooting scores.

Upon his graduation in mid-March, Quentin received a high-level commendation from the gunnery school's French captain: "Very good pilot—very regular landings—very good shot—much military spirit."[346]

About the same time, Theodore wrote, "You can't imagine the constant pride and satisfaction with which we think of you and talk of you. . . . I am out of the hospital."[347]

Then Archie got shot. The 25-year-old, freshly-promoted captain was hit by wayward shrapnel while leading a platoon toward German lines northwest of Toul. The projectiles shattered his left kneecap and fractured his left arm at the elbow, severing a key nerve. Bleeding gravely and in great pain, Archie was evacuated to the Sebastopol Hospital at Toul, and later to a Paris hospital where he would remain for four months of rehabilitation. There he was comforted by Eleanor and cheered with news that his month-old son, Archibald Jr., was thriving nicely in Boston under his wife Grace's care.

Word of Archie's wounding reached Sagamore Hill on March 13 when a news reporter informed Theodore that his son had received the French *Croix de Guerre* "under dramatic circumstances." A War Department cable and a subsequent letter from Ted filled in some of the details. Once the family was certain that Archie would survive, his parents, his sister, Ethel, and a visitor toasted him at a Sagamore Hill luncheon. Theodore recalled the ceremony in a letter to his wounded son: "Mother ordered some Madeira [from the basement reserve], all four of us filled the glasses and drank them off to you; then Mother, her eyes shining, her cheeks flushed, as pretty as a picture and as spirited as any heroine of romance, dashed her glass on the floor, shivering it in pieces, saying, 'that glass shall never be drunk out of again'; and the rest of us followed suit and broke our glasses too."[348]

"And there were tears in Father's eyes," Ethel added.[349]

About a month later, Theodore learned more about Archie's wounding from Dr. O. H. L. Mason, foreign secretary of the Y.M.C.A., who was visiting Sagamore Hill to drum up support for a Liberty Loan bond drive. According to *The New York Times*, Dr. Mason, who had fought under Colonel Roosevelt in the Spanish-American War, stunned Theodore when he "tenderly drew from his inner coat a small bag which Captain Roosevelt asked him to give to his father. It contained the projectile that shattered the bone in his left arm."

Nearly overcome with emotion, Theodore could only respond, "That is bully."[350]

Archie was determined to return to the fight but doctors ordered him back to the States during the summer of 1918; eventually he was discharged with full disability. He would thrive, however, to battle another day in a later war.

The chirping birds of spring made virtually the only sounds at Issoudun base early in the morning of March 30, the Saturday of Easter weekend. Quentin and Hamilton Coolidge took a couple of planes from the hangars, fitted overnight bags into their cockpits and flew to Romorantin. "Side by side we flew in our little buses, making faces at each other just for amusement," Hamilton recalled.

In a field about a mile from their residence, the Normant family was waiting in their automobile to whisk the arriving soldiers away for a weekend of relaxation and "civilization" at their luxurious home. Before leaving, Hamilton said he needed to escape from the stress of running the aircraft testing department and trying out new planes. Quentin was equally ready for a break from his emotional rollercoaster.

"They have a palatial house and are dears," Hamilton wrote of the Normants in a series of descriptive letters to his mother. "We had a huge room, nice soft beds and a real American-type tile bathroom to ourselves."[351] Morning hospitality rarely varied from the optimum: warm, welcoming hugs and engaging French repartee. Then, hot, soaking baths in a real porcelain tub, fluffy terrycloth robes, and seats of honor at the breakfast table where Edithe Normant presented a robust country breakfast of eggs, bacon, and biscuits.

"This afternoon, we all took bikes and rode out to look at a superb little chateau belonging to an aunt," Hamilton relayed on Sunday. "The chateau is of the fifteenth century. It is a diminutive affair, but the most perfect specimen imaginable . . . solid stone with towers at the corners. It is surrounded by a moat, has a fine little stone bridge over it with the family crest carved on the key of the arch. Inside you see these grand old ceilings of hand-hewn beams, tiled floors, and very pure Renaissance furniture."

By 5:30 p.m., as ominous storm clouds closed in, Quentin and Hamilton returned to their planes and darted back to base, relaxed and refreshed. They planned to attend an Easter "after supper" service at the Y.M.C.A. "I think I'll look it over, though I seldom get up much enthusiasm over them ordinarily," Hamilton confessed.[352]

Quentin certainly had reason to say a prayer of thanks. He had experienced a terrifying scare in the air the day before. He was descending into Romorantin in his Nieuport, making difficult headway against heavy winds, "feeling as if I were in a delivery cart on a cobblestone road." Quentin executed the landing successfully but told Flora that he had been "really scared" on his approach to the airfield. "We were just about five miles [out], and I was getting ready to nose her down and come through the clouds to land when, for some unknown reason, I began to feel faint and dizzy."

Quentin, left, and Hamilton having Sunday breakfast
at the Normant home, Romorantin, France; May 1918.

(MS Am 2925 (99), Theodore Roosevelt Collection, Houghton Library,

Harvard University)

He later expanded on the sensation, admitting to Flora that, "I was feeling queerer and queerer all the time and came down in a rush." Fearing that the experience might recur with serious consequences, he checked with a doctor who offered a plausible explanation. Quentin relayed it: "A couple of days ago, I had a couple of warts taken out of my lips," he told Flora. "They filled it up with cocaine and then proceeded to chop a cross section of it, and then sew it together. According to the doctor, my fainting was the result of cocaine in my system."[353]

Quentin in Doc Yak near Romorantin, France.

(Photo from Ethel Roosevelt Derby Album, Sagamore Hill National Historic Site, via Alan D. Toelle.)

The incident added to what Quentin called "a streak of bad flying" that had included landings that had gone "all to the bad." He reported smashing a plane "beautifully" on March 26. "It was really a very neat job," he recalled cynically, "for I landed with a drift, touched one wing and then, as there was a high wind, did three somersaults, ending up on my back. I crawled out of it with nothing more than a couple of scratches."

Notwithstanding his erratic landings of late, Lieutenant Roosevelt was given a personal plane, a new Nieuport 27, shortly thereafter. It was a perk for a popular officer now serving as training chief at Issoudun's Field 7, near the village of Saint Valentin, where formation and combat flying were taught.

"Every morning, promptly at seven o'clock, a gaudily painted plane could be seen circling the camp," Hamilton Coolidge later remembered, "sometimes ducking in and out of low-flying clouds, at other [times] diving, twisting and rolling in an extravagant demonstration of nice handling."[354] It was Quentin, the "Go and Get 'em Man," on display in a plane that he had nicknamed "Doc Yak" after the popular cartoon of the time. It seems that a team of mechanics surprised their chief by decorating the Nieuport with white wings and rudder, a huge American shield, and red and blue spiral stripes. Colorful characterizations of Doc Yak in his speeding auto covered both sides of the fuselage. Quentin declared his plane "v. sporty;" it was an attraction that drew crowds to his side wherever he landed.

From the evidence in letters and the observations of those close to Quentin, these were among his happiest days at Issoudun. Spring arrived on warm southwesterly winds, and the ever-present mud was drying into hard soil—and the promise of green grass. He was flying daily, if not always deftly, with the admiration and respect of the men training under him, showing them how it should be done. There was, however, still an aching hole in Quentin's heart for his Foufie. The hardest hours were the darkest and quietest when a weary man, alone in the stillness of his room, would feel deeply about whom and what he was missing.

"The one thing I want most is to have you here, to know you are near and to be able to go with you to Paris and visit Cartier's looking for rings," he wrote. "It's terribly lonely here with you so far away, dear."[355]

Quentin had hatched a plan. "Wouldn't it be better all-around if you could come over here this summer?" he asked. "I used to think it would be unfair to you to marry now in these times, but I've changed now to your views, even if things did go wrong. . . . You could get a job with the Y.M.C.A., either as secretary . . . or canteen worker. Then once you get over here, we could get married, and you could live in the other half of Eleanor's house or at the [art] studio if Hon. Ma [Gertrude] wanted. . . . Do think it over and talk it over with [your family]."[356]

A few weeks earlier, Miss Givenwilson had issued an invitation to Flora to come to Issoudun: "I think of you ever so much, and often wonder if it would not be possible for you to come over and work in my canteen."[357] At the same time, Ethel was encouraging Quentin to write to Flora's parents, demanding that she come over to marry him. "Flora is one of those people who rise up higher by every trial," Ethel explained. "She has a very valiant spirit and reserves of strength and patience and courage which she will develop to their full when called upon. . . . She is really an extraordinary person."[358]

Quentin was skeptical that Flora's parents would support her needs: "They are gumps, aren't they?" he told his sister. "I always feel as if the W's, not so much Mrs. as Mr., feel as if their children were nice, occasionally-amusing dolls, to be taken up when there is nothing better to do or, if there is anything else, to be left absolutely to their own devices. No wonder it's tough on Fouf."

Quentin's mother spoke for herself and her husband: "If Flora agrees to be married, Father will apply for a passport for her and me to go across and be there for a specified time."[359]

For the moment, all the dreaming and scheming among those with a unified intent could not overcome complicating events on the war's western front. A significant amount of French territory now was in German hands, and the enemy had mounted a series of spring ground offensives in northeastern France, hoping to splinter British and French forces with advances and ploys before General Pershing could get the mass of American forces in place. Theodore Roosevelt biographer Edmund Morris wrote of a case in point: "A bombardment of unbelievable intensity battered Allied artillery emplacements around Arras [in northern France], while poisonous phosgene fumes spilled like fog into every bunker."[360]

The enemy had thrust to within 50 miles of Paris, terrifying the outer communities with round after round of artillery from the *Paris-Geschütz* (the Paris Gun), sending refugees fleeing, and prompting the French to consider evacuating their government from the capital.

Back home, Theodore Roosevelt worried. "Our army is small; of good material except, among many of the older officers, completely without field guns, machine guns and air planes, except what it has obtained from the French . . . with little prospect of making it a formidable or, indeed, ponderable military force in the war for many months to come. I suppose all peoples tend to be foolish and shortsighted when danger is not pressing. . ."[361]

Eighteen

Qualities of Courage

The question was preoccupying the Roosevelt and Whitney families in the mid-spring of 1918: should Flora Payne Whitney journey to France to marry Quentin Roosevelt before he goes off to battle? The War Department was reporting that German U-boat harassment of vessels in the North Atlantic had been curbed by the convoys, and spring had brought favorable ocean crossing weather. It was now or never.

Quentin desperately wanted Flora to come to Paris, and her letters made clear that she yearned to make the voyage. Moreover, she had an open invitation from Miss Givenwilson to work with the Red Cross at Issoudun. Eleanor offered a room at her Paris home and the likelihood of a job with the Y.M.C.A. Theodore and Edith Roosevelt were as supportive as could be, encouraging Flora during her visits to Sagamore Hill. The only wildcard was a crucial one: Gertrude and Harry Whitney, Flora's parents.

"I wonder if the family will ever let you come over here," Quentin wrote Flora May 2 from Paris. "I dream of it more now and then, to make plans about it; but down in my heart I know it's impossible no matter how much I want it."

His desire for Foufie had deepened as the fateful day of his assignment to the war zone approached. "I want you so much. [I] think of the time when I could come into your room and hold out my arms and kiss you, and know that the time was our own and that there was no ocean between us."[362]

The Whitneys were continuing to invest their influence in a scheme to keep their newly-commissioned airman son, Sonny, stateside and out of harm's way. Harry even had approached Colonel Roosevelt for advice. Wary of such an attempt, yet eager to keep the Whitneys in good graces for Flora's sake, Theodore advised Harry to approach some influential third parties. "I will get hold of the men you suggest on Monday and let you know the results as soon as possible," Harry wrote. He signed off his letter, "Yours in haste, Harry P. Whitney."[363]

Gertrude and Harry were apprehensive about Flora's future. What assurance did they have that their 20-year-old daughter would be secure in wartime Paris? Would she have the necessary resolve to manage the challenges that were sure to confront an attractive heiress on her own? What if something should happen to Quentin?

On May 5, Edith reported to Quentin that Flora was ready for a face-off at home. "Flora arrived yesterday, looking so pretty and full of enthusiasm, looking to get across. She is to break it to her mother, and then the family will counsel her as best they can."[364]

Apparently the face-off did not go well. "I got a telegram [from Flora] three days ago saying that it wasn't possible at the moment, and saying why," Quentin told his father. "The trouble is that the French telegraph service had mangled the message beyond hope of recognition, and so I am waiting for the letter that will explain it." Quentin speculated on the outcome: "I suppose that her family is the reason. I wonder if they will ever let her. They must see that the war is going to be an awfully long proposition by now." He solicited his father: "If you see Mrs. W., do see if she's the one. I bet it is Mr."[365]

Three days later, Harry accepted an invitation to dine with Theodore at Sagamore Hill. We cannot be sure of what transpired, but around that time Theodore announced to Kermit that "Flora has obtained the permission of her father and mother to cross over and marry Quentin at once." The optimism in his words was tempered, however, by the reality that hard conditions governed overseas travel during wartime. "Of course, we are not at all certain whether she can get a passport, but I most earnestly hope she can carry out her plan."[366] In what may have been a condition of the Whitneys' acquiescence, Theodore and Edith had agreed that they, too, would apply for passports if it became necessary for them to accompany their future daughter-in-law overseas.

Virtually concurrent with the hopefulness alive in New York, seeds of despair were germinating in Washington. President Wilson raised a pen at the White House and affixed his cramped and slanted signature to an act of Congress popularly known as the Travel and Passport Control Act. Effective May 22, 1918, it would restrict any citizen's departure from the U.S. that was "contrary to the public safety." Further, it codified the existing practice that required anyone leaving or entering the country to have a valid passport or face a $10,000 fine.

More specifically, hard-nosed regulations prohibited women younger than 25 from going to do war work in France, even if they intended to help the Red Cross or the Y.M.C.A. Female relatives of soldiers were denied permission to visit their loved ones in French hospitals.

The "Under 25 Rule" alone seemingly would ground Flora. But especially ruinous to Quentin's and her dreams was a related provision that barred travel by young women who happen to have brothers in service. It would come to be known as the "Sisters of Soldiers Rule." And we know that Flora's brother, Sonny, was a commissioned officer in the U.S. Air Service. (In the end, the Armistice would be signed before Sonny could go abroad, leaving him "sorely disappointed." He would, however, serve overseas with distinction during the Second World War.)

The rationale for the restrictions, viewed from the 21st century, sheds discomforting light on how young women were perceived at the time by many of those who made laws in Washington. "We should only have those who are steady, those of well-balanced mental equilibrium," they claimed. "The war zone is no place for emotional 'flibbety-gibbets.'" Besides, they reasoned, thousands of young women bound for France would surely swamp the ocean transportation service.[367]

Within days, critics pounced. One of the most vocal and influential was Major Alexander Lambert, surgeon-in-chief of the American Red Cross in Paris. Lambert was, perhaps not coincidentally, the well-respected personal physician of Theodore Roosevelt and his family.

"The boys are lonely, and they want and ought to have the opportunity now and then of getting the companionship of the girls who go over to do canteen work," he argued. "Practically every self-respecting girl of the right age for the work now, has or will soon have a brother in the Army in France. To bar them for this reason is to rule out the active, vigorous young girls who are on a par with the active, vigorous young men in our draft Army." Dr. Lambert urged that the restrictive rules be rescinded.[368]

The ban on travel by sisters of soldiers would be relaxed by the end of July 1918, but that would be too late for Quentin and Flora. In the future, sisters would be permitted to go abroad as workers, ordered Army Chief of Staff General Peyton C. March, under six conditions. Number six was: If a woman married an officer or soldier in the American Expeditionary Force after her arrival abroad, she automatically would be sent back to the U.S. by the organization in which she is serving.

Theodore Roosevelt was outraged. Venting to his sister, Bamie, he wrote: "Under the idiotic ruling about the sisters of soldiers, poor Flora was not allowed to go across. It is wicked; she should have been allowed to go and marry Quentin; then, even if he were killed, she and he would have known their white hour; it is part of the needless folly and injustice with which things have been handled."[369]

In the end, Theodore had only good things to say about the Whitneys, telling Archie that Flora's father and mother had behaved "splendidly" during the episode. "I hope [Flora] can get over sooner or later," he added.[370]

When he learned of their fate, Quentin expressed remorse for Flora and lamented the lost opportunity: "Oh sweetheart. Poor, poor you. . . . I feel as though Father and H.P.W. [might have been] able to do it. It was taken from us when it was almost within our grasp."[371] He wondered to Ethel whether the outcome was permanent or a temporary impossibility. "I see no prospect of any of us over here getting back [to the States] short of getting shot or smashed up." He added, "It is terribly hard being separated for so very long. We'll have to start-in to know each other all over again."[372]

Eleanor was enjoying a quiet summerlike Sunday in her Paris home when the voice bellowed through the opening door. "Why are you still here? Don't you know the Germans are advancing on Paris? You must leave at once." It was her husband Ted.

Eleanor and Ted Roosevelt in 1918.

(570.R67.t, Theodore Roosevelt Collection, Houghton Library, Harvard University)

"I have never seen anyone look so ghastly," Eleanor remembered. "His face was scorched and inflamed; the whites of his eyes were angry red. He was thickly covered with dust and shaken by a racking cough."[373] Ted told of being gassed and temporarily blinded by the Germans during a clash at Cantigny a few days earlier, and how he had refused to abandon his command. Later, once his men were safe, he had commandeered a car and driver, signed his own pass, and set out for Paris. *The New York Times* reported on Ted's battlefield clash and his subsequent citation for "conspicuous gallantry in action" during the capture and defense of Cantigny: "During an enemy raid, he displayed high qualities of courage and leadership in going forward to supervise, in person, the action of one of the companies of his battalion which had been attacked."

Ted's commanding general added to the citation: "On the day of our attack on Cantigny, although gassed in the lungs and gassed in the eyes to blindness, Major Roosevelt refused to be removed and retained the command of his battalion under a heavy bombardment throughout the engagement."[374]

Eleanor remembered, "I did not know until later that [Ted] and his unit had taken part in a battle that was the first proof to the Allies and to the enemy that 'the half-trained, poorly-disciplined American troops' could overcome Germans steeled to combat by four years of warfare."[375] There were more than a thousand American casualties in three days of horrific fighting at Cantigny.

Ted rebounded quickly in Paris following a hot bath, Eleanor's tender care and a change into a new uniform and boots. He was resting and reading at her place when Quentin bounded into the apartment unexpectedly. Quentin could not conceal his astonishment at seeing his oldest brother. They hugged and exchanged wartime stories. Following dinner, Eleanor and the brothers visited Archie in the hospital and brought him up to date on recent weighty events. A few weeks earlier, Quentin and Archie had reconciled. Perhaps many days in traction in a hospital bed had awakened Archie to the truth of his brother's determination to reach the front. "He's taking a more charitable view of me," Quentin reassured their mother.[376]

Early the next morning, despite Eleanor's pleading, Ted departed Paris for the front, laughing as he left, and claiming that he needed no further care because he was "fit as a fiddle."

Western Union Cablegram to Mrs. Theodore Roosevelt from Quentin Roosevelt: "Moving out at last with Ham; very glad. Love to all."[377]

With just 12 hours' notice, Quentin and a detachment of fellow aviators were ordered out of Issoudun. It had been ten protracted months at the training base for Quentin, and he and Hamilton felt sure that their sudden dispatch was the first step toward real action. "We got into the truck and started to leave [Field 7] for the main camp to get our clearance papers," Quentin related to Flora. "Then they did one of the nicest things I've ever had happen. Our truck driver . . . took us down the line of hangars and, as we went past, all the mechanics lined up in front and cheered us goodbye. As we passed the last hangar, one of the sergeants yelled after us, 'Let us know if you are captured, and we will come after you.' So I left with a big lump in my throat, for it's nice to know that your men have liked you."[378]

The pair's enthusiasm waned when they arrived at the French ferry pilot station at Orly Airport near Paris. They learned that no one there expected them or had any idea why they had come. It took a couple of days of animated bi-lingual conversation and investigation for Quentin and Hamilton to figure out that they were in a holding pattern, awaiting assignment to a French squadron, or *escadrille.*

When she learned of Quentin's new station, Flora wrote, "If only I could be in Paris. It would be at least near you . . . and then after you went to the front, the feeling that I was right there would make all the difference in the world. If you are wounded, I would be able to go to you and perhaps be of some comfort to you . . . perhaps in September I will be able to come."[379]

"Ham and I raised a howl that could be heard in New York," Quentin said of their assignment to Orly. Testing French planes was not their idea of fighting at the front.

"So they finally gave in," Hamilton reported. Along with eight other flyers, he and Quentin were ordered to a base at Chartres, about a hundred miles southwest of Paris, a French staging area for pilots awaiting assignment to an *escadrille.* "I am one of the happiest men on earth," Hamilton swaggered to his mother. But he cautioned, "One can never tell when the grasping claws may try to steal me back again."[380]

For Quentin, the transfer to Chartres alongside active flyers represented a promise fulfilled. Back at Issoudun in February, Colonel Walter Kilner, then the base commander, had vowed to him, "I will send you out to the front . . . in a real squadron, either English or French." Now, in June, he kept his word—at last.

At Chartres, Quentin and Hamilton tested the Spad, a single-seat, French-made plane. "They seem rather crude," Hamilton thought initially, but later he judged the Spad "a sweet machine."

Hamilton updated his mother on their spare living conditions at Chartres: "We are billeted in a tiny hamlet and have for quarters the attic of a tiny farmhouse." Notwithstanding the rudimentary arrangements, he projected optimism: "We are with old hands at the game who can teach us much in the gentle art of aerial battle tactic."[381]

The best news was yet to come. "I am doing what I came over here for," Quentin announced with satisfaction to Flora on June 18. Finally, his boots were on the ground at the front. While training at Chartres, he had received an unexpected telegram ordering him to report at once to an American unit, the First Pursuit Group, where he was immediately assigned to the 95th Aero Squadron, known as "The Kicking Mules." "I'll be working in Germany, as my flight is on for regular planes' protection," he wrote to Flora. "It's much nicer to be with Americans."[382]

Hamilton was assigned to the companion 94th Aero Squadron. "Thank goodness they have left us together, Q. and me," he told his sister. "They've been mighty decent about that."[383]

Although he had realized his long-sought goal, Quentin could not clear Flora from his mind. Now with danger an everyday threat, he seemed to hunger more deeply for her: "I want you always, always, and there's never a moment, work or play, when there isn't an ache in my heart that only Fouf can cure."[384] Noting the June 23rd date, he reminded Flora that they had been engaged nearly a year and a month. "And we haven't seen each other for eleven of those months."[385]

The Kicking Mules were headquartered temporarily at Gengoult Airfield, 160 miles distant from Paris near Toul on the Moselle River. The Moselle was a left tributary of the Rhine, evidence, if it were needed, that the base was closer to Germany than it was to the French capital. From the airstrip at Toul, American flyers would stage reconnaissance forays over the border, safeguard their own observation aircraft, and strafe enemy ground forces, all when wind and cloud conditions permitted.

Quentin's fluency in French became a genuine asset at the Toul aerodrome. Almost every day for an hour or so, he would help other American officers translate secret French aerial intelligence reports on German aircraft and their sky tactics.

Although he did not see actual air combat at Toul, Quentin reported to Flora on his first aerial conflict, "a sort of a private Boche hunting party."[386]

We started up at about eight o'clock and lit the lines at about 4,800 meters. It was a bully day, the wind blowing out of Germany and just enough clouds to make it interesting. With just my usual luck, though, there was no Boche to be seen anywhere. The only thing we managed to scare up was a perfect flock of archies [anti-aircraft fire]. We dodged around pretty actively, and they didn't get very near as I only felt one once, which was all I wanted. It felt as if it had gone under my tail. . . . The disturbance it caused hit me and just about turned me inside out. One of those Boche gunners must have been a mighty good shot from the way I felt. The mechanic reported to me that I had a hole through my wing. . . . We spotted two photographers [enemy reconnaissance planes] well below us and chased them, but as they dove for home we found ourselves about 20 miles in Germany, a most disturbing state of affairs, so we had to beat it for home. . . . We lost two fellows yesterday. One got lost and landed in Switzerland and the other got shot down in Germany.[387]

Theodore, just returned to Sagamore Hill from a Midwest speaking tour with Edith, hurried a letter to his son: "A couple of days ago, we were thrilled by your cable. . . . I know well how hard the long delay has been. . . . My joy for you and pride in you drown my anxiety. . . . You are at the front, and I am satisfied."[388]

Edith was the first of the family at home to learn that the Kicking Mules were being reassigned out of Toul—deemed to be a relatively quiet sector—to what was termed "a hot spot" east of Paris. "From all we can gather, there are Boche here all the time," Quentin told her. He recounted that he had flown six or seven hours over the lines so far and was beginning to get an idea of what the front was about. "At first, you don't see the Boche at all, but gradually you begin to get onto them. . . . The real thing is that I am on the front— cheers, oh cheers—and I'm very happy."[389]

The sector did indeed fire up in intensity a few days later. It was blistering enough, Quentin reported to Flora, "to make even the most war-like satisfied. . . . The Boche took it upon themselves to bomb our field [at 3 a.m.]. . . . The bombs landed about 500 yards from our barracks which is plenty close enough for yours truly."[390]

Hamilton Coolidge took up the narrative:

Our flight leader tapped on my door and said, 'I guess we had better get up. It looks as if the Huns were starting something.' When we came over the [German] lines, we could see hundreds of brilliant little flashes out of the twilight here and there. . . . For an hour and a half, we circled round over the place amid an incessant storm of shrapnel bursts. Sometimes they came so close that I could feel my whole plane give a great bounce from the concussion, tho no fragments actually hit me. We circled, twisted, squirmed and dived, and always the black bursts appeared at the spot where we had been only a fraction of a second before. It was absolutely thrilling.[391]

For the benefit of his family in Massachusetts, Hamilton listed the main responsibilities of an airborne pilot: "1) Keep a continual watch out for Boches; 2) Continually watch your patrol leader; 3) Look at the ground to see where you are going and where you want to go; 4) Watch out for anti-aircraft shrapnel; and, 5) Watch your instruments which give you the dope on your motor, your altitude, etc." He added, "No longer are any of these trips [made] alone over the lines. A lone man is practically certain to be nailed. On all our voluntary patrols, we must go at least six strong in formation."[392]

To Ethel, Quentin explained the nature of reconnaissance patrols: "We have one high patrol and one low patrol regularly. . . . High patrol is generally the least pleasant, for that means around 5,500 meters where it is cold and the air bothers you. I generally get a headache for a couple of hours after I am down from one. You meet more Boche up high though. . . . They send over their planes *chasse* in groups of 15 or so which makes it pretty hot when you shake them. Down on low patrols, on the 3,500 meter level, it's a lot warmer and the air is okay but you're right in among the worst of the archies. You meet all the Boche photographers around that level. . . . So far, I have had good luck and haven't run into much. But I am due for better luck, I hope."[393]

There were rumors that the squadrons would be changing base again, so Quentin took advantage of down time to journey to Paris. A Brentano's store receipt that inexplicably has survived shows that Quentin spent the equivalent of $55.53 on a host of reading and writing materials. He chose works by O. Henry, Oscar Wilde, and Dickens; issues of *Cosmopolitan*, *Vogue*, and *Vanity Fair* magazines, stationery, stamps, and a fountain pen. Around that time, he also dropped in on Archie at the hospital. "When he found out I was really going [to the front], he became most affectionate," Quentin related to Flora. "He evidently felt that he was saying a last fond farewell to me."[394]

Near the end of June, the 94th and 95th Aero Squadrons and two others were indeed on the move, this time to Touquin, in the Marne region southwest of Château-Thierry, 30 miles east of Paris. Their assignment was to give air support to a corps of division-sized ground forces that General Pershing had assembled.

Before they departed Toul, there was a memorable farewell celebration at Café Stanislas in nearby Nancy. Quentin was recalled as "the life of that party" for generously enhancing the evening's cold rum punch with cognac. Armed with a sturdy bottle in lieu of a gavel, he served as toastmaster for a raucous program that saluted a departing commander and other officers who were staying behind. Fellow pilots looked back on the noisy, happy evening as "the best party they had in France."[395]

While waiting to fly a mission from the new Touquin field, Hamilton described his dwelling conditions at *Le Chateau Mirabeau*, given over to the men of the 94th Aero Squadron: "We are living in a château with wonderful lawns, gardens, pine groves and a small lake full of fish," he exclaimed. "Did you ever hear of such luxury?"[396]

Quentin told Flora about his unlikely new billeting—at the remote but luxurious *Château de Malvoisine* (The Bad Neighbor Estate), owned before the war by a rich olive oil merchant.[397]

"I am in a room about as large as that of [your mother's], next to yours. There are three other fellows in it . . . but you've no idea of the other-worldly sensation involved in going *upstairs* to bed, then in the morning getting up with a carpet under your feet. . . . There are two bully sitting rooms downstairs with a piano, attached to a dining room of the oak-paneled, tall chairs sort."[398]

The American flyers had little time to enjoy their newfound comfort. On Monday, July 1, Quentin went up on patrol in his Nieuport 28, in support of an American infantry offensive:

There was a lot of *chasse* work to be done what with protecting our own biplanes and keeping off the Boche. . . . Altogether, there was lots doing, and I was glad to be comfortably above it all with no worries but two cold fingers and a mad magneto [generator]. When we got in, we found that tho we hadn't seen any Boche, the top flight had—and then some. . . . They had bad luck with machine gun jams, and the Boche made it pretty hot for them. One man got back here with his plane so shot up that it was nothing short of a miracle that he escaped. He had one center section shot away and to hit it, the bullet must have gone within an inch of his head. The whole fuselage and one gas tank were riddled with bullets and, as the Boche use explosive bullets, that fellow can thank his stars.[399]

A forecast of what lay just ahead for the squadrons was revealed in a 27-page, unpublished manuscript attributed to Philip Roosevelt, Quentin's cousin. Entitled *Quentin at the Front*, it was later sent to Theodore and Edith at Sagamore Hill:

> It became evident that we were up against a very different problem in meeting the German aviation there [at the Château-Thierry sector] than we had faced at Toul. A new German attack was expected almost hourly, and the 6th French Army staff was so fearful of the consequences that a note of almost-panic often crept into the summaries of bulletins and intelligence which it issued. [One summary] described the German pursuit aviation as extremely aggressive and tenacious in its attacks on our planes. . . . They carried the battle far into our lines, rarely withdrawing until their efforts were crowned with success.[400]

For Quentin and Hamilton, the days of wine and roses at their respective chateaux were resting in the hands of fate.

Nineteen

A Gallant Foe

The front was ominously still, and Quentin Roosevelt seemed apprehensive and reflective. From the patio at *Château de Malvoisine*, he began the first of what would be an almost daily series of letters to Flora. Trying to reassure himself as well as his fiancée, he wrote, "War is only an interlude, and our lives will go on as they did before. This will be only a memory."[401]

Quentin, foreground, writing from
Château de Malvoisine, 1918.

(James Knowles photo collection, via Charlie Woolley and

Alan D. Toelle)

In his Nieuport, at altitudes low and high, Quentin had been patrolling his sector on the front lines, along the Marne River, about 30 miles north of the aerodrome. For the first few days of July, no German aircraft appeared. Even his "two hours of frozen discomfort at 5,500 meters" had not yielded sight of a menacing Boche. "Outside of my patrols, I've been doing nothing but working on my plane and resting all day," he reported.

The perplexing interlude had given him pause to plan for the unthinkable, something to which all warriors rightfully are disposed. "I think you might rather hear more often from me where there is a chance of my getting into trouble," Quentin alerted Flora. "In case I do get it, Ham is going to look after my things and send them home to the family." He added, "I'm leaving a letter for you in my trunk that he will find when he goes through it." As he wrote on his mood seemed to brighten, and he vowed, "I love you too much not to come back, my darling."[402]

Onward, from the day after a July Fourth observance at the Touquin field, Quentin would have no further respite. While on routine patrol inside the lines at 3,500 meters, he experienced motor trouble with his Nieuport, causing him to drag far behind others in his formation. As he struggled to keep up, he spied a patrol of six Boche above him. "The next thing I knew, a shadow came across my plane," he recounted to Flora. "And there, about two hundred meters above me, and looking as big as all outdoors, was a Boche! He was so near, I could make out the red stripes around his fuselage. I'm free to confess that I was scared blue."

As the young aviator leaned on his stick and "prayed for motor," the threatening enemy pilot scattered a few shots, then retreated unexpectedly. Quentin could only imagine that the German did not want to brawl over Allied territory. "He had every kind of advantage over us," Quentin believed. "Lord, but I was glad when he left."

The next day, equipped with a fresh Nieuport, Quentin "went hunting for trouble" with the rest of his flight. They soon found it. At 5,000 meters, just inside the German lines, the Americans dove on six enemy fighters half a mile below. "They never saw us until we started shooting, so we had them cold," Quentin recalled. Again he had what he described as miserable luck. "I had my man just where I wanted, was piquing down on him . . . and after getting good and close, set my sight on him and pulled the trigger. My gun shot twice and then jammed. I couldn't fix it. The feed box had slipped, and she only fired one shot at a time and then quit. I did everything I could but finally had to give up and come home."

Nonetheless, the others in his flight knocked down three enemy planes. However, they lost one man. He was captured when his motor failed, and he landed in enemy territory. "I've had my first real fight," Quentin crowed to Flora. "I was doubtful before—for I thought I might get cold feet, or something, but you don't. You get so excited that you forget everything except getting the other fellow and trying to dodge the tracers when they start streaking past you."[403]

On the ninth of July, the airmen relocated their base of operations from Touquin to the edge of a farmer's field, known as *Les Aulnois*, in the village of Saints, three miles to the northeast. Quentin and a roommate moved their belongings about half a mile west of Saints to a dwelling at the corner of *rue des Noyers* and *rue Bricot* in the village of Mauperthuis. There, Melina Thibault, a widowed mother of three soldiers, opened a guestroom to them.[404] "It's one of those white plaster houses with tile roofs that sag in between the rafters," Quentin informed Flora in one of his delightfully descriptive passages. "It's spotlessly clean with a red tiled floor and a huge grandfather's clock ticking solemnly in the corner. The old lady who owns the house is equally delightful. She's a little bit of a dried up person, at least as old as the hills, with gold-rimmed spectacles that all these country folks have. . ."[405] Mme. Thibault would later praise Quentin as *"un vrai mécanicieu"*—a true mechanic. It seems that he had deftly repaired the big clock which had not run for more than 30 years.

On the ground, northwest of where the squadrons were operating, heavy Allied resistance had halted the German ground advance toward Paris. Four Australian Imperial Force divisions had arrived on site to help two American divisions blunt the offensive. Enemy supply lines were stretched, and the Germans found themselves short of tanks and motorized artillery. Elsewhere, quietly, the Kaiser's forces were assembling for what would become the Second Battle of the Marne with the goal of encircling the historic city of Reims, about 75 miles northeast of Saints and Mauperthuis.

"Isn't it thrilling about Quentin?" Flora exclaimed to Ethel after learning about her fiancé's subsequent airborne duel. "I almost died of excitement and can hardly wait till letters arrive about it."[406]

Two days earlier *The New York Times* had headlined a dispatch from the front, "Quentin Roosevelt Wins Aerial Fight."[407] The story was the immediate buzz of the Roosevelt family.

Theodore declared himself "immensely excited."[408]

Hamilton Coolidge, a family intimate by now, called it a "splendid *coup de main*."[409]

Quentin, himself, announced to his father, "I think I got a Boche."[410] It would be his first—and last.

Flora learned much more, from a long letter, of the "great excitement" in Quentin's life.

On July 10th, he was the top man in a flight of 15 patrolling the sector high up at 5,200 meters in frigid, blustery winds. North of the city of Château-Thierry, he reported suddenly getting "pretty well mixed up" in the clouds and losing sight of his formation. He related what happened next:

> So I began circling about, keeping a sharp watch out for any other planes. Three planes appeared quite a bit off from me and a little below. I seriously started for home but as they didn't follow, I decided they must be part of my old formation. So I swung around and chased them. We went on and on—with me drawing slowly nearer. They were going directly north into Germany, but as I had plenty of gas, I wandered a little further. . . . Then I got up pretty close and discovered to my perfect horror that they had white tails and black crosses and were a Boche patrol going home.

As the Germans raced on, already about ten miles inside their territory, they failed to notice the American hot on their tail.

Quentin was alone and hard to spot in the bright summer sun. More from him:

> I was scared perfectly green but then I thought to myself that I was so near that I might as well take a crack at one of them. So I pulled up a little nearer, got a line on the end man, and pulled the trigger. The gun never jammed, and he kept straight ahead. My tracers were going all around him, and I guess that he was so surprised that for a bit he couldn't think what to do. Then his tail shot up, and he went down in a [turn]. I wanted to follow him, but at that moment his two companions lit after me so I had to hustle for base.

The enraged German pilots chased Quentin all the way to the French border, then turned for home. As he retreated, pushing his Nieuport toward its 124-miles-per-hour-limit, Quentin saw the downed plane in a death spiral, cutting into the clouds at 3,000 meters below.

Because the kill occurred inside Germany and the wreckage would be out of reach of the Allies, formal confirmation would not occur until later when it was verified by the French and credited to Quentin. Satisfied with his achievement, Quentin considered it a joke on the Boche. "Think of having an enemy plane flying in your formation for ten minutes then shooting you down."[411]

In letters to Kermit and Ethel, Theodore gloated. "The last of the lion's brood has been blooded!" he crowed to Kermit.[412] To his daughter: "Whatever now befalls Quentin, he has now had his crowded hour and his day of honor and triumph."[413]

Flora, though sharing in Quentin's delight, lamented to Ethel, "Oh, how I wish it was all over."[414]

Quentin hopped a motorcycle to Paris to celebrate his big score. He surprised Eleanor at the Y.M.C.A., and the two went out to hunt for sweets for Archie who had just undergone another operation. "We went on a search for wild strawberries and Normandy cream for Archie," Eleanor remembered in her memoir. "The *Café de la*

Régence sold us some in a china dish tied up with paper and string. I was carrying it as we walked along the *avenue de l'Opera* when the string broke and the package crashed to the pavement, oozing strawberries and cream in all directions. All we could do was walk hurriedly away."[415]

Archie certainly would have enjoyed the treat. Doctors had just cut into his left arm, repositioning vital nerve endings that had shrunk after being severed in battle. They told him that it might be eight months before the strands grew together and restored some degree of feeling to the limb.

"Quentin blew in yesterday," Archie informed Flora from his hospital room on July 13. He surely was thrilled to see Quentin and revel in his brother's tale of a downed Boche. Yet Archie was wary. "With so many of our family over here," he wrote, "I confess, since I have been in the hospital, that I never take up the paper without a tremor."[416]

That evening, Quentin and Eleanor dined at Ciro's and took in a horror show at the *Grand Guignol.* Eleanor recalled, "He left the next morning, and I never saw him again."[417]

Humidity-laden clouds had moved in, and it was raining in Paris July 14 as Allied soldiers paraded smartly down the *Avenue des Champs-Élysées* to mark Bastille Day, the French Independence Day holiday. The Germans were at bay, and it was safe for people to mark the storming of the fortress-prison in 1789 and the dawn of the French Revolution.

At the aerodrome at Saints, the *Tricoleur* flew alongside the Stars and Stripes to signify the nations' unity of purpose, and French airmen prepared a celebration that was to include the staging of American musical numbers organized by Quentin Roosevelt.

At rehearsal the night before, Quentin was once again "the life of the party, inspiring everybody with his enthusiasm," in the words of Captain Henry Lyster, adjutant of the 94th Aero Squadron. He recalled, "I appointed Quentin to get up the entertainment. He racked up all the musical talent—the French are very fond of American ragtime and banjos—and the night before he came into my room and sat on my bed telling, with a great sense of humor, of what he had done. The next day [July 14], I called up to arrange about getting his party into town when I heard that he was reported missing."[418]

The air was thick and hazy, and cloud patches blanketed the wide sky above Saints early on that holiday morning. At 8:20 a.m., First Pursuit Group biplanes from the 95th Aero Squadron climbed into the wind. At 3,500 meters, the pilots crossed into German-occupied territory, along the Marne River near Dormans, northeast of Château-Thierry, their twin machine guns loaded and ready.

Less than an hour after departure, Quentin and his mates were climbing in their Nieuports through 4,300 meters, fighting the bitter wind and cold, when a formation of seven enemy Fokker *chasse* planes appeared suddenly above them. They were dark brown and steel gray with white elevators and tails. "One had a black cross on the fuselage outlined in white, [and] another two diagonal black stripes on the fuselage," historian Alan Toelle reported.[419]

Lt. James Knowles of the American pursuit patrol described what happened next:

> Lt. Ted Curtis signaled that he saw [the] enemy formation and fired his guns in their direction. At the same time, French anti-aircraft batteries pointed out the Boche by firing an arrow-shaped barrage of white smoke shells. We all turned toward our own lines, climbing steadily to gain the advantage of altitude and maneuvering into the sun so that the Huns could not see us. After reaching 4,600 meters, we turned back to attack. The Boche were 450 meters below us. . . . We dove on them with every advantage except the wind which was blowing us straight into Germany. Quentin and I picked a machine apiece and immediately attacked. Our opponents dove and we followed them, not realizing that they were luring us down into a position from which we could be attacked by the remaining Huns above us.[420]

Lt. Edward Buford, Jr., another patrol member, recalled the encounter this way:

[The Germans] attacked before we reached the lines and, in a few seconds, had completely broken up our formation, and the fight developed into a general free-for-all. I tried to keep an eye on all of our fellows, but we were hopelessly separated and outnumbered. . . . About a half mile away, I saw one of our planes with three Boche on him, and he seemed to be having a pretty hard time with them, so I shook the two I was maneuvering with and tried to get over to him, but before I could reach them [the] machine turned over on its back and plunged down out of control. . . . Of course, at the time of the fight, I did not know who the pilot was I had seen go down, but as Quentin did not come back, it must have been him.[421]

Whatever the true sequence of events, the fateful dogfight lasted only five or six minutes but it would be recalled in fact and lore for a century because Quentin Roosevelt was at its center.

Hamilton Coolidge, whose squadron did not fly on that fateful Sunday, dutifully took charge of Quentin's belongings two days later. He packed everything into a trunk, he told Flora, including "your picture in a large pigskin frame and your letters, all neatly arranged and numbered in a green leather case." He found no final letter from Quentin. Hamilton promised to ship the trunk to Paris in care of Eleanor.

Although that act suggested closure, Hamilton sought to reassure Flora that Quentin could have survived. "An observer in one of the French balloons did see a Nieuport come down at the place and time of the combat," he told her, "but it was not in flames and did not appear to be out of control. Surely this was Quentin."

Hamilton speculated that Quentin was wounded in the dogfight and had had the presence of mind to put his plane into a steep dive so he could land before fainting from loss of blood. "My conclusion is that Quentin was wounded and is a prisoner," he declared. "All you can do, Flora, is to use every ounce of courage and patience you possess and, above all, keep busy constantly." He added, "I know that he was more than ever in love with you at the time of his disappearance. . . . All we can do is use our utmost faith and courage and trust in his great goodness."[422]

Later that day Hamilton wrote to Edith: "In this awful period of suspense when we don't know whether Quentin is dead or alive . . . the best thing I can do is tell you in detail the circumstances of his disappearance." He went on to describe what he had heard from the American combatants. "The fact that his plane was neither spinning nor in flames as it came down makes me believe that [Quentin] landed safely. I have talked to all the men on his patrol, and almost all seem to think that he is a prisoner and was not shot down."[423]

Other Roosevelt family members in France dispatched similar encouraging news back to Sagamore Hill. Ethel's husband, Dr. Dick Derby, cabled Theodore that Quentin's fellow aviators believed that he had landed safely behind enemy lines. Eleanor struggled to be upbeat in her cable but reported glumly that Quentin's plane was seen to strike the ground. Nevertheless, she wished, "The chance exists that he is a prisoner."[424]

Theodore received distressing news on July 16 when Philip Thompson, an Associated Press reporter, knocked on the door at Sagamore Hill. He showed Theodore a news directive from Paris that read cryptically, "Watch Sagamore Hill in the event of . . ." The final word of the message had been deleted by censors. Closing the door behind him so as not to alarm Edith, Theodore whispered under his breath, "Something has happened to one of the boys."

The reporter returned to the Roosevelt estate the next morning with confirmation from abroad that Quentin had been killed. Theodore's first thought was of Edith. "Mrs. Roosevelt—how am I going to break it to her?"

Appearing on the piazza a half hour later, he read a griefless, one-line statement to reporters who had gathered: "Quentin's mother and I are very glad that he got to the front and had a chance to render some service to his country, and to show the stuff that was in him before his fate befell him."[425] He retreated to telephone Flora.

That morning's edition of *The New York Times* quoted *Havas*, the semi-official French News agency, that Quentin indeed had been killed in an airborne fight and that an American patrol was working behind German lines to find the wreckage of his plane. "He appeared to be fighting up until the last moment," the *Times* noted.[426] Yet the War Department still had no confirmation that it could pass along to the family. In fact, General Pershing would wire Theodore as late as the 19th, saying: "Regret very much that your son is reported missing. . . . I hope he may have landed safely. [I] will advise you immediately on receipt of further information."[427]

Further word of Quentin's heroics came from a German communiqué that was intercepted by the Allies in France: "After a stubborn fight, one of the [American] pilots—Lieutenant Roosevelt— who had shown conspicuous bravery during the fight by attacking again and again without regard to danger, was shot in the head by his more experienced opponent and fell at Chaméry."[428]

The body of Quentin Roosevelt lies beside his crashed plane in Chaméry, France, July 14, 1918, in a photo apparently taken by German troops.

(Courtesy Michael J. O'Neal, Golden Air Age Museum)

A German newspaper, the *Kölnische Zeitung*, reported that Quentin met a hero's death. "A lively air battle began in which one American in particular persisted in attacking," it recounted. "The principal feature of the battle consisted of an air duel between the American and a German fighting pilot, Sgt. [Carl-Emil] Gräper. After a short struggle, Gräper succeeded in bringing the brave American before his gun sights. After a few shots, the plane apparently got out of his control; the American began to fall and struck the ground near the village of Chaméry, about 10 kilometers north of the Marne. The American flyer was killed by two shots through the head. . . . He was buried by German aviators with military honors."[429]

While going through Quentin's things at the crash site, the Germans discovered letters from Flora that positively identified him as the son of Theodore Roosevelt, appreciated even by enemy troops as one of the world's most notable men. Out of military tradition, respect for the Roosevelt family, and Quentin's gallantry as a foe, the Germans gave him a ceremonial burial.

There is a surviving eyewitness account of Quentin's graveside funeral on July 16, authored by Army Lt. James Edgar Gee, a Pennsylvanian from the 110th Infantry, who had been captured and, by chance, was being evacuated near the scene. He reported that about a thousand German soldiers stood stiffly in a hollow square around the grave, and that officers stood at attention before the ranks. "Near the grave was the smashed plane, and beside it was a small group of officers, one of whom was speaking to the men. I did not pass close enough to hear what he was saying; we were prisoners and did not have the privilege of lingering, even for such an occasion as this. At the time I did not know who was being buried, but the guards informed me later. The funeral certainly was elaborate."[430]

A few days after Quentin fell, American forces launched a counteroffensive to push the enemy east toward Reims and beyond. They would quickly reclaim the Château-Thierry region, including Quentin's resting place at Chaméry. When troops came upon the grave, they noticed that someone had placed a wooden cross there with the inscription:

Lieutenant Roosevelt
Buried by the Germans

Americans further decorated the site, mindful of the sorrow of Colonel and Mrs. Roosevelt. Daniel J. Martin, a captain with the 2nd Battalion of the 128th Infantry, said he built a cross made from parts of Quentin's plane and placed it at the head. He claims, as well, to have ordered a guard from his unit to watch over the gravesite.

Quentin's gravesite at Chaméry, France, July 1918.

(Courtesy the Groton School Archives)

Later, other soldiers encircled the earth mound with stones that they had found nearby and erected a larger wooden cross with the message:

Here rests on the Field of Honor
Quentin Roosevelt
Air Service U.S. A.
Killed in Action, July 1918

About 20 feet away, a few remains of the crumpled Nieuport were left to rust in their place, only to be carried off later by souvenir hunters.

A French tribute to their fallen ally was remembered by an unidentified American officer who, in a letter to his family, described the arrival of an elaborate grave marker:

> Down the road came a big open truck loaded with something that looked like a gigantic wooden bed—perhaps 12 feet long and eight feet wide. At the head of it there was a large shield, and above this a carved wooden cross. Did I not know the French idea of homage to the dead, I would not have recognized what it was. As we went by, I looked at the shield—in large carved letters I saw the words, "Quentin Roosevelt." You see, he is buried not far from our rear. It was a bit of French tribute for to these people, there is no man like Roosevelt. They still talk about him, and their eyes snap whenever his name is mentioned. He commands their profound respect. They consider him their friend. This was the only way they could show it."[431]

Quentin's death was officially confirmed to Theodore on July 20th when a telegram of condolence arrived from President Wilson: "I had hoped for other news," he wrote.[432] It was one of hundreds of letters, wires, and other tributes from important people and everyday citizens that flooded somber Sagamore Hill as the Roosevelts grieved for their fallen son.

From the French family that had befriended Quentin while he was at Issoudun, Edithe Normant praised Quentin's "passion for his work," his "young, daring strength" and "the sensitivity of his heart and spirit which had made [him] a very dear friend." She concluded, "We will cherish his memory."[433]

Irene Givenwilson wrote, "Your boy has proved his mettle, done his glorious part in the Great War and laid down his life for his ideals."[434]

Rector Endicott Peabody of the Groton School dwelled on his disappointment "from the thought of what [Quentin] might have done for his country had he survived the war."[435]

The president of Allegheny College, the Rev. William H. Crawford, recalled Quentin's pride when he was asked earlier about the four sons of Theodore Roosevelt at war. "It is rather up to us," Quentin responded to him at the time, "to practice what Father preaches."[436]

Quentin's gravesite, with French crib, at Chaméry, 1918.

Theodore surely treasured one letter in particular—that of the Rev. C. A. White of Chicago—which arrived some weeks later. It seemed that the writer had motored past Quentin's "noble resting place" and felt compelled to correspond, one father to another. In part, he wrote, "There are no other marked graves near. . . . The very isolation and immediate calmness of the scene seemed to me splendid. . . . The grave is in the midst of a broad rolling country, at the foot of a gentle slope which, beyond the grave, drops rather sharply to a more level field. . . . Here, where he fell doing his whole duty, your son sleeps in the bosom of France."[437]

Twenty

Aftermath

Flora's grief was absolute. Her face paled and sunk as she retreated within herself to brood over the unthinkable that had come to pass. How often had she and Quentin written to each other about the possibility—this eventuality of death—considering it only in fleeting, painless abstraction before casually moving on to the next thought? But now, Quentin's loss was authentic, and her anguish was deep. Flora would face the rest of her long life without her true love, a war hero to be sure, one who was gruesomely dead in a remote place an ocean away.

The depth of Flora's heartache moved her mother, the usually self-absorbed Gertrude, to take up her tools of sculpture and preserve the moment. Within months, she would finish a small bronze of the disconsolate Flora, seated limply, her shoulders bent, a sullen head bowed, dolefully staring downward.

As the news of Quentin's death took root, Flora fled her immediate family to share in the close-knit broken-heartedness of the Roosevelts at Sagamore Hill. "Poor darling Flora has been spending the night here," Theodore wrote to Kermit on mourning stationery, the day after receiving President Wilson's telegram. "It is Flora and [Quentin's] mother for whom I feel most." The always-loquacious father allowed, "There is not much to say." Then seemingly righting himself in the next line, he paid tribute to his fallen son: "No man could have died in finer or more gallant fashion, and our pride equals our sorrow."

Theodore and Edith left the mournful house for a couple hours to row in isolation on the glassy waters of nearby Long Island Sound. "There was a little haze," he reported to Kermit, "and it all soothed her poor, bruised and aching spirit. . . . Mother has been as wonderful as she always is in great crisis. She has the heroic soul." [438]

Flora's downcast days captured by Gertrude's
bronze sculpture.

(Courtesy of Flora Miller Biddle.)

Edith's stalwartness was about to face another unanticipated test.
A messenger rapped on the screen door at Sagamore Hill with a
cablegram from Paris. It was from Eleanor: "Ted wounded. Not
seriously. Here with me. Not any danger. No cause for anxiety."[439]
The oldest Roosevelt son who had been gassed and nearly blinded
just seven weeks earlier had been shot twice by an enemy machine
gunner. The projectiles pierced a leg, just above and behind the
knee.

"I got wounded this morning, and here I am," Ted announced
to his wife as corpsmen lifted him from a car and carried him up
to their home. It happened in battle at Ploisy, near Soissons, he
said, as Allied forces severed German supply lines to precipitate
their retreat from the Marne region. Following emergency surgery,
Ted recovered but would limp and have no feeling in his heel for
the rest of his life. His wounding, of course, made headlines and

prompted another round of worried calls and letters to Sagamore Hill.

It was Edith who recognized that the family must remove itself from the specter of war and the house that held so many lingering ghosts of Quentin. A change of scenery was needed, and it would have to be immediate and dramatic, to a venue remote and isolated. Edith asked Ethel if it would be all right if they encamped for a fortnight at the Derby family cottage along the coast of Maine.

On July 25, Theodore and Edith boarded a sleeper and sped north from New York. Ethel and her two children, Richard, four, and Edie, just turned one, went on ahead. The grandchildren would be a loving and cheerful diversion for the duration, Ethel knew.

Dark Harbor, a village on the secluded island of Islesboro, was authentic Maine, separated largely from civilization and accessible only by steamer—an idyllic retreat at which to grieve and recover strength and purpose. The Derby cottage was "a cheery place, pale yellow with scarlet awnings and a view of Penobscot Bay."[440] From that "dear little house" on a knoll by the bay, Theodore wrote letter after letter to family, giving expression to his pain and further memorializing Quentin's sacrifice. "Nothing is more foolish and cowardly than to be beaten down by sorrow while nothing we can do will change," he advised his sister Corinne. "I dread when Edith receives the letters [Quentin] wrote before his death—the letters from her dead boy." Ethel tried to lift her parents' spirits by holding prayer services in the parlor each evening.

Theodore asked Flora to join them in Maine, and she willingly accepted the opportunity to go to her adopted family for their final four days there. "Flora is here; really, she has the heroic quality in her," Theodore wrote to Corinne. "She is so brave and cheerful, although it has been a shattering blow."[441]

With bowed head Flora recalled what Quentin said was his favorite prayer, sent to her from Paris shortly after his arrival there: "O Lord, protect us all the daylong of our troublous life on earth until the shadows lengthen and the evening comes, and the busy world is hushed, the fever of life is over, and our work is done."[442]

As anticipated, Quentin's last letters to Flora and his parents began arriving in Dark Harbor, forwarded from post offices in New York. "He was at the fighting front," Theodore explained to

Kermit's wife, Belle, after reading them. "[He was] very proud and happy—and singularly modest, with all his pride and his pleasure at showing his mettle."[443] Still, Theodore allowed to Corinne, "The letters from the dead open the wounds of the living, and yet one would not miss them for anything."[444]

As the Roosevelts and Flora headed back to Sagamore Hill on August 10, Hamilton Coolidge was making a pilgrimage to his friend's gravesite in the tiny hamlet of Chaméry. Acknowledging to Edith that he was "fighting an awfully empty feeling inside," Hamilton revealed that he was writing "a little sketch," a remembrance of Quentin's days in France, "in the hope that I may be able to tell you some things about him [that] you would never have learned from his letters."[445] Edith and Flora would not see the sketch until several months later when it was discovered among Hamilton's things by a friend and mailed to Sagamore Hill.

As the immediate pain of the hero's death receded in the cooling weeks of fall, friends and colleagues of Quentin began to assess his manner as an aviator. Some of his men at Issoudun knew him to be "both selfless and voracious in his search for victory . . . a daredevil who courted risk and glory."[446] Others wondered whether he had been overconfident as a flyer, foolishly averse to danger. Captain Eddie Rickenbacker, the decorated flying ace and commander of the 94th Aero Squadron, acknowledged that Quentin was easily the most popular man in the 95th. Yet, in his memoir, Rickenbacker was harshly judgmental of him: "[Quentin] was reckless to such a degree that his commanding officers had to caution him repeatedly about the senselessness of his lack of caution. His bravery was so notorious that we all knew that he would either achieve some great, spectacular success or be killed in the attempt. Even the pilots in his own flight would beg him to conserve himself and wait for a fair opportunity for a victory. But Quentin would merely laugh away all serious advice."[447]

Even Quentin's best buddy began to question cause and effect. In a candid note to Flora, Hamilton Coolidge wrote, "His daring was difficult to understand. His utter fearlessness perhaps caused his death. But it is a death that makes us thrill."[448]

In the end, the French government would award Quentin the *Croix de Guerre avec Palme*, an honor bestowed to warriors who distinguish themselves by acts of heroism involving combat with the enemy. The citation praised him as an *"Excellent pilote dé, possedant les plus belle qualities de courage et de devoument."*[449]

Additionally, Quentin would receive the unprecedented honor of having a French war vessel named for him during the war. A former Russian torpedo boat and destroyer was rechristened the *Quentin Roosevelt* in September out of respect for his sacrifice and his father's service as U.S. president.[450]

Among the many tributes Quentin would receive at home was a War Department resolve that "the flying field on Long Island, now known as Westbury Plateau [in Mineola], is hereby named Roosevelt Field in memory of Quentin."[451] And within a year of his death, Quentin would be awarded an undergraduate degree from Harvard College for honorable service in the war, "though deficient seven and one half courses of the requirements."[452]

From the Red Cross canteen at faraway Issoudun, Irene Givenwilson strove to fortify Flora. From a talk they had had while he was in France, she paraphrased Quentin's words about death. "In case I die," she recalled him saying, "[Flora] must just live, and if she must drink the cup, then drink it with thankfulness for what we have already had, and then she must live it again. Life is glorious."[453]

By now, Theodore had assumed a role as Flora's interim protector. "Dearest Flora," he wrote, "Just a line of love, dearest girl; and to tell you again how I admire and respect you because of the way you took your engagement to Quentin and because of your fine and gallant bearing in your hour of bitter trial. You made him very, very happy. . . . Remember, Flora, that as long as I live, I shall love you as if you were my own daughter . . ."[454]

Theodore's affection for Flora was mixed with deep resentment that wartime bureaucracy had prevented her marriage. He told Kermit, "The War Department now lets sisters of soldiers go abroad. I shall always feel the most intense bitterness at the red tape stupidity which refused to permit this last spring. I would not feel nearly so sad about gallant Quentin if he had been able to marry Flora; and if Flora had been his wife and perhaps had his baby. It would have made a world's difference to her."[455]

Still, Theodore expressed hope for her future when he wrote to his daughter-in-law Belle from Dark Harbor: "There is nothing to comfort Flora at the moment, but she is young. I most earnestly hope that time will be very merciful to her and, in a few years, she will keep Quentin as only a long memory of her golden youth, as the love of her golden dawn, and that she will find happiness with another good and fine man. . . ."[456] Perhaps that would prove true, but as the first-month anniversary of Quentin's death passed, Flora remained deeply pained: "Everything else just hurts nearly all of the whole time," she confided to Ethel. "There is no one I can talk to who half understands. It is all so lonely. . . ."[457]

Flora would soon learn that another young woman of about the same age could empathize with her emotional state. It was the budding artist Kay Sage, now 20, her close friend from the Foxcroft School. Kay brought comfort to Flora through her expressive poetry:

-To Quentin Roosevelt-
A moment past, he soared above the land
On golden wings—not as his thoughts had soared,
But with a fierce intent of purpose. And
Beneath, the tortured beast of battle roared.
There, hand in hand and side by side, men gave—
He gave alone. No heart however crude
Was near to help his fight—superbly brave,
He faced the peril in his solitude—
He gave the greatest gift—a gift sublime—
Unflinchingly he played a losing game
But won the right to live through endless time
An honor to his country and his name
Above a bit of France in which he lies
A spot, beyond man's reach, is set apart.
There, through the darkest clouds, a star shall rise
As fearless, true and perfect as his heart.[458]

In the weeks following Quentin's death, Hamilton Coolidge would assume command of a flight within the 1st Pursuit Group. On October 8, he was promoted to captain—during a period in which his kills were coming "thick and fast." It was said that he once had three in one hour. Hamilton's commanding officers acknowledged that by his daring, aggressiveness and courage, he had become a master of aerial attack and defense. In all, he was credited with shooting down eight enemy planes and balloons.[459]

Capt. Hamilton Coolidge, October 1918,
shortly before his death.

(Laurence LaTourette Driggs Collection, National Air

& Space Museum, courtesy Alan D. Toelle.)

The War Department's adjutant general would later describe the "extraordinary heroism in action" that Hamilton showed on October 27, 1918: "Leading a protection patrol, he went to the assistance of two observation planes which were being attacked by six German machines. Observing this maneuver, the enemy sent up a terrific barrage from anti-aircraft guns on the ground. Disregarding the extreme danger, [Hamilton] dived straight into the barrage, and his plane was struck and sent down in flames."[460] He came down in a no man's land, southeast of Grandpré in the Argonne Forest, and was buried where he fell by Rickenbacker and others. His friendship was cherished by both Quentin and Flora, and a role model of "clean thinking and clean living" among the men in his squadron, Hamilton Coolidge was honored posthumously with the French *Croix de Guerre avec Palme* and the U.S. Distinguished Service Cross for "extreme gallantry."

Coincidentally, October 27, 1918, was Theodore Roosevelt's 60th birthday. When he learned of Hamilton's death, Theodore told Edith that he wished Hamilton would be buried alongside Quentin. He cited their close friendship dating to their adolescence at the Groton School. Theodore raised the idea with Hamilton's mother, but later set the idea aside because of his own deteriorating health.

Flora, at work in Washington, D.C., in the spring of 1919.

(Courtesy of Flora Miller Biddle.)

Since perfecting her typing and stenography, Flora had been accepting work on and off from associates. Now, in the fall of 1918, those skills would prove therapeutic and time-absorbing as she endeavored to get on with her life. Earlier in the year, she had prepared a card index and rash of file folders for a Navy post in New York after first having signed a security oath. Now, Theodore was asking if she would accept some of his dictation and turn it into typed manuscripts. With enthusiasm and skill, she obliged the man who had comforted her so kindheartedly in the days immediately following Quentin's death. Her first product, dated Armistice Day, November 11, 1918, was a three-page typed letter, virtually error free. She kept a copy and documented it with a handwritten note at the top, "1st letter, written for the Colonel while he was in the hospital."

Theodore had checked himself into Roosevelt Hospital in New York in early November, suffering the lingering aftereffects of the tropical forests of Cuba and Brazil. His joints ached and swelled from rheumatism, and he could hardly walk. Edith wondered whether he had pushed himself too hard in the preceding weeks when he had campaigned tirelessly for Republican congressional candidates in states as far away as Montana. Although his crowds were huge and enthusiastic then, often chanting "We Want Teddy," Theodore usually looked fatigued and weak of spirit when the cheering subsided. Longtime associates observed that his old exuberance had faded under the weight of years, exhaustion, and sorrow. "Quentin's death shook him greatly," Edith wrote to Kermit around this time. "I can see how constantly he thinks of [Quentin], and not the merry, happy, silly thoughts which I have, but sad thoughts of what [he] would have counted for in the future."[461]

While Theodore lay in his hospital bed—with Edith staying in an adjoining room—the Great War was coming to a decisive end in Europe. Bells pealed from church tops throughout Paris, and people celebrated in the boulevards with abandon. A succession of Allied offensives in eastern France during the second half of 1918 had shattered Germany's positions and destroyed its morale. Devastated by a soaring number of casualties and with little hope for future success, German leaders lost their will to fight. They asked President Wilson and other Allied leaders for an armistice. It was signed, ceremonially, at the 11th hour of the 11th day of November in a railcar in France's Compiègne Forest. It was the day, Belle Roosevelt later remarked with hyperbole, that Quentin had made possible.

Theodore argued for abject German capitulation. He ridiculed Wilson's plan for a negotiated surrender based on his earlier-announced Fourteen Points of peace. "Let us dictate peace by the hammering of guns," Theodore implored, "and not chat about peace to the accompaniment of the clicking of typewriters."[462]

There was increasing talk in Republican circles and in the newspapers about the certainty of Theodore's nomination to succeed Wilson in 1920. It grew, in part, from people's empathy with Theodore over Quentin's death and their eagerness to help him rebound. Theodore responded uncaringly, saying he would not lift a finger for the nomination. "I am not eager to be president again. . . . Since Quentin's death, the world seems to have shut down on me."[463] Those who saw him at the time knew that the idea of a Roosevelt restoration was a fanciful dream. He was a very sick man, and he knew it.

On Christmas Day, Theodore shuffled out of the hospital "stiff, weak and very pale." Edith had arranged for Sagamore Hill to be gaily decorated, layering over the gloom of Quentin's absence. Theodore reveled at the giant evergreen tree twinkling with lights, and the array of colorful packages beneath it, marked for the grandchildren. Archie was there with his family, albeit evidencing a gaunt look and a limp arm. Eleanor was home safely, too.

"Lord, how beautiful, even its sad, frozen winter landscape looked," Theodore wrote to Kermit a few days afterward, perhaps while gazing out a window at Sagamore Hill. "Inflammatory rheumatism, slightly complicated by sciatica, means a long period of getting better, and I am still a cripple, unable to do anything but hobble a few yards," he acknowledged. Still, he consented to being "very happy, for all of you have made me so very proud."[464]

As he wrote, Theodore surely thought of Kermit; Ethel's husband, Dick; and Ted, all of whom were still mopping up in France. Ted had recently been promoted to colonel—Theodore's rank a generation ago, coming out of the Spanish-American War. As Edmund Morris observed, "Two Colonel Roosevelts in one family, plus two decorated captains and one dead hero, added up to plenty of honor."[465]

James Amos, Theodore's longtime valet, arrived at Sagamore Hill on January 4, 1919, to help Edith care for him. Amos recalled being shocked by how poorly Theodore looked. "His face bore a tired expression," Amos wrote in his memoir. "There was a look of weariness in his eyes. It was perfectly plain he had suffered deeply."[466]

Within two days, the 26th President of the United States was dead. He went quietly to the ages in his sleep, ultimately succumbing to an embolism that, most likely, had lodged in a coronary artery. "Theodore darling," Edith pleaded at his bedside in the dark of the early morning. There was no response.[467]

"The old lion is dead," Archie cabled to his family abroad.[468]

Joseph Bucklin Bishop, Theodore's authorized biographer, wrote soon thereafter, "He died as he would have wished to, in the home that he loved, with his family about him, in the full possession of his faculties, in the midst of work that was nearest to his heart, and at the summit of his fame."[469]

Weeks earlier, Theodore and Edith had spoken of going abroad in the spring to see where Quentin rested. Now, the sad duty would fall to his mother alone. Within a month of Theodore's funeral, on February 5, Edith sailed for Le Havre where Ted, Kermit and Belle were waiting. Her sister, Emily Carow who lived in Italy, joined them in Paris.

Sylvia Jukes Morris, Edith's biographer, penned a poignant portrayal of the valiant mother's mission in a remote commune about 80 miles southeast of Paris: "The sky was overcast, but rain held off as she made the ten-minute walk from the village [of Chaméry] to the hillside grave. In her arms she carried great bunches of while lilac, lilies of the field, violets and anemones, and Emily marveled at her tearless self-control as she knelt and recited the Lord's Prayer."[470]

Edith wanted a permanent marker at Quentin's grave site, and arranged for a large marble slab to be engraved and laid upon the tomb. She chose a passage from the 40th stanza of Shelly's *Adonais*: "He has outsoared the shadow of our night."

The dwellers of Chaméry and its parent commune of Coulonges-Cohan, some of whom were tending to Quentin's grave site, wanted something more substantial, a monument to Quentin that would be visible from the street. Edith, too, wanted a memorial that would be both commemorative and functional. Upon returning home, she enlisted the French-born architect Paul Philippe Cret, who had distinguished himself in uniform during the war, to design the monument.[471] Drawing inspiration from ancient Roman villas, Cret conceived a broad stone structure, nearly ten feet wide and more than seven feet tall. It was configured with a central fountain and seats on either side where people could rest and contemplate Quentin's sacrifice. To symbolize his attachment to the people of France, the memorial was sited in the heart of Chaméry, hugging a winding farm road.

There is no evidence that Flora ever visited Quentin's grave, even though she journeyed to France in August 1919. She sailed with her aunt, Dorothy Straight, who had recently lost her husband. According to B. H. Friedman, Flora spent her days hobnobbing in Paris with artists who knew her mother and went shopping for Chanel and Poiret fashions. "I wish you could see the clothes!" she wrote to Gertrude at the time. "They are getting shorter and shorter, & as for the evening dresses, there is nothing to them at all—literally nothing above the waist in the back, and cut entirely out under the arms—it's too awful."[472]

The boisterous 1920s were dawning in America. Prohibition would bring the spread of defiant speakeasies and the rollicking Jazz Age. Babe Ruth would play winning baseball for the New York Yankees. Jack Dempsey would hold the world heavyweight boxing title, and Edith Wharton would prepare to earn a Pulitzer Prize for literature, the first for a woman.

In this milieu Flora was, indeed, getting on with her life. From the Adirondacks in November, Gertrude sent off an urgent letter to her husband who was tending to his mining interests in Montana: "Something has happened about Flora that you won't like—I don't. It's Rod [Roderick Tower, Quentin's Air Service mate at Mineola]. They informed me the other afternoon that they were engaged. . . . I have been trying in subtle ways to influence Flora. . . . I don't really think she is very much in love. . . . I don't see that there is anything to do except give her time and hope she will get over it. Knowing Flora, I think there is a very good chance that she will."[473]

"I think she has just done it in desperation," Ethel said. "She was so unhappy."[474]

Mindful perhaps of Quentin's insistence that "she must live life again," Flora married Rod Tower at 4 p.m., Monday, April 19, 1920 in St. Bartholomew's Church on Park Avenue in Manhattan. A huge crowd of notables attended. Edith Roosevelt stayed home.

Quentin's memorial at Chaméry, France, as seen in 2013.

(Photo by Chip Bishop.)

Twenty One

Life after Quentin

On a steamy July day in 1986, a bevy of granddaughters and other family intimates gathered at Flora's Old Westbury home. They had come with sundry mindsets: sorrow to be sure, but also with anticipation that comes with any family ritual. The women recently had buried their aged matriarch. It was now time to distribute Flora's extraordinary wardrobe, relics of her life that had been saved in crowded closets and bulging dressers for decades. There were proper Chanel suits and gay party dresses, Balenciaga ball gowns, and an elegant black pant suit once owned by Gertrude.

"What is this?" a voice surely asked. It was Flora's familiar jacket that she wore on shooting expeditions.

"Look here," another undoubtedly exclaimed. "There's a pair of buckskin pants and a fringed, beaded jacket, probably from a jaunt out West."

Flora Miller Biddle, Flora's younger daughter, recalled the animation in the room: "They wept a bit, and laughed with each other too, as they preened in all the finery: huge ostrich fans, fine leather pocketbooks, silk and chiffon scarves, kidskin gloves in white and dazzling colors, negligees, bed jackets trimmed in swans' down, and dozens of hats—veiled, feathered, sequined, beribboned with tassels and furbelows."[475]

The participants surely appreciated that the objects of their fascination were more than just examples of Flora's wardrobe. They were artifacts of her life, manifestations from almost every facet of it: from her youth and the Quentin years, from later marriages, and from stylish museum parties to the retirement years at home. Through her myriad of costumes, Flora's life story came alive from the clouds of time. Mother, grandmother, and aunt, she was recalled as an extraordinary woman who lived a long and accomplished life, extravagant at times, often heartbroken but never dull.

He was the ruggedly handsome son of Charlemagne Tower, Jr., former ambassador to Germany and Russia. A few years older than the bride, Roderick Tower was, like Quentin, a Harvard man and Air Service officer, but one who had remained safely stateside during the war. Surviving snapshots showed that he had trained with Quentin at Mineola and socialized with him in off times. Then, in 1920, as a postwar stockbroker in New York, he magnetized Flora with his good looks and urbane charm.

Following a honeymoon in Hawaii and Japan, Rod and Flora Tower settled in Los Angeles where he ventured into oil and gas exploration, and she raised their two children, Pamela, born in the year following their wedding, and Whitney, who came along in 1923.

To fuel his new career, Rod traveled widely in search of accessible natural resources. His recurring business trips throughout the west and to Mexico—some for as long as a month—placed a considerable strain on the young family. Responsibility for the children's care fell to Flora and the help that she hired. Yet when Rod was at home, the husband's and wife's schedules clashed. "Horrible," Flora wrote. "I sleep all night, and he sleeps all day."[476]

Those who read Flora's Line-a-Day diary entries of the period noted expressions of loneliness and nostalgia. There were commemorations of Theodore Roosevelt's birth and Quentin's death. There was evidence that she tried to make the marriage work, even delving into dry geology texts in a struggle to comprehend Rod's work. But he was increasingly unstable, temperamental, and withdrawn.[477] In reaction, Flora and the children often fled to her family in New York.

By the spring of 1925, following five years of marriage, Flora and Rod contemplated divorce. Quietly, and with the help of Gertrude, she traveled to a court in the 19th century spa town of La Bourboule, in the Auvergne region of France. There she would end the marriage. She was confident that it was the right move for her and for the children. The divorce was granted promptly on the grounds of Rod's desertion, and custody of the children was split: Pamela to Flora, and Whitney to Rod. In a short time, however, young Whit was returned, without contest, to his mother.

202

Flora wrote around that time, "If married people were more intimate—more openly honest—more willing to allow the other to participate in innermost thoughts, there would be a better knowledge of human nature and therefore less misunderstanding."[478] Now, freed from her vows, Flora returned to sculpture, practicing that summer at Gertrude's elbow. She proudly exhibited her work at the Waldorf Astoria. A small bronze statuette, a female nude dubbed "South Wind," sold for $200, more than $2,500 in value today.

Bereft of the life she had planned with Quentin, and with a failed marriage behind her, the Flora of that period searched for her own muse. She continued to sculpt with some success and studied writing for a while at Columbia University. Seeking further grounding, she moved into the French House on the Old Westbury campus, an inspiring residence designed by the prominent architect William Adams Delano. It was marked by a round tower, 9.2 acres of English gardens and chestnut trees, and an inviting cobblestone drive. A friend said she lived and loved well from there, "zestfully and deeply," enjoying the rhythms of her life.

In her memoir, *Embers*, Flora Miller Biddle wrote, "With no real commitment to work, my mother's ambition was partly, if not wholly, satisfied by her daily life which included her family, decorating her houses, games, books, entertaining, fishing, shooting and a number of male admirers. She had, like her mother, a kind of pride in being able to attract desirable men."[479]

The most noteworthy of those was G. Macculloch Miller, an elegant and debonair bachelor of about 40. Cully, as he was called, was a product of St. Paul's School and, for a while, the Art Students League of New York. He shared the Whitney family's interest in American art and felt comfortable joining their place in society. He charmed Flora with his attentiveness to her, his finely-tailored attire, a love of Prohibition-era dry martinis, and silkiness on the dance floor in the manner of his friend, Fred Astaire. "[I] haven't been so happy in months and months and more months," Flora confided to her journal in 1926. "[I] lay in bed all morning and drifted on a lovely pink cloud. I hope he lets me stay there just for a little while."[480]

Flora delighted in Cully's art, "lovely evocations of nature, people, flowers and still lives," by her daughter's description. Often, Flora was the adored subject of his work, depicted lounging, sun bathing or fishing. Flora Miller Biddle allowed that her father's love of art later infused her lifetime appreciation of creative works.

Early in 1927, Gertrude took a cruise to Egypt to build up her health and study ancient architecture and sculpture in preparation for a major commission. Flora, Cully and the children booked passage too, full of excitement and anticipation. Following a leisurely tour of the Mediterranean, the party arrived in Cairo on January 28. Flora and Cully began making arrangements for a wedding that they had been planning. Since their meeting, their courtship had matured steadily into love and mutual commitment. This time, Flora assured herself, it was for real.

Cully's local friends promptly threw a bachelor dinner for him in Cairo and, on the following day, February 23rd, he and Flora were wed. It was a brief and simple ceremony, performed at the height of the day's heat at the home of North Winship, the American consul. During the vows, the tanned, blue-eyed groom surprised Flora by placing a stylish, African-made elephant hair ring on the third finger of her left hand. According to legend, the elephant hair—observable from a small window in the gold band—would protect the wearer from illness, keep her out of harm's way and ensure a life of great fortune.

The *Scarab*, a double-decked dahabeah, was awash in swaying palm fronds when the wedding party and their guests arrived for a dockside reception lunch. An American flag waved smartly from above the vessel's smokestack. Following a meal and celebratory toasts, Flora and Cully cleared their guests from the houseboat and embarked on a honeymoon cruise down the Nile.

Perhaps their most notable wedding gift was a hand-me-down from Gertrude: *Le Petit Boulay*, a small, turreted château near Tours on the River Loire in central France. It would become Flora's and Cully's summer getaway in later years, before occupying German officers used it as a billet. "There were deep underground passages with wine stored in wooden casks," the younger Flora would recall years later. She found the "cavernous spaces filled with the rich odors of fermenting grapes and chalky earth" a terrifying but irresistible playground.[481]

Flora and Cully at the New York World's Fair, 1939

(Courtesy Flora Miller Biddle)

On returning home, the couple moved into the French House. Cully was a patient and supportive husband, encouraging Flora's eclectic pursuits and mixing well with the family, qualities that Flora surely had been seeking since she lost Quentin. Cully applied his draftsman's training by partnering with Auguste Noël to form the architectural firm of Noël and Miller. The firm specialized in the design of dignified residences on the northern shore of Long Island and throughout the East Coast.

Within a year, Flora and Cully started a family of their own, to share the good life with Pamela, now seven, and Whit, five. Flora Macculloch Miller (later Flora Miller Biddle), was born in 1928, and Leverett Saltonstall Miller in 1931. But another loss loomed. On October 26, 1930, Flora's father, Harry Payne Whitney, died suddenly. Flora and Gertrude were at his bedside at the family's Fifth Avenue mansion when Harry, at 58, succumbed to pneumonia after coming down with a cold and slight fever. Harry was remembered in news accounts as a passionate sportsman and shrewd capitalist who had built up one of the nation's great fortunes.

Flora had worked hard to stay close to her father during her childhood, keeping up with his business pursuits, international polo competitions, and thoroughbred racing. In time, she would benefit, through her mother's bequest, from his success.

While overseeing the care of her young children, Flora also kept an eye on the widow Gertrude as she took a major step toward the creation of what would become the Whitney Museum of American Art. By 1930, Gertrude had collected nearly 700 works of mostly unrecognized American artists which she had shown from time to time at other museums. She had been considering a permanent home for the collection, and had offered it to the Metropolitan Museum of Art which declined. Undaunted, she created her own showcase. With the aid of Cully's firm, she renovated her studio and adjoining row houses on 8th Street in Greenwich Village. On November 17, 1931, the museum opened to 5,000 early guests and encouraging newspaper reviews.

The Whitney, as it was popularly known, bought and showed works by American artists. "Its primary purpose," Gertrude declared, was to "discover fresh talents and stimulate the creative spirit of the artist before it is deadened by old age . . ."[482] The displayed works represented the taste of Gertrude Vanderbilt Whitney, pure and simple. There was no need for an institutionalized board of trustees, she said. The family would watch over the museum, and she would underwrite all costs. To ensure that its works were accessible to all, Gertrude decided that there would be no admission fee to the museum. And, about the same time, she gave Joye Cottage, the family's beloved retreat in Aiken, South Carolina, to Flora. It soon became a haven where Flora, Cully, and the children could enjoy collective seclusion and ward off the dreadful news of Depression-era newspaper headlines.

The care of the children was left, in good measure, to paid staff to make certain, in the younger Flora's words, "that we were learning what they thought we needed to know, in order to someday have the same sheltered lives that [my parents] were leading."[483] To provide for the children's education, Flora and two other mothers organized the Aiken Day School at the squash court near Joye Cottage and recruited a young teacher from her one-time New York school, the Brearley, to act as headmistress and instructor.

From daughter Flora's written remembrances, a reader may conclude that the young family's social ecosystem at Joye Cottage was akin to a genteel cocoon, a "unique American utopia,"[484] of the privileged life and *au courant* style.

In 1936, as she neared 40, Flora acceded to a request from Gertrude that would serve as a prologue to the rest of her professional life. She agreed to join the museum's new board of trustees to secure its future as a family institution. Within six years, she would become its president.

On April 18, 1942, Gertrude died of a heart infection, "sad, weak and very thin," according to friends. Flora was grief stricken. Sharing her mother's lifelong preoccupation with art and frequent excursions aboard, the two had become close. "Mama was not only my mother but my best friend," Flora wrote to her brother, Sonny. ". . . There was very little we had not discussed together. . . . We not only had the tragedies together, but we had fun together—more fun than I have ever had with anyone else."[485] Out of respect for Gertrude's memory, the Whitney Museum closed its doors, if only temporarily.

Flora occupied herself, as she had during the Great War, as a Red Cross volunteer. She donned the starched, gray and white uniform of the Gray Lady Corps and offered recreational diversions to wounded veterans of the Second World War in New York hospitals. Her cheeriness and compassionate manner, no doubt, helped boost the morale of scores of injured soldiers. That was, she said, her most worthy contribution to the war effort.

During the Depression and following America's sudden entry into World War II, the family's wealth eroded. At her death, Gertrude's estate was valued at $11 million ($153 million today), much of which was left to charity. The museum received $2.5

million, and the balance went to Flora and her siblings. Of more long-term significance, Gertrude bequeathed the museum itself to Flora with permission to retain it or sell it, as she wished.

Flora accepted the museum, ensuring that it would stay within the family's control. It was the right decision but an intimidating obligation, one for which she said she was not fully prepared. After all, she had no training or experience in institutional policy-making and fund raising, just the priceless family name and a flock of friends who wanted to see her succeed.

"Undaunted and energetic at about 50 years old, my mother embarked on a new career," the younger Flora recalled.[486] On her mother's shoulders rested the obligation not only to carry on Gertrude's mission but to keep the Whitney afloat financially.

With nearly single-handed generosity and a personal manner of "privileged assurance," Flora guided the museum for the next 20 years, beyond survival through the crucial stages of its growth and sustenance. During the 1950s and early 60s, the Whitney evolved from a pioneer establishment, with no support outside the family, to an organization with broad and deep backing from its board and friends. That enabled it to relocate, in 1954, to a larger and better midtown location on West 54th Street in a building designed by Cully's firm. The museum's collection expanded to more than 19,000 works of art, and attendance quadrupled.

An alluring personal portrait of Flora emerged during those years. "Even in her early sixties," author B. H. Friedman remembered, "Flora was still an unusually attractive woman, still something of a flapper. Though her hair was graying, she wore it short as she had in the 20s, and she remained slim, suggesting the stem-like elegance of a flower."[487]

Her board leadership was not without its critics. Barklie Henry, a nephew, trustee and Flora devotee, recommended an activist approach to museum policies and finances. "In long, thoughtful letters that followed board meetings, he often criticized what he saw as weakness in my mother's running of those meetings and her reluctance to accept what new [board] members were offering. . . ," Flora Miller Biddle wrote.[488] She recalled him saying that the museum could never lose by being daring and taking risks—only by conservatism and fear of change. "It has most to do with your mother and the embarrassment and modesty she naturally feels as [head] of that high-powered group," Barklie told the younger Flora.[489]

Flora persevered by subsidizing the museum's annual deficit for years while quietly gifting money to her children and grandchildren, and paying for their education. "If we built a house, she'd help so we wouldn't need a mortgage," her daughter remembered. The unplanned consequence of Flora's munificence was an acute erosion of her fortune. "I'm sure she never dreamed that her money could ever run out," the younger Flora later observed.[490]

Within a decade of moving to West 54th Street, the museum's exhibition space was once again inadequate. A desirable parcel of land, uptown at East 75th Street and Madison Avenue, became available, and Flora and the other trustees raised the funds to buy it. Hungarian-born architect Marcel Breuer, a master of modernism, was retained to design what turned out to be a rugged structure of concrete and glass.

Flora pledged $500,000 toward the construction, conditioned on the sale of a painting, Manet's "Smoker," that had hung for years in Gertrude's living room at Old Westbury. As she dedicated the new Whitney with a flourish, in the fall of 1966, Flora declared, "It is the culmination of a dream that my mother had nearly sixty years ago."[491]

By the next year, while professionals were running the Whitney, Flora was elevated to chairman of the board, serving alongside Jacqueline Kennedy who had joined in 1962 while she was first lady. The chairmanship was largely titular and awarded for life; Flora would have little responsibility except to attend meetings from time to time and turn up at museum celebrations in her usual gracious manner.

To offset the dissipated Whitney and Vanderbilt fortunes, the family had been selling off chunks of the original 630-acre Old Westbury estate to real estate developers. In 1964, the New York Institute of Technology, a private research school, bought 310 acres for use as a campus for Long Island commuter students. The family preserved only Gertrude's studio and about 10 acres of land for use by Flora's elder daughter, Pamela.

Flora's life was a succession of hills and valleys. She relished the hills and survived each valley. Cully's death from emphysema and pneumonia at 85, in the summer of 1972, devastated her. Flora and Cully had been married, more-or-less contentedly, for 45 years. She responded by withdrawing into herself, and fighting off bouts of loneliness and despair. She grew increasingly distant from museum business and politics, turning over more and more to her daughter, Flora Miller Biddle.

"Activities and friends filled Mom's days and nights," the younger Flora recalled, "until late in life when television took the place of companionship."[492] She settled in at home on Long Island, in front of the TV, to enjoy boxing, horse racing, and baseball. From time to time, she emerged for social events, appearing in her "slightly flirtatious but dignified manner, polished nails, and black evening suit covered with shiny paillettes."[493]

The generational torch passed again in the spring of 1977 when Flora Miller Biddle accepted the presidency of the museum. Overcoming the same feelings of inadequacy and intimidation that her mother had felt 35 years before, Flora temporarily set aside her family obligations. "It became about art," she said, acknowledging that she yearned to get involved with the change, diversity, and excitement that was buzzing in the art world at that moment.[494]

Three years later, her mother, now 82, made a final, grand gesture to ensure the Whitney's future by turning to one of the family's remaining prime assets. The trustees had a plan to expand the building at East 75th and Madison but were short of funds to pay for the design. Flora resolved to sell J. M. W. Turner's "Juliet and her Nurse," an early 19th Century pre-Impressionism masterpiece that had been treasured by the Whitney family since her grandfather's generation. The decision to dispose of her favorite work was a practical one. Not only would the Whitney benefit from the auction proceeds, she would get a welcomed infusion of cash as well.

Flora with her daughter, Flora, in 1978.

(Courtesy Flora Miller Biddle)

It was May 29, 1980 when Sotheby's chairman and chief auctioneer John Marion stepped up to the lectern in New York: "A hush fell over the room as I began the auction," he remembered. Continuing:

> Rather quickly, the bidding passed the $2.5 million mark. The silence in the auction room was punctuated only by the sound from the two bidders: one over the telephone, calling from London, the other present in the sales room. In six minutes and four seconds, I brought the hammer down for a record $6.4 million . . . the highest price at that time ever paid at auction for any work of art. . . .[495]

The proceeds paid for the architect's fees but to Flora's everlasting disappointment, the new museum wing was never built.

In the Florida springtime of 1986, New York Mets manager Davey Johnson surveyed his roster of talent on the sun-kissed training field. Afterward, he told his baseball team that they were going to win it all for their fans that season. Moreover, he said, they would blow away the opposition. No one was more thrilled at that prospect than #1 Mets fan Flora Whitney Miller. Now 88, with keen interest but failing eyesight, she was a fixture in front of her TV, following games intently and smoking from inning to inning through a long, elegant cigarette holder. When the Mets were not televised, she would clip newspaper accounts of the games and paste them into her scrapbook, reserving extra pages for her favorite player, the good-looking All-Star first-baseman Keith Hernandez.

Flora's enthusiasm for the team may have been at its height, but her health was declining. She was mostly housebound now, diminished in strength and ambition, and dependent on her children. Daughter Flora recalled at the time, "She looked tiny and ate very little—just a few bites."[496] When doctors told her that she had an aneurism that might burst at any time, she accepted her fate with "radiant courage," deflecting conversations about it to happier developments in her grandchildren's lives.

"I told her about things at the museum," the younger Flora said. "I read aloud to her and talked of family and old friends. She always pretended interest but I could see that she was really somewhere else much of the time."[497]

In July, as her beloved Mets drove for the pennant, Flora was taken by ambulance to the hospital where she was admitted into intensive care. Still, the family spoke of plans to celebrate her 89th birthday later that month. But, suddenly, in the early hours of July 18th, Flora closed her weary green eyes and died quietly. Doctors said it was cardiac arrest.

Her children scrambled to make arrangements, and concluded that a private family funeral was what she would have wanted. Her daughter recalled, "We chose things for her to wear, [including] her Cairo wedding ring—the elephant hair encased in thin gold."[498]

The woman whose sturdy will had nurtured one of New York's great art museums was laid to rest solemnly under a flat stone marker in a Quaker cemetery not far from Old Westbury. Many of her 18 grandchildren and nine great-grandchildren paid their respects. Subsequently, the family sold many of her things to pay estate taxes.

Flora did not live to witness the mammoth victory parade down Broadway, a confetti-showered celebration to mark the greatest Mets season ever. Manager Johnson's springtime prediction was on the mark. The team rewrote the record books, winning 108 games in the season, taking the league championship, and beating the Boston Red Sox in one of the most memorable World Series ever. The Mets were the World Series champs. Flora Whitney Miller would not complete her scrapbook for 1986 but my, oh my, would she have cheered the outcome.

So what, then, is Flora's legacy? On a personal level, she had four children who loved her deeply and found ways to use what they had inherited to contribute to the world. Professionally, she ensured the Whitney Museum of Art's survival as a pre-eminent museum of 20th century American art. Her daughter, Flora, asserted that her mother's vision "enabled the museum to grow and change from a family enterprise to a broadly-based professional institution with non-family trustees and a much larger footprint in New York City."[499]

The years had stretched on to nearly 70 from the day young Quentin Roosevelt died in wartime battle over the lush fields of France to the quiet passing in New York of the aged and exhausted Foufie, his sole true love. Quentin adored her more than anything, and she worshipped him passionately from across a forbidding ocean, but his death denied them the great prizes of marriage and children. They were just 20 when all of that happened.

Had he lived, would he have continued to love the mature woman of purpose, grace, and riches? Could he have stayed home willingly during the long museum meetings and smiled contentedly as he held her arm during the many receptions?

If he had become a successful writer or celebrated political heir to the House of Roosevelt, would she have stood comfortably beside him in the role of the adoring wife, basking in audience applause? Would youthful Quentin have become the Roosevelt who valiantly guided the nation through the Second World War? What would living in the White House have meant to a woman whose genes overflowed with the DNA of the Vanderbilts and Whitneys? These are riveting fantasies, impossible questions with no answers.

Flora's daughter recalls that her mother would occasionally speak of Quentin. But near the end of her life, her recollection faded and she lost all memory of him and other loved ones.

One fact is certain: the exemplary love that Quentin and Flora shared for an eventful 18 months before and during the world's Great War was authentic and full-bodied. Against great temptation, they remained faithful to each other. From all the indicators, their loyalty and selfless love surely would have strengthened and endured through the decades, if they had only been given the chance to live it.

Quentin's rain-soaked crash-site marker, against the backdrop of Chaméry, as seen in 2013.

(Photo by Chip Bishop)

Epilogue

Edith and Theodore Roosevelt about 1918.

(541.9 - 010, Theodore Roosevelt Collection, Houghton Library,

Harvard University)

It was October 25, 1918, and Colonel Roosevelt was dictating a letter on a matter that had been weighing on his mind since Quentin had died in July. "Mrs. Roosevelt and I wish to enter a most respectful but most emphatic protest against the proposed course, so far as our son, Quentin, is concerned. We have always believed that where the tree falls, there let it lie. . . . We greatly prefer that Quentin shall continue to lie on the spot where he fell in battle and where the foeman buried him."[500]

He sent the letter off to General March, the Army chief of staff, in opposition to a plan to remove Quentin from his grave in France and send him back to the U.S. for permanent burial. It was

War Department policy, dating to the Spanish-American War, to repatriate the remains of American soldiers who died on foreign soil. Fortunately, General March was empathetic to the Roosevelts' appeal. "I am sending an order to General Pershing to carry out your wishes," he replied.[501] Like-minded demands from relatives of other fallen men also would be honored.

Quentin's solitary repose in rural Chaméry, amid the wide rolling fields of central France, had become "the epicenter of his commemoration," in the phrase of Steven Trout whose book, *On the Battlefield of Memory*, chronicles Quentin's story in the years that followed his death. A growing "cult of remembrance," prompted, in part, by the publication of the shocking image of Quentin's body lying on the ground, face-up aside his crashed Nieuport, made his Chaméry resting place one of the most visited sites on the Great War's western front.

After the Armistice—and following Theodore Roosevelt's death in January 1919—France gifted the land to the Roosevelt family. They, in turn, hired a Madame Fouquet, a Chaméry shopkeeper, to clean the grave site every Sunday and to lay down fresh flowers. She was paid ten dollars annually.[502] Nonetheless, inside a decade and a half, conditions at the site had deteriorated, and it became an eyesore. A report by the American Battle Monuments Commission (ABMC) in 1932 disclosed that the old wooden railing around the grave, installed in tribute by the French, was falling apart, and the stone marker was in need of refurbishing. Soon after the German invasion of France in 1940, an Army inspection turned up no war damage to the gravesite but noted continued worsening of conditions.

Soon after the Second World War, Archie and Ethel asked the U.S. to assume responsibility for Quentin's plot, but the government showed little interest—ostensibly because it was not in a veterans' cemetery. Ultimately, it fell to Ted's wife, Eleanor, to give refuge to Quentin in death, as she had done many times in his lifetime. By 1954, the widow of highly-decorated Brigadier General Theodore Roosevelt, Jr., had won appointment to the ABMC board and, using her influence, had asked that Quentin be moved to rest beside her husband at the American Cemetery in Normandy. The commission agreed, and plans were made to disinter Quentin.

It was a cool and damp Thursday, September 22, 1955, when ABMC workmen exhumed Quentin from the place where he had lain for more than 37 years. His remains were passed up from the ground respectfully and placed on a sheet that lay in a truck bed. Then, they were placed in a casket. Trout relayed the observations of Daniel Gibbs, chief of the ABMCs Burial Records Branch, who supervised the procedure: "The skeleton is, as far as I could judge, complete—lower jaw and one leg broken, probably at the time of death. . . . There were no clothes except for a few buttons and scraps of material; the leather aviator's boots were in fair shape. . . . A small metal cross that Lt. Roosevelt either had around his neck or in his breast pocket was found, and I asked Mr. Darois [a local official] to take it to Paris for a decision on its disposition."[503]

The following day, Quentin's remains were reinterred at the American Cemetery in Normandy next to those of his brother Ted "without ceremony." The brothers lay at the edge of a long row of tall marble crosses on a bluff overlooking Omaha Beach. Quentin rests there to this day, in Plot D, Row 28, Grave 46, the only combatant from the Great War to lie with the American heroes of the Second World War in Europe.

The Congressional Medal of Honor that was awarded in 1944 to **Ted Roosevelt** cited his "gallantry and intrepidity, at the risk of his life, above and beyond the call of duty" on D-Day in France. The senior man on Utah Beach during the invasion, Brigadier General Roosevelt led the Fourth Infantry Division's landing in what General Omar Bradley later called the single most heroic action he had ever seen in combat.

In 1941, Ted had volunteered for active duty with the Army following an ambitious and sometimes controversial career between the wars as a statesman and business executive. His résumé was eerily familiar: service in the New York State Legislature, an unsuccessful campaign for governor of New York, three years as assistant secretary of the Navy, governor of Puerto Rico, and a short stint as governor general of the Philippines. Leaving public service in 1934, Ted embraced the private sector. He served as chairman of the board of American Express Co. and later, as vice president of Doubleday.

Five weeks after D-Day, while serving in the war zone, Ted Roosevelt succumbed to an untreated heart condition. He was 56.

"It was like the magnificent climax to a great play," his son would write. Ted was laid to rest in Normandy on Bastille Day 1944, the 26th anniversary of Quentin's death.

American and French flags decorate the final resting places of Quentin, left foreground, and his brother Ted, right, at the Normandy American Cemetery in France.

(Photo by Chip Bishop 2013)

Following the Great War, Ted's wife, **Eleanor Alexander Roosevelt**, relished life as the first lady of Puerto Rico and the Philippines; she also was a senior Red Cross organizer in Europe, an author, a needlepoint artist, and photographer.

The New York Times characterized Eleanor's life as one of "energy, resourcefulness, adventurousness and high spirits."[504] She stumped for Ted during his 1919 campaign for the New York State Assembly and helped to break the taboo against women speaking in public.

There was a complex, private side to Eleanor as well. She

soothed a nervous condition by fashioning museum-quality needle crafts and by using her state-of-the-art camera to create expert photographs of family members and other famous people. She provided newspapers and magazines with examples of her work which, at the time, "helped to lower privacy expectations for prominent families."[505] Her 478-page memoir, *Day Before Yesterday*, was read widely at the time of its publication in 1959.

Eleanor and Ted had four children between 1911 and 1919. The youngest, Quentin, a decorated World War II hero, and namesake of Flora's fiancé, was killed in 1948 in a private plane crash in China. He was 29.

Eleanor Alexander Roosevelt died at Old Orchard, her home on the grounds of Sagamore Hill, on May 29, 1960, at age 71.

Archie Roosevelt was discharged from the Great War with full disability and "mental wounds more severe than physical ones."[506] Depression aggravated a prickly personality which his mother once described as "most contrary and autocratic in nature."[507] After the war, he went to work for Sinclair Consolidated Oil where he skirted the edges of the Teapot Dome scandal.

Volunteering for the Army during World War II, Lt. Colonel Archie Roosevelt commanded a combat unit in New Guinea in the Pacific Theater. During fighting, an enemy grenade smashed the same knee that had been damaged during the Great War. Again, he was awarded full disability, along with multiple citations for bravery. The Roosevelt family believes Archie was the sole American soldier to be fully disabled in both world wars.

Returning home after the war, Archie founded the investment firm of Roosevelt and Cross and got caught up in multiple, extremist right-wing political organizations. Some of his political writings and speeches were disavowed publicly by the family.

In 1971, Archie was behind the wheel of a car that collided with a bus in Cold Spring Harbor, New York. Grace, his wife of more than 50 years, was killed. Archie faulted himself for her death and withdrew to their home in Florida where he later died of a stroke, in 1979, at age 85.

Ethel Roosevelt Derby, Quentin's sister with whom he had a special bond, devoted her life to others. She went to France early during the Great War to nurse wounded soldiers, alongside her surgeon husband, Dick. She later returned to Oyster Bay to raise four children and organize local Red Cross and community nursing chapters.

Ethel put her "capable, charming and determined personality" to work for other local civic organizations, advocating for civil rights and public housing, largely out of the limelight.

Her long and tireless "charge up Sagamore Hill to preserve the family landmark"[508] was perhaps her most significant accomplishment. Following her mother's death, Ethel convinced the National Park Service to take over the estate, restore it, and open its doors for public appreciation. When the time came to have her own portrait done, Ethel eschewed dressy clothes and jewelry, and put on her Red Cross uniform.

The woman known respectfully as the First Lady of Oyster Bay died peacefully in her home town on December 10, 1977 at age 86.

Kermit Roosevelt, the president's second son, appears in this narrative chiefly as his father's favored family correspondent. For most of the period he was living in South America, working in engineering and banking.

During the Great War, Kermit fought with the British army in Mesopotamia, and later transferred to the U.S. Army in Europe. He re-entered service with the British in World War II, serving in Scandinavia.

Kermit is remembered most often as his father's resolute companion during their long hunting trip in Africa (1909-1910) and his savior during the treacherous 1913-1914 expedition along the River of Doubt in the Brazilian rainforest.

Kermit and his wife, Belle Wyatt Willard, had four children between 1916 and 1925.

Three years after Quentin died, Kermit edited and had published *A Sketch with Letters*, an affectionate tribute that introduced many of Quentin's letters home. In the foreword, Kermit wrote, "Quentin Roosevelt was not yet 21 when he was shot down; still, years count for but little in the record of a life; one man, at 20, may have accomplished more and leave more behind to mourn his loss than another who saw a century out."[509]

Plagued by depression and alcoholism during much of his later life, Kermit died in 1943 while on active duty in Alaska. At the time, the cause of death was reported as natural causes; his elderly mother was told it was a heart attack. Later, it was revealed that Kermit died of a self-inflicted gunshot wound. He was 53.

Having tragically lost her youngest child and husband within six months in 1918-19, **Edith Kermit Roosevelt** carried on stoically despite lingering grief. She would live 30 more years, most of them at Sagamore Hill in the company of her surviving children and a budding clutch of grandchildren. Edith found great reward in travel and embarked on frequent journeys to Europe, Asia, Africa, and South America. Upon returning home, she often would chronicle her travels, then settle down to volunteer countless hours for the local needlework guild that supplied clothing to the poor of Oyster Bay.

Essentially a private person, she did emerge in 1920, following the ratification of the 19th Amendment, to urge women to vote. During the Great Depression, again she came out of her comfort zone to speak for Herbert Hoover and against the presidential candidacy of Franklin D. Roosevelt. She said she wanted people to know that Franklin, a Democrat, was not her son.

To the eternal lament of historians, Edith sealed her domestic privacy by burning a lifetime's worth of intimate letters with Theodore.

She once said that nothing would please her more than to have an inscription on her tombstone that read: "Everything she did was for the happiness of others."[510] She would not get her wish. Edith is recalled on their memorial in the family plot at Oyster Bay simply as the wife of Theodore Roosevelt. She died at Sagamore Hill, September 30, 1948, at age 87.

Two of Flora Whitney Miller's four children survive as of this writing. *The New York Times'* upbeat review of **Flora Miller Biddle's** book,

The Whitney Women and the Museum They Made, characterized it as having "a complete lack of malice." That must be said of Flora herself. A warm and welcoming personality at 86, she divides her time and family activities between a residence near New Haven and her artistically-unique home on a hilltop in western Connecticut. Flora served as the Whitney Museum's president until 1985 when she became honorary chairman, a post she holds today. Besides authoring *The Whitney Women*, in 2011 she published *Embers*, an endearing memoir of her life growing up as a Vanderbilt and Whitney. Flora also was instrumental in helping B. H. Friedman research his book, *Gertrude Vanderbilt Whitney*, in the late 70s, and she was active in producing *Flora*, a "memorial scrapbook" to her mother, published by the Whitney Museum in 1987.

Pamela Tower LeBoutillier was Flora's first born. Growing up "clever, beautiful and bold with many friends and admirers,"[511] she volunteered for many years at New York's American Museum of Natural History (co-founded by Theodore Roosevelt, Sr., and supported by generations of her family). Pamela preserved her grandmother's studio and garden on the Old Westbury estate and lived there for many years. She died July 16, 2013 at age 91. Her *New York Times* obituary remembered her as "the indefatigable leader of a large and disparate family."

Like their maternal grandfather, **Leverett Saltonstall Miller** and **Whitney Tower** were ardent horsemen. An architect and retired horse breeder, Lev is a founder and board member of the National Museum of Polo and Hall of Fame of Lake Worth, Florida. For many years, he owned T-Square Stud, a thoroughbred horse farm in Fairfield, Florida. At 83, Lev retains the Whitney family's storied Eton blue and brown racing colors.

Whitney, remembered for "his courtly manner and rich personal pedigree," died in 1999 at age 75. According to *The New York Times*, he was "one of the most visible leaders in thoroughbred racing, both as a newspaper and magazine writer, and later, as an official of the National Museum and Hall of Fame."[512] For 22 years, he excelled as turf editor of *Sports Illustrated* and later co-founded *Classic* magazine, a publication devoted to thoroughbred racing. He served eight years as president of the National Museum of Racing in Saratoga Springs, New York.

The Whitney Museum of American Art is growing once again. In 2015, it will occupy a new 200,000 square foot, tiered structure, adjacent to the Hudson River, in Manhattan's meatpacking district. Designed by the Italian architect Renzo Piano, it will feature 13,000 square feet of outdoor exhibition space on a series of rooftops facing the High Line Park. The board of directors' successors to Gertrude Vanderbilt Whitney, Flora Whitney Miller, and Flora Miller Biddle promise an unsurpassed collection of modern and contemporary art in downtown Manhattan.

A Closing View

The astute contemporary biographer, Kate Buford, once said that your subject must die a second time at your typing hands. In that act, she said, the writer is obliged to reveal the larger truth of his life. Thus, for Quentin Roosevelt, a determination of the sum of his short, eventful life is upon us.

Major Warwick Greene, the executive assistant to Lt. Colonel Bolling during the Great War, observed that "Quentin was a splendid boy, genial, energetic, intelligent and honest—a real American-bred youngster full of activity, humor, 'sand,' and a force of personality that promised plenty of accomplishment later in life."[513] Indeed. But why did he have to die so young and so violently? For what reason was he denied an extended life with Flora and personal achievements outside of his father's reflected glory?

Was Quentin's alleged recklessness as a flier a deliberate ploy to show his bravado, to put the lie to the allegation of his skeptical brothers, Ted and Archie, that he was an *embusqué*? Perhaps. Was he showing off his daring-do to Flora so he could boast of his exploits in letters to her? That would have been extraneous to their relationship; she clearly loved him unconditionally.

Quentin's best friend, Hamilton Coolidge, thought that his death made us thrill by its courageous and brutal end, when engines raced high in enemy skies and machine guns blazed their ammunition. It was the stuff of real legend—and, at Sagamore Hill, paternal satisfaction.

Historian Alan Toelle has asserted that Quentin sealed his future in September 1917 when, at Issoudun, he refused an initial call to the front. He was stuck in an existential predicament, Toelle contends, to be remembered for what he actually did, not what he thought he might do, if only he had accepted the opportunity. It is this writer's view that there and then, Quentin purposefully deferred to the judgment of superior males in his life, as he did many times at home with his father and, later at school, before

Rector Peabody. Quentin was someone who believed in promises and in the honorable men who made them to him. He believed that he would eventually get an assignment to the front.

Throughout Quentin's brief and episodic life—from childhood gang leader in the White House, through salad days at Groton, to his few but eventful weeks at the front—there was something deeper, more inevitably Rooseveltian at work. He was the model of performance and conduct, always characteristic of his need to meet his father's high expectations and prove worthy of his adulation— and the family name.

Quentin was the product of an irrepressible force of nature: an exceptional man's man of a parent who had a distorted, romanticized view of war. Quentin was, in that respect, the next-generational life force of Theodore Roosevelt. He knew what was expected of him, the final son. He understood his obligation to embody valor and guts and the mettle that flowed through the family bloodline. In France, during the fateful summer of 1918, with the aggressive enemy in close, his actions gave heroic testimony to his own expectations and to his family's.

When Quentin died, Theodore's lingering lust for combat glory expired with him. As Edmund Morris observed, "Quentin's death hit T. R with such cosmic force that he never recovered."[514] In fact, the colonel was dead inside of 26 weeks of Quentin's death—from physical causes to be sure, but also from unbearable melancholy and guilt—a self-inflicted broken heart.

If you journey to France today to see where Quentin lived and died, you must seek out the torch bearers, as we did. They are the descendants of those who knew him well nearly 100 years ago, and the committed, contemporary historians who keep his story alive. They will point with earnest pride to the farmer's field in Saints from which Quentin's plane once soared, to the gated château at Touquin where he billeted comfortably, to the brass plaques here and there that memorialize his sacrifice, to the modest winery near Château-Thierry that bottles Quentin Roosevelt Brut from local grapes, and, ultimately, to the Normandy gravesite on a bluff above Omaha Beach, where he rests—his marble headstone facing west, toward America.

Quentin Roosevelt remains the enduring, ever-youthful symbol of American salvation and martyrdom during both world wars. The French have resolved never to forget his sacrifice. It is incumbent on us, as well, to keep his memory burning brightly.

Acknowledgements

The book you are reading is the end product of contributions by many people who helped to bring Quentin's and Flora's story back to life. Jane Nichols Bishop, the love of my life, encouraged and supported me for many months as I researched sources and ground out the manuscript at home, usually at very early hours. She read the manuscript innumerable times, always finding ways to cleanse and improve it.

Arlene Kirsch, my expert Cape Cod copy editor, corrected many errors in an early draft and suggested words and phrases that smoothed out the roughest of my passages.

Alan Toelle, a faithful correspondent from the West Coast, continually challenged me to be incisive and accurate about Quentin's months in wartime France; he helped me significantly to achieve what I hope is a good measure of both. Alan's magnum opus, "One of Us: Quentin Roosevelt–a Hero's Journey," for the League of World War One Aviation Historians, is a must-read for anyone who wants to fully appreciate Quentin's service.

Quentin's and Flora's heartfelt letters to each other are the foundation of this tale. And, thankfully for history, most of the correspondence has been saved and conserved. At the Theodore Roosevelt Collection at Harvard University's Houghton Library, retired curator Wallace F. Dailey and current curator Heather Cole were extraordinarily helpful by giving me full access to the original letters and photographs. When I needed to see other documents I deemed vital to the story, they obliged promptly and cheerfully.

The Theodore Roosevelt Center at Dickinson State University in North Dakota has undertaken an indispensable project to digitize a trove of documents including Quentin's papers that are held at the Sagamore Hill National Historic Site in Oyster Bay, New York. Sharon Kilzer and her team went above and beyond to make it easy for me to review these; significantly, they granted me access to previously-unpublished material.

I feel privileged to know Flora Miller Biddle, the daughter of Flora Payne Whitney. She took an instant interest in my work and was unendingly supportive and hospitable.

The Roosevelt family has been equally supportive, especially Dick Williams, Ethel Roosevelt Derby's grandson, and his wife Mary Kongsgaard. In 2013, they generously guided Jane and me on an illuminating tour of the tiny villages in France where Quentin lived during his momentous weeks at the front. That tour was made special by the hospitality of Pierre-Mary and Flo Bachelet, and enriched by the elegance and expertise of Claudine Thibault Barrière whose great grandmother billeted Quentin in Mauperthuis nearly a century ago. And my deep appreciation extends to her son Narayan Sengupta for introducing me to Claudine and for keeping the flame of Quentin's memory burning intensely here and in France.

Our Memorial Day pilgrimage to Quentin's final resting place at the American Cemetery in Normandy was enabled by the irrepressible John Flaherty of Hand Maid Tours. Thank you, John, for the fresh-cut lilacs that I laid at the base of Quentin's headstone.

In Massachusetts, the very accommodating Doug Brown gave me access to the extensive archives at the Groton School and opened a window on Quentin's student years there. At the Episcopal High School in Alexandria, Virginia, archivist Laura Vetter helped with useful materials and fact-checking.

Whenever I needed hard-to-find reference books, Janet Trask of the Mashpee, Massachusetts Public Library magically located them with unruffled professionalism.

A special nod goes to the late Earle Looker whose wonderful 1929 chronicle, *The White House Gang*, enables us to experience vividly the mischievous young Q. in locomotion at the Executive Mansion during his father's terms. I drew heavily on his ebullient tales of frolic and fun in the marbled hallways—and attics—of power.

Thanks to Alan Nevins for first suggesting the idea of a dual biography of Quentin and Flora. To Anthony Mattero, my current literary agent and friend, thank you for your persistence and for never losing faith in the worthiness of this story.

Thomas Salvas of Chatham, New Jersey, my college roommate in the 1960s, volunteered his time to bring old photographs of Quentin and Flora back to life for new generations to appreciate. Alexander Horn and Sarah Nichols were helpful research assistants.

And finally, any narrator of a Roosevelt family saga is obligated to salute the still-vibrant memory of Theodore Roosevelt and his wife, Edith Kermit Roosevelt. They not only parented Quentin during his all-too-brief life, and loved and sustained Flora in her days of grief, the Roosevelts left us with a rich legacy of warmth and wisdom that radiates through virtually everything they said and wrote.

To all of you and to the others I have inadvertently overlooked, a great big Teddy Bear of a hug.

Mashpee, Mass., February 2014

About the Author

C hip Bishop is an accomplished writer and speaker. His debut book, *The Lion and the Journalist – The Unlikely Friendship of Theodore Roosevelt and Joseph Bucklin Bishop*, was hailed by historians, reviewers, and readers alike. The e-book was a *New York Times* bestseller in March 2014.

Chip grew up in Woonsocket, R.I. and was graduated from Boston University. His lifetime of achievements includes time as a campaign and administration aide to President Jimmy Carter, Capitol Hill lobbyist, business entrepreneur, local elected official, and disc-jockey during the 1960s British Invasion.

Chip is a member of the board of directors of the Biographers International Organization, a member of the Theodore Roosevelt Association and the executive committee of its New England chapter.

He serves his community as an elected member of the board of trustees of the Mashpee Massachusetts Public Library. He loves doo-wop music, old German stamps and the 2013 World Series Champion Boston Red Sox.

Chip lives on Cape Cod with his wife and business partner, Jane Nichols Bishop, and their two black, rescue cats.

He is the great-grandnephew of Joseph Bucklin Bishop, Theodore Roosevelt's authorized biographer, who was profiled in his first book.

Bibliography

Aldrich, Jr., Nelson W. 1988. "Old Money: The Mythology of the American Upper Class." New York: A. A. Knopf.

Amos, James. 1927. "Hero to his Valet." New York: The John Day Co.

Ashburn, Frank D. 1944. "Peabody of Groton." New York: Coward McCann, Inc.

Biddle, Flora Miller. 1999. "The Whitney Women and the Museum They Made." New York: Arcade Publishing.

—. 2011. "Embers." New York: Plumley Press.

Bishop, Chip. 2011. "The Lion and The Jouralist: The Unlikely Friendship of Theodore Roosevelt and Joseph Bucklin Bishop." Guilford, Conn.: Lyons Press.

Bishop, Joseph Bucklin (ed.). 1919. "Theodore Roosevelt's Letters to His Children." New York: Charles Scribner's Sons.

Bishop, Joseph Bucklin. 1920. "Theodore Roosevelt and His Time." New York: Charles Scribner's Sons.

Coolidge, Hamilton. 1919. "Letters of an American Airman: Being the War Record of Capt. Hamilton Coolidge, U.S.A., 1917-1918." Boston: Privately Printed by the Plimpton Press.

Cooper, Jr., John Milton. 2009. "Woodrow Wilson: A Biography." New York: Alfred A. Knopf.

Duffy, Christopher. 2006. "Through German Eyes: The British and the Somme 1916." London: The Orion Publishing Group.

Fontoney, Paul E. 2005. "Convoy System." *The Encyclopedia of World War I: A Political, Social and Military History.* Santa Barbara, Calif.: ABC-CLIO.

Friedman, B. H. 1978. "Gertrude Vanderbilt Whitney." Garden City, New York: Doubleday and Co.

Hagedorn, Hermann. 1954. "The Roosevelt Family of Sagamore Hill." New York: The MacMillan Company.

Hale, Richard W. (ed.). 1931. "Letters of Warwick Greene 1915-1928." New York: Houghton Mifflin.

Kinsolving, Arthur Barksdale. 1922. "The Story of a Southern School: The Episcopal High School of Virginia." Baltimore: Norman Remington Co.

Klepper, Michael and Gunther, Robert. 1996. "The Wealthy." New York: Citadel Press.

Kuniegel, R. J. (n.d.). "The Life and Work of Theodore Roosevelt Memorial." *www.TRAmericanPatriot.com.*

Looker, Earle. 1929. "The White House Gang." New York: Fleming H. Revel, Co.

Mason, Jr., Herbert Malloy. 1976. "The United States Air Force: A Turbulent History." New York: Mason/Charter.

Maureer, Maurer (ed.). 1978. "The U.S. Air Service in World War I." Darby, Penna.: Diane Publishing.

Merrill, W. Earl. 1975. "One Hundred Echoes from Mesa's Past." Mesa, Ariz.: W. Earl Merrill.

Morris, Edmund. 2010. "Colonel Roosevelt." New York: Random House.

—. 2001. "Theodore Rex." New York: Random House.

Morris, Sylvia Jukes. 2001. "Edith Kermit Roosevelt: Portrait of a First Lady." The Modern Library edition.

O'Toole, Patricia. 2005. "When Trumpets Call: Theodore Roosevelt After the White House." New York: Simon & Schuster.

Renehan, Jr., Edward. 1999. "The Lion's Pride: Theodore Roosevelt and His Family In Peace and War." New York: Oxford University Press.

Richards, Henry Howe. 1925. "Groton School in the War." Groton, Mass.: The Groton School.

Rickenbacker, Eddie. 1919. "Fighting the Flying Circus." New York: Frederick A. Stokes, Co.

Roosevelt, Eleanor Alexander. 1959. "Day Before Yesterday: The Reminiscenses of Mrs. Theodore Roosevelt, Jr." Garden City, N.Y.: Doubleday and Company.

Roosevelt, Jr., Theodore. 1929. "All in the Family." New York: G. P. Putnam's Sons.

Roosevelt, Kermit. 1921. "Quentin Roosevelt: A Sketch with Letters." New York: Charles Scribner's Sons.

Roosevelt, Theodore. *The Forum.* February 1895.

—. 1913. "An Autobiography." New York: Da Capo Press, 1985 edition.

Rowley, Hazel. 2010. "Franklin and Eleanor." New York, N.Y.: Farrar, Strauss and Giroux (Picador).

Seale, William. 1986. "The President's House." Washington, DC: the White House Historical Association and the National Geographic Society.

Thomas, Capt. Shipley. 1920. "The History of the American Expeditionary Force." New York: George H. Doran, Co.

Toelle, Alan D. "One of Us: Quentin Roosevelt—A Hero's Journey." *Over the Front*. Plymouth, Minn.: League of World War I Aviation Historians, Vol. 27, No. 4, Winter 2012.

Trout, Steven. 2010. "On the Battlefield of Memory: The First World War and American Remembrance 1919-1941." Tuscaloosa, Ala.: The University of Alabama Press.

Vanderbilt, Jr., Cornelius. 1935. "Farewell to Fifth Avenue." New York: Simon and Schuster.

Vaughan, David K. (ed). 1998. "Flying for the Air Service - The Hughes Brothers in World War I." Bowling Green, Ohio: Bowling Green University Popular Press.

White, John. 1989. "Chronicles of the Episcopal High School: 1839-1989." Peterborough, N.H.: Bauhan Publishing.

Whitney Museum of American Art. 1987. "Flora Whitney Miller, Her Life, Her World." New York: Whitney Museum of American Art.

Willmott, H. P. 2009. "World War I." London: Dk Publishers.

Letter Sources and Endnotes

Letters cited in the manuscript may be found in the following locations:

- TGS – Archives of the Groton School, Groton, MA.

- TRC-DSU – Quentin Roosevelt's papers are held at the Sagamore Hill National Historic Site in Oyster Bay, N.Y. and may be accessed through the Theodore Roosevelt Digital Library at Dickinson State University, Dickinson, ND. Online access is available at: http://www.theodorerooseveltcenter.org/Research/Collections.aspx?colID=c578. Most of the Theodore Roosevelt letters cited in this book are available online as well.

- TRC-HU – Letters from Quentin Roosevelt to Flora Payne Whitney are archived at the Theodore Roosevelt Collection, Harvard University, Cambridge, MA, in MS Am 2925; some cablegrams are in *87M-100. Flora Payne Whitney's letters to Quentin Roosevelt are accessible at *87M-100. Roosevelt family letters are available here as well. At the time these materials were first consulted by the author in 2012, they were un-cataloged. Additional material is available online at http://hcl.harvard.edu/libraries/houghton/collections/roosevelt.cfm.

Endnotes

1 Quentin Roosevelt to Ambler Blackford, August 1909. (TRC-DSU)

2 *You're The Top*, words and music by Cole Porter, 1934. Available online at http://www.allthelyrics.com/lyrics/cole_porter/youre_the_top-lyrics-120385.html.

3 Whitney Museum of American Art, *Flora Whitney Miller: Her Life, Her World*, New York: Whitney Museum, 1987, p. 38.

4 *The New York Times*, August 5, 1916.

5 Friedman, B. H., *Gertrude Vanderbilt Whitney*, Garden City, New York, Doubleday & Company, 1978, p. 380.

6 Whitney Museum of American Art, *Flora Whitney Miller: Her Life, Her World*, p. 48.

7 Quentin Roosevelt to Flora Payne Whitney, April 7, 1916. (TRC-HU)

8 Ibid., July 25, 1916. (TRC-HU)

9 Theodore Roosevelt to Anna Roosevelt Cowles, November 19, 1897. (TRC-DSU)

10 Kuniegel, R. J., *The Life and Work of Theodore Roosevelt Memorial*, available online at www.TRAmericanPatriot.com.

11 Hagedorn, Herman, *The Roosevelt Family of Sagamore Hill*, New York: The Macmillan Company, 1954, p. 49.

12 Morris, Sylvia Jukes, *Edith Kermit Roosevelt: Portrait of a First Lady*, New York: The Modern Library, 2001, p. 171.

13 Theodore Roosevelt to Archibald Butt (n.d.). (TRC-HU)

14 Morris, *Edith Kermit Roosevelt: Portrait of a First Lady*, p. 196.

15 Edith Kermit Roosevelt to Theodore Roosevelt, January 11, 1901. (TRC-HU)

16 Ibid., January 13, 1901. (TRC-HU)

17 Ibid., January 14, 1901. (TRC-HU)

18 Aldrich, Jr., Nelson W. *Old Money: The Mythology of the American Upper Class*, New York: A. A. Knopf, 1988.

19 *The New York Times*, "Harry Payne Whitney, Youthful Guard," (n.d.), 1904.

20 Biddle, Flora Miller. *The Whitney Women and the Museum They Made*, New York: Arcade Publishing, p. 32.

21 Whitney Museum of American Art, *Flora Whitney Miller: Her Life, Her World*, pp. 45-46.

22 Biddle, *The Whitney Women and the Museum They Made*, p. 11.

23 Ibid., p. 31.

24 Ibid., p. 40.

25 Whitney Museum of American Art, *Flora Whitney Miller: Her Life, Her World*, p. 14.

26 *The New York Times*, "Vanderbilt Grandchildren," August 13, 1899.

27 Biddle, Flora Miller. *Embers*, New York: Plumley Press, 2011, p. 17.

28 Friedman, B. H., *Gertrude Vanderbilt Whitney*, p. 205.

29 Ibid.

30 Edith Kermit Roosevelt to Emily Carow, September 18, 1901. (TRC-HU)

31 Hagedorn, *The Roosevelt Family of Sagamore Hill*, p. 127.

32 Seale, William. *The President's House*, Washington, D.C. and New York: White House Historical Association and National Geographic Society, Vol. II, 1986, p. 650.

33 Bishop, Joseph Bucklin (ed.), *Theodore Roosevelt's Letters to His Children*. New York: Charles Scribner's Sons, 1919, pp. 31-32.

34 Ibid., p. 35.

35 Edith Kermit Roosevelt to Theodore Roosevelt, September 21, 1901. (TRC-HU)

36 Seale, *The President's House*, Vol. II, p. 669.

37 Ibid., p. 648.

38 Theodore Roosevelt to Kermit Roosevelt, November 28, 1902. (TRC-DSU)

39 Theodore Roosevelt to Master James A. Garfield, December 26, 1902. (TRC-HU)

40 *Hartford Courant*, December 1902.

41 Theodore Roosevelt to Master James A. Garfield, December 26, 1902. (TRC-HU)

42 Morris, Edmund. *Theodore Rex*. New York: Random House, 2001, p. 142.

43 Flora Payne Whitney to Quentin Roosevelt, July 31, 1917. (TRC-DSU)

44 Roosevelt, Theodore. *The Forum*, February 1895.

45 History of Vanderbilt University, available online at www.Vanderbilt.edu/about/history.

46   Vanderbilt, Jr., Cornelius, *Farewell to Fifth Avenue*, New York: Simon and Schuster, 1935, p. 15.

47   Ibid., pp. 29-31.

48   Roosevelt, Theodore. *An Autobiography*, New York: Da Capo Press edition, 1985, p. 439.

49   *The Washington Post*, "To Battle Wall Street, Obama Should Channel Teddy Roosevelt," April 4, 2010.

50   Roosevelt, *An Autobiography*, p. 452.

51   Renehan, Jr., Edward J. *The Lion's Pride: Theodore Roosevelt and his Family in Peace and War*, New York: Oxford University Press (paperback ed.), 1999, p. 72.

52   Looker, Earle. *The White House Gang*, New York: Fleming H. Revell Company, 1929, pp. 13-14.

53   Ibid., p. 14.

54   Ibid., pp. 45-46.

55   Virginia J. Arnold to Edith Kermit Roosevelt, December 8, 1922. (TRC-DSU)

56   Theodore Roosevelt to Kermit Roosevelt, October 19, 1903. (TRC-DSU)

57   Theodore Roosevelt to Kermit Roosevelt, January 17, 1903. (TRC-DSU)

58   Ibid. (TRC-DSU)

59   Theodore Roosevelt to Kermit Roosevelt, February 19, 1904. (TRC-DSU)

60   Theodore Roosevelt to Quentin Roosevelt, May 10, 1903. (TRC-DSU)

61   Seale, *The President's House*, Vol. II, pp. 699-700.

62   Theodore Roosevelt to Kermit Roosevelt, February 27, 1904. (TRC-DSU)

63   Ibid., April 9, 1904. (TRC-DSU)

64   Theodore Roosevelt to Archie Roosevelt, March 8, 1908. (TRC-DSU)

65   Morris, *Edith Kermit Roosevelt: Portrait of a First Lady*, p. 266.

66   Theodore Roosevelt to Kermit Roosevelt, May 28, 1904. (TRC-DSU)

67   Theodore Roosevelt to Quentin Roosevelt, June 12, 1904. (TRC-DSU)

68   Ibid., June 21, 1904. (TRC-DSU)

69   Hagedorn, *The Roosevelt Family of Sagamore Hill*, p. 137.

70   Quentin Roosevelt to Edith Kermit Roosevelt, July 30, 1904. (TRC-DSU)

71 Hagedorn, *The Roosevelt Family of Sagamore Hill*, p. 144.

72 Roosevelt, Jr., Theodore. *All in the Family*, New York: G. P. Putnam's Sons, 1929, pp. 23-24.

73 Looker, *The White House Gang*, p. 160.

74 Biddle, *The Whitney Women and the Museum They Made*, p. 37.

75 Ibid., p. 17.

76 Ibid., p. 18.

77 Ibid., p. 19.

78 Biddle, *Embers*, pp. 40-41.

79 Biddle, *The Whitney Women and the Museum They Made*, p. 46.

80 Whitney, Flora Payne. Diary entry from late 1915 or 1916, as recounted in "*The Whitney Women and the Museum They Made*," p. 47.

81 Friedman, *Gertrude Vanderbilt Whitney*, pp. 411-12.

82 Biddle, T*he Whitney Women and the Museum They Made*, p. 47.

83 *The New York Times*, December 7, 1913.

84 History of the Foxcroft School, available online at www.Foxcroft.org.

85 Irene Givenwilson to Flora Payne Whitney, January 16, 1915. (TRC-HU)

86 Gertrude Vanderbilt Whitney to Flora Payne Whitney, July 30, 1915, as cited in Friedman, *Gertrude Vanderbilt Whitney*, p. 371.

87 Looker, *The White House Gang*, p. 13.

88 Bishop (ed.), *Theodore Roosevelt's Letters to His Children*, pp. 148-49.

89 Looker, *The White House Gang*, p. 24.

90 Ibid., pp. 24-26.

91 Theodore Roosevelt to Kermit Roosevelt, August 18, 1906. (TRC-DSU)

92 Ibid., April 11, 1908. (TRC-DSU)

93 Looker, *The White House Gang*, p. 22.

94 Morris, *Edith Kermit Roosevelt: Portrait of a First Lady*, pp. 315-16.

95 Hagedorn, *The Roosevelt Family of Sagamore Hill*, p. 146.

96 Renehan, Jr., *The Lion's Pride: Theodore Roosevelt and His Family in Peace and War*, p. 80.

97 Roosevelt, Quentin. Available online at http://www.theodorerooseveltcenter.org/Research/Digital-Library/Record.aspx?libID=o275945.

98 Theodore Roosevelt to Alice Roosevelt Longworth, June 29, 1908. (TRC-DSU)

99 Looker, *The White House Gang*, p. 230.

100 Ibid.

101 Morris, *Theodore Rex*, p. 527.

102 TIME *Magazine*, Education: High School's Looth, September 12, 1938.

103 White, John. *Chronicles of the Episcopal High School – 1839-1989*, Peterborough, New Hampshire: Bauhan Publishing, 1989, p. 84.

104 Quentin Roosevelt to Edith Kermit Roosevelt, September 18, 1908. (TRC-HU)

105 Ibid., September 19, 1908. (TRC-HU)

106 Roosevelt, Quentin, September 28, 1908. (TRC-HU)

107 Theodore Roosevelt to Kermit Roosevelt, January 10, 1909. (TRC-DSU)

108 Theodore Roosevelt to Archie Roosevelt, November 8, 1908. (TRC-DSU)

109 White, *Chronicles of the Episcopal High School – 1839-1989*, p. 302.

110 Theodore Roosevelt to Archie Roosevelt, December 3, 1908. (TRC-DSU)

111 Seale, *The President's House*, Vol. II, p. 738.

112 Theodore Roosevelt to Quentin Roosevelt, April 16, 1909. (TRC-DSU)

113 Kinsolving, Arthur Barksdale. *The Story of a Southern School: The Episcopal High School of Virginia*, Baltimore: The Norman Remington Co., 1922, p. 226.

114 Quentin Roosevelt to Ambler Blackford, August 1909. (TRC-DSU)

115 Ibid. (TRC-DSU)

116 Ashburn, Frank D., *Peabody of Groton*, New York: Coward McCann, Inc., 1944, p. 83.

117 Ibid., p. 37.

118 Rowley, Hazel. *Franklin and Eleanor*, New York: Farrar, Strauss and Giroux, Picador Imprint, 2010, p. 18.

119 Quentin Roosevelt's Groton School report card, October 23, 1909. (TGS)

120 Ted Roosevelt to Quentin Roosevelt, October 1, 1908. (TRC-DSU)

121 Quentin Roosevelt to Ethel Roosevelt, (n.d.), circa. Fall 1909. (TRC-DSU)

122 Hagedorn, *The Roosevelt Family of Sagamore Hill*, p. 296.

123 Quentin Roosevelt to Held Promoting Co., (n.d.). (TRC-DSU)

124 *Boston Post*, June 4, 1911.

125 Quentin Roosevelt's Groton School report card, June 17, 1911. (TGS)

126 Quentin Roosevelt to Theodore Roosevelt, March 13, 1912. (TRC-DSU)

127 Hagedorn, *The Roosevelt Family of Sagamore Hill*, p. 293.

128 Theodore Roosevelt to Anna Roosevelt Cowles, July 28, 1911. (TRC-DSU)

129 Morris, *Edith Kermit Roosevelt: Portrait of a First Lady*, p. 373.

130 Theodore Roosevelt to Endicott Peabody, October 6, 1911. (TGS)

131 Ibid., October 10, 1911. (TGS)

132 Endicott Peabody to Theodore Roosevelt, October 19, 1911. (TGS)

133 Quentin Roosevelt's Groton School report card, October 21, 1911. (TGS)

134 Jacob Riis to Theodore Roosevelt, November 7, 1911. (TRC-DSU)

135 Groton School stenographer's notes, November 29, 1911. (TGS)

136 Theodore Roosevelt to Archie Roosevelt, December 23, 1911. (TRC-DSU)

137 Betty Kilral to Edith Kermit Roosevelt, July 18, 1932. (TRC-DSU)

138 Morris, Edmund. *Colonel Roosevelt*, New York: Random House, 2010, p. 170.

139 Renehan, Jr., *The Lion's Pride*, p. 80.

140 Archie Roosevelt to Endicott Peabody, June 5, 1912. (TGS)

141 Theodore Roosevelt to Endicott Peabody, April 23, 1912. (TGS)

142 Edith Kermit Roosevelt to Endicott Peabody, June 2, 1912. (TGS)

143 Endicott Peabody to Edith Kermit Roosevelt, June 6, 1912. (TGS)

144 Edith Kermit Roosevelt to Endicott Peabody, June 13, 1912. (TGS)

145 Endicott Peabody to Edith Kermit Roosevelt, June 15, 1912. (TGS)

146 Theodore Roosevelt to Ethel Roosevelt, August 21, 1912. (TRC-DSU)

147 O'Toole, Patricia. *When Trumpets Call: Theodore Roosevelt After the White House*, New York: Simon & Schuster, 2005, p. 243.

148 Quentin Roosevelt to Edith Kermit Roosevelt, November 15, 1912. (TRC-DSU)

149 Theodore Roosevelt to Endicott and Fannie Peabody, October 27, 1912. (TGS)

150 The Groton School Log, January 9, 1913. (TGS)

151 Theodore Roosevelt to Kermit Roosevelt, January 21, 1913. (TRC-DSU)

152 Ibid., March 7, 1913. (TRC-DSU)

153 Theodore Roosevelt to Quentin Roosevelt, February 14, 1913. (TRC-DSU)

154 Merrill, W. Earl. *One Hundred Echoes from Mesa's Past*, Mesa, Arizona: W. Earl Merrill, 1975, p. 93.

155 Theodore Roosevelt to Ethel Roosevelt Derby, April 7, 1913. (TRC-HU)

156 O'Toole, *When Trumpets Call: Theodore Roosevelt after the White House*, p. 242.

157 Renehan, Jr., *The Lion's Pride*, p. 79.

158 Theodore Roosevelt to Kermit Roosevelt, July 11, 1913. (TRC-HU)

159 Roosevelt, Theodore. Remarks at the Grand Canyon, May 6, 1903.

160 Theodore Roosevelt to Kermit Roosevelt, July 27, 1913. (TRC-DSU)

161 Renehan, Jr., *The Lion's Pride*, p. 79.

162 Theodore Roosevelt to Kermit Roosevelt, August 28, 1913. (TRC-DSU)

163 Quentin Roosevelt's Groton School report cards, October 20, 1914 and November 14, 1914. (TGS)

164 Theodore Roosevelt to Belle Roosevelt, November 7, 1914. (TRC-DSU)

165 Gertrude Vanderbilt Whitney journal, November 16, 1914, as reported in Friedman, *Gertrude Vanderbilt Whitney*, p. 349.

166 Ibid.

167 Gertrude Vanderbilt Whitney to Flora Payne Whitney, October 30, 1914, as reported by Friedman, *Gertrude Vanderbilt Whitney*, p. 348.

168 Friedman, *Gertrude Vanderbilt Whitney*, p. 358.

169 Ibid., p. 361.

170 Ibid., p. 364.

171 Ibid., p. 363.

172 Willmott, H. P. *World War I*, London: Dk Publishers, 2009, p. 307.

173 Bishop, Chip. *The Lion and the Journalist: The Unlikely Friendship of Theodore Roosevelt and Joseph Bucklin Bishop*. Guilford, Connecticut: Lyons Press, 2011, pp. 248-49.

174 *The Grotonian*, January 1915.

175 Quentin Roosevelt to Endicott Peabody, April 1915. (TGS)

176 Dr. Robert Lovett to Endicott Peabody, June 7, 1915. (TGS)

177 Quentin Roosevelt's Groton School report card, June 8, 1915. (TGS)

178 Theodore Roosevelt to Kermit Roosevelt, June 26, 1915. (TRC-HC)

179 Ibid., April 8, 1915.

180 Theodore Roosevelt to Kermit and Belle Roosevelt, July 10, 1915. (TRC-DSU)

181 Ibid. (TRC-DSU)

182 Morris, *Colonel Roosevelt*, p. 434.

183 Quentin Roosevelt's Groton School certificate of completion, August 8, 1915. (TRC-DSU)

184 Theodore Roosevelt to Kermit Roosevelt, August 26, 1915. (TRC-DSU)

185 Theodore Roosevelt to Belle Roosevelt, October 1, 1915. (TRC-DSU)

186 Theodore Roosevelt to Kermit Roosevelt, October 24, 1915. (TRC-DSU)

187 *The New York Times*, September 10, 1915.

188 Quentin Roosevelt to Flora Payne Whitney, October 25, 1915. (TRC-HU)

189 Quentin Roosevelt to Flora Payne Whitney, May 26, 1916. (TRC-HU)

190 Theodore Roosevelt to Kermit Roosevelt, January 24, 1916. (TRC-DSU)

191 Harvard University Class of 1919 yearbook, Harvard University Archives.

192 Theodore Roosevelt to Anna Roosevelt Cowles, July 23, 1916. (TRC-DSU)

193 Bishop, *The Lion and the Journalist*, p. 252.

194 Theodore Roosevelt to Anna Roosevelt Cowles, July 23, 1916. (TRC-DSU)

195 Quentin Roosevelt to Flora Payne Whitney, March 8, 1916. (TRC-DSU)

196 Ibid., April 7, 1916.

197 Ibid., April 25, 1916.

198 Ibid., May 26, 1916.

199 Ibid., July 1916.

200 *The New York Times*, July 21, 1916.

201 Theodore Roosevelt to Anna Roosevelt Cowles, July 23, 1916. (TRC-DSU)

202 Duffy, Christopher. *Through German Eyes: The British and the Somme 1916*, London: The Orion Publishing Group, 2006.

203 Ashburn, *Peabody of Groton*, p. 83.

204 Biddle, *Embers*, p. 54.

205 *The New York Times*, October 11, 1916.

206 H. W. Broughton to Quentin Roosevelt, June 10, 1916. (TRC-DSU)

207 An abstract from a Quentin Roosevelt Groton School mathematics examination, February 1916. (TRC-DSU)

208 Quentin Roosevelt to Flora Payne Whitney, October 7, 1916. (TRC-DSU)

209 Ibid., October 16, 1916.

210 Ibid., November 1, 1916.

211 Ibid., January 7, 1917.

212 Ibid., February 22, 1917.

213 Ibid., November 16, 1916.

214 *The New York Tribune*, October 12, 1910, p. 1.

215 Mason, Jr., Herbert Malloy. *The United States Air Force: A Turbulent History*. New York: Mason/Charter, 1976, p. 7.

216 America Declares War on Germany – 1917, Available online at www.eyewitnesstohistory.com/wilsonwar.htm.

217 Edith Kermit Roosevelt to Ethel Roosevelt Derby, 1912. (TRC-HU)

218 Quentin Roosevelt to Flora Payne Whitney, April 1917, unmailed. (TRC-DSU)

219 Roosevelt, Kermit. *Quentin Roosevelt: A Sketch with Letters*, New York: Charles Scribner's Sons, 1921, p. 34.

220 Quentin Roosevelt to Flora Payne Whitney, April 10, 1917. (TRC-DSU)

221 Quentin Roosevelt to Flora Payne Whitney, (n.d.), April 1917. (TRC-HU).

222 Ibid., May 12, 1917.

223 Ibid., May 28, 1917.

224 Ibid., May 29, 1917.

225 Cooper, Jr., John Milton. *Woodrow Wilson: a Biography*, New York: Alfred A. Knopf, 2009, p. 394.

226 Morris, *Edith Kermit Roosevelt: Portrait of a First Lady*, p. 411.

227 Morris, *Colonel Roosevelt*, p. 489.

228 Ibid., p. 495.

229 Lt. Col. Cuthbert G. Hoare to Brigadier General Lionel Charleton, April 20, 1917, as reported by Alan Toelle in One of Us: Quentin Roosevelt – A Hero's Journey, *Over the Front* magazine, League of World War I Aviation Historians, Winter 2012, Vol. 27, No. 4.

230 Vaughan, David K., (ed.), *Flying for the Air Service - The Hughes Brothers in World War I*, Bowling Green, Ohio: Bowling Green University Popular Press, 1998, p. 20.

231 Ibid., p. 21.

232 Ibid., p. 16.

233 Ibid., pp. 22-23.

234 Renehan, Jr., *The Lion's Pride*, p. 138.

235 Vaughan, (ed.), *Flying for the Air Service-The Hughes Brothers in World War I*, p. 33.

236 Ibid., p. 38.

237 Quentin Roosevelt to Flora Payne Whitney, May 31, 1917. (TRC-DSU)

238 Quentin Roosevelt and Flora Payne Whitney to Kermit and Belle Roosevelt, June 1917.

239 Theodore Roosevelt to Kermit Roosevelt, July 1, 1917. (TRC-DSU)

240 Flora Payne Whitney to Quentin Roosevelt, July 19, 1917, pp. 2-3. (TRC-HU)

241 Ibid., p. 3.

242 Quentin Roosevelt to Edith Kermit Roosevelt, while at sea, July 25, 1917. (TRC-HU)

243 Flora Payne Whitney to Ethel Roosevelt Derby, July 24, 1917. (TRC-HU)

244 Quentin Roosevelt to Flora Payne Whitney, while at sea, July 29, 1917. (TRC-HU)

245 Quentin Roosevelt to Flora Payne Whitney, July 23, 1917. (TRC-HU)

246 Hamilton Coolidge to Mrs. J. Randall Coolidge, July 22, 1917, as reported in *Letters of an American Airman: Being the War Record of Capt. Hamilton Coolidge, U.S.A., 1917-18*, Boston: Privately printed by the Plimpton Press, 1919, p. 1.

247 Quentin Roosevelt to Edith Kermit Roosevelt, July 27, 1917. (TRC-DSU)

248 Quentin Roosevelt to Flora Payne Whitney, July 31, 1917. (TRC-HU)

249 Flora Payne Whitney to Quentin Roosevelt, July 31, 1917. (TRC-HU)

250 Quentin Roosevelt to Flora Payne Whitney, August 3, 1917. (TRC-HU)

251 Hamilton Coolidge to Mrs. J. Randall Coolidge, (n.d.), *Letters of an American Airman*, p. 2.

252 Ibid., July 31, 1917.

253 Fontenoy, Paul E. "Convoy System," in *The Encyclopedia of World War I: A Political, Social and Military History*, Spencer C. Tucker and Priscilla Roberts, (eds.), Santa Barbara, Calif.: ABC-CLIO, 2005, Vol. 1, pp. 312-314.

254 Coolidge, Hamilton, A Sketch of Quentin Roosevelt, p. 1, enclosed in a letter from Ethel Roosevelt Derby to Flora Payne Whitney, June 4, 1919. (TRC-HU)

255 Quentin Roosevelt to Flora Payne Whitney, August 1, 1917. (TRC-DSU)

256 Quentin Roosevelt to Edith Kermit Roosevelt, August 6, 1917. (TRC-DSU)

257 Flora Payne Whitney to Quentin Roosevelt, July 31, 1917. (TRC-DSU)

258 Theodore Roosevelt to Quentin Roosevelt, July 28, 1917. (TRC-DSU)

259 Theodore Roosevelt to Flora Payne Whitney, July 28, 1917. (TRC-DSU)

260 Edith Kermit Roosevelt to Flora Payne Whitney, July 28, 1917. (TRC-DSU)

261 Theodore Roosevelt to Quentin Roosevelt, July 28, 1917. (TRC-DSU)

262 Hamilton Coolidge to Mrs. J. Randall Coolidge, August 15, 1917, *Letters of an American Airman*, pp. 2-3.

263 Quentin Roosevelt to Flora Payne Whitney, August 18, 1917. (TRC-DSU)

264 Ibid.

265 Ibid.

266 Flora Payne Whitney to Quentin Roosevelt, August 14, 1917. (TRC-DSU)

267 Quentin Roosevelt to Flora Payne Whitney, August 18, 1917. (TRC-DSU)

268 Toelle, "One of Us: Quentin Roosevelt – A Hero's Journey," *Over the Front*, p. 296.

269 Quentin Roosevelt to Flora Payne Whitney, August 20, 1917. (TRC-DSU)

270 Ibid.

271 Quentin Roosevelt to Flora Payne Whitney, August 22, 1917. (TRC-DSU)

272 Edith Kermit Roosevelt to Warrington Dawson, (n.d.), circa 1917. (TRC-HU)

273 Theodore Roosevelt to Quentin Roosevelt, September 1, 1917. (TRC-DSU)

274 Theodore Roosevelt to William Allen White, August 3, 1917. (TRC-HU)

275 Flora Payne Whitney to Quentin Roosevelt, September 16, 1917. (TRC-DSU)

276 Quentin Roosevelt to Flora Payne Whitney, August 22, 1917. (TRC-DSU)

277 Flora Payne Whitney to Quentin Roosevelt, September 16, 1917. (TRC-DSU)

278 Sgt. Orrin A. Gardiner, Jr., to his parents, (n.d.). (TRC-DSU)

279 Quentin Roosevelt to Flora Payne Whitney, August 28, 1917. (TRC-DSU)

280 Ibid., September 5, 1917.

281 Ibid., September 7, 1917.

282 Ibid., August 31, 1917.

283 Eleanor Alexander Roosevelt to Flora Payne Whitney, September 13, 1917. (TRC-HU)

284 Quentin Roosevelt to Flora Payne Whitney, September 9, 1917. (TRC-DSU)

285 Ibid., September 13, 1917.

286 Ibid.

287 Ibid.

288 Toelle. One of Us: Quentin Roosevelt–A Hero's Journey, *Over the Front*, p. 293.

289 Ibid., p. 300.

290 Quentin Roosevelt to Flora Payne Whitney, September 20, 1917. (TRC-DSU)

291 Flora Payne Whitney to Quentin Roosevelt, September 30, 1917. (TRC-DSU)

292 Quentin Roosevelt to Edith Kermit Roosevelt, October 3, 1917. (TRC-DSU)

293 Quentin Roosevelt to Flora Payne Whitney, September 27, 1917. (TRC-DSU)

294 Quentin Roosevelt to Edith Kermit Roosevelt, November 1, 1917. (TRC-DSU)

295 Ibid., October 3, 1917.

296 O'Toole, *When Trumpets Call: Theodore Roosevelt after the White House*, p. 344.

297 Theodore Roosevelt to Ted Roosevelt and Archie Roosevelt, August 17, 1917. (TRC-DSU)

298 Maurer, Maurer (ed.), *The U.S. Air Service in World War I*, Darby, Pennsylvania: Diane Publishing, 1978, Vol. II, p. 412.

299 Thomas, Captain Shipley. *The History of the American Expeditionary Force*, New York: George H. Doran Co. 1920, p. 386.

300 Quentin Roosevelt to Flora Payne Whitney, October 31, 1917. (TRC-HU)

301 Ibid., November 11, 1917. (TRC-HU)

302 Ibid., December 8, 1917. (TRC-HU)

303 Quentin Roosevelt to unknown recipient, December 18, 1917. (TRC-HU)

304 Quentin Roosevelt to Flora Payne Whitney, December 8, 1917. (TRC-HU)

305 Ibid., December 10, 1917. (TRC-HU)

306 Hamilton Coolidge to Roger Coolidge, December 27, 1917, *Letters of an American Airman*, p. 64.

307 Quentin Roosevelt to Flora Payne Whitney, December 9, 1917. (TRC-HU)

308 Theodore Roosevelt to Archie Roosevelt, October 14, 1917. (TRC-HU)

309 Edith Kermit Roosevelt to Ethel Roosevelt Derby, October 22, 1917. (TRC-HU)

310 Flora Payne Whitney to Quentin Roosevelt, November 27, 1917. (TRC-DSU)

311 Quentin Roosevelt to Flora Payne Whitney, November 26, 1917. (TRC-DSU)

312 Flora Payne Whitney to Quentin Roosevelt, December 18, 1917. (TRC-DSU)

313 Quentin Roosevelt to Edith Kermit Roosevelt, December 18, 1917. (TRC-DSU)

314 Quentin Roosevelt to Flora Payne Whitney, December 8, 1917. (TRC-DSU)

315 Irene Givenwilson to Flora Payne Whitney, February 23, 1918. (TRC-DSU)

316 Ibid., December 20, 1917.

317 Quentin Roosevelt to Theodore Roosevelt, December 16, 1917. (TRC-DSU)

318 Roosevelt, Eleanor Alexander. *Day Before Yesterday: The Reminiscences of Mrs. Theodore Roosevelt, Jr.,* Garden City, New York: Doubleday and Company, 1959, pp. 89-90.

319 Quentin Roosevelt to Edith Kermit Roosevelt, December 29, 1917. (TRC-DSU)

320 Quentin Roosevelt to Theodore Roosevelt, December 16, 1917. (TRC-DSU)

321 Quentin Roosevelt to Flora Payne Whitney, December 28, 1917. (TRC-HU)

322 Roosevelt, Theodore, remarks delivered at *la Sorbonne*, Paris, April 23, 1910, available online at http://www.theodore-roosevelt.com/trsorbonnespeech.html.

323 Quentin Roosevelt to Edith Kermit Roosevelt, December 29, 1917. (TRC-DSU)

324 Quentin Roosevelt to Flora Payne Whitney, December 30, 1917. (TRC-HU)

325 Edith Kermit Roosevelt to Quentin Roosevelt, January 19, 1918. (TRC-DSU)

326 Ethel Roosevelt Derby to Quentin Roosevelt, January 18, 1918. (TRC-HU)

327 Quentin Roosevelt to Flora Payne Whitney, February 2, 1918. (TRC-DSU)

328 Quentin Roosevelt to Ethel Roosevelt Derby, February 1, 1918. (TRC-HU)

329 Quentin Roosevelt to Flora Payne Whitney, February 9, 1918. (TRC-DSU)

330 Quentin Roosevelt to Ethel Roosevelt Derby, probably mid-February 1918. (TRC-HU)

331 Theodore Roosevelt to Quentin Roosevelt, February 16, 1918. (TRC-DSU)

332 Flora Payne Whitney to Quentin Roosevelt, February 12, 1918. (TRC-HU)

333 Quentin Roosevelt to Flora Payne Whitney, February 13, 1918. (TRC-HU)

334 Ethel Roosevelt Derby to Quentin Roosevelt, February 26, 1918. (TRC-HU)

335 Theodore Roosevelt to Quentin Roosevelt, February 28, 1918. (TRC-DSU)

336 Flora Payne Whitney to Quentin Roosevelt, (n.d.). (TRC-DSU)

337 Theodore Roosevelt to Quentin Roosevelt, probably early March 1918. (TRC-DSU)

338 Quentin Roosevelt to Flora Payne Whitney, March 5, 1918. (TRC-DSU)

339 Friedman, *Gertrude Vanderbilt Whitney*, p. 401.

340 Quentin Roosevelt to Flora Payne Whitney, February 16, 1918. (TRC-DSU)

341 Ibid., February 21, 1918.

342 Ibid., February 23, 1918.

343 Ibid., February 20, 1918.

344 Ibid., March 7, 1918.

345 Ibid., March 1918.

346 Quentin Roosevelt's evaluation sheet from *L'école de tir Aerien*, Cazaux, France, March 1918. (TRC-DSU)

347 Theodore Roosevelt to Quentin Roosevelt, March 5, 1918. (TRC-DSU)

348 Theodore Roosevelt to Archie Roosevelt, March 13, 1918. (TRC-DSU)

349 Ethel Roosevelt Derby to Richard Derby, March 12–13, 1918. (TRC-HU)

350 *The New York Times*, April 15, 1918.

351 Hamilton Coolidge to Mrs. J. Randall Coolidge, February 17, 1918, *Letters of an American Airman*, pp. 89-92.

352 Ibid., March 31, 1918, pp. 107-109.

353 Quentin Roosevelt to Flora Payne Whitney, March 30–31, 1918. (TRC-HU)

354 Coolidge, Hamilton, as reported in *Quentin Roosevelt: A Sketch with Letters*, p. 222.

355 Quentin Roosevelt to Flora Payne Whitney, February 13, 1918. (TRC-HU)

356 Ibid., March 27, 1918. (TRC-HU)

357 Irene Givenwilson to Flora Payne Whitney, February 23, 1918. (TRC-DSU)

358 Ethel Roosevelt Derby to Quentin Roosevelt, March 11, 1918. (TRC-DSU)

359 Edith Kermit Roosevelt to Quentin Roosevelt, April 28, 1918. (TRC-DSU)

360 Morris, *Colonel Roosevelt*, p. 521.

361 Theodore Roosevelt to Kermit Roosevelt, March 24, 1918. (TRC-DSU)

362 Quentin Roosevelt to Flora Payne Whitney, May 2, 1918. (TRC-HU)

363 Harry P. Whitney to Theodore Roosevelt, May 4, 1918. (TRC-HU)

364 Edith Kermit Roosevelt to Quentin Roosevelt, May 5, 1918. (TRC-DSU)

365 Quentin Roosevelt to Theodore Roosevelt, May 12, 1918. (TRC-DSU)

366 Theodore Roosevelt to Kermit Roosevelt, May 12, 1918. (TRC-DSU)

367 *The New York Times*, "Her Share in War," June 2, 1918.

368 Ibid.

369 Theodore Roosevelt to Anna Roosevelt Cowles, July 6, 1918. (TRC-DSU)

370 Theodore Roosevelt to Archie Roosevelt, circa June 1918. (TRC-DSU)

371 Quentin Roosevelt to Flora Payne Whitney, June 2, 1918. (TRC-HU)

372 Quentin Roosevelt to Ethel Roosevelt Derby, July 1, 1918. (TRC-DSU).

373 Roosevelt, *Day before Yesterday: The Reminiscences of Mrs. Theodore Roosevelt, Jr.*, p. 97.

374 *The New York Times*, June 25, 1918.

375 Roosevelt, *Day before Yesterday: The Reminiscences of Mrs. Theodore Roosevelt, Jr.*, p. 97.

376 Quentin Roosevelt to Edith Kermit Roosevelt, April 7, 1918. (TRC-DSU)

377 Cablegram from Quentin Roosevelt to Edith Kermit Roosevelt, June 8, 1918. (TRC-DSU)

378 Quentin Roosevelt to Flora Payne Whitney, June 8, 1918. (TRC-HU)

379 Flora Payne Whitney to Quentin Roosevelt, June 17, 1918. (TRC-HU)

380 Toelle, One of Us: Quentin Roosevelt—A Hero's Journey, *Over the Front*, p. 329.

381 Hamilton Coolidge to Mrs. J. Randall Coolidge, June 9, 1918, *Letters of an American Airman*, pp. 139-142.

382 Quentin Roosevelt to Flora Payne Whitney, June 18-26, 1918. (TRC-HU)

383 Hamilton Coolidge to Lu Coolidge, June 15, 1918, *Letters of an American Airman*, pp. 142-143.

384 Quentin Roosevelt to Flora Payne Whitney, June 18, 1918. (TRC-HU)

385 Ibid., June 23, 1918.

386 Boche was an Allied pejorative for German forces during the Great War.

387 Quentin Roosevelt to Flora Payne Whitney, June 25, 1918. (TRC-HU)

388 Theodore Roosevelt to Quentin Roosevelt, June 19, 1918. (TRC-DSU)

389 Quentin Roosevelt to Edith Kermit Roosevelt, June 25, 1918. (TRC-DSU)

390 Quentin Roosevelt to Flora Payne Whitney, June 29, 1918. (TRC-HU)

391 Hamilton Coolidge to Mrs. J. Randall Coolidge, June 19, 1918, *Letters of an American Airman*, pp. 143-146.

392 Hamilton Coolidge to Lu Coolidge, June 30, 1918, *Letters of an American Airman*, pp. 151-153.

393 Quentin Roosevelt to Ethel Roosevelt Derby, July 1, 1918. (TRC-DSU)

394 Quentin Roosevelt to Flora Payne Whitney, June 28, 1918. (TRC-HU)

395 Attributed to Philip Roosevelt, *Quentin at the Front*, circa 1918. (TRC-DSU)

396 Hamilton Coolidge to Lu Coolidge, June 30, 1918, *Letters of an American Airman*, pp. 151-153.

397 Toelle, One of Us: Quentin Roosevelt—A Hero's Journey, *Over the Front*, p. 331.

398 Quentin Roosevelt to Flora Payne Whitney, July 1, 1918. (TRC-HU)

399 Toelle, One of Us: Quentin Roosevelt—A Hero's Journey, *Over the Front*, p. 332.

400 Attributed to Philip Roosevelt. Available online at www.ThedoreRooseveltCenter.org.

401 Quentin Roosevelt to Flora Payne Whitney, July 1, 1918. (TRC-HU)

402 Ibid., July 3, 1918.

403 Ibid., July 6, 1918.

404 Toole. One of Us: Quentin Roosevelt—A Hero's Journey. *Over the Front*, p. 337.

405 Quentin Roosevelt to Flora Payne Whitney, July 11, 1918. (TRC-HU)

406 Flora Payne Whitney to Ethel Roosevelt Derby, July 13, 1918. (TRC-HU)

407 *The New York Times*, July 11, 1918.

408 Theodore Roosevelt to Ethel Roosevelt Derby, July 12, 1918. (TRC-DSU)

409 Hamilton Coolidge to Mrs. J. Randall Coolidge, July 10, 1918, *Letters of an American Airman*, pp. 154-157.

410 Quentin Roosevelt to Theodore Roosevelt, July 11, 1918. (TRC-DSU)

411 Ibid.

412 Theodore Roosevelt to Kermit Roosevelt, July 13, 1918. (TRC-DSU)

413 Theodore Roosevelt to Ethel Roosevelt Derby, July 12, 1918. (TRC-DSU)

414 Flora Payne Whitney to Ethel Roosevelt Derby, July 13, 1918. (TRC-HU)

415 Roosevelt, *Day before Yesterday: The Reminiscences of Mrs. Theodore Roosevelt, Jr.*, p. 100.

416 Archie Roosevelt to Flora Payne Whitney, July 13, 1918. (TRC-HU)

417 Roosevelt, *Day before Yesterday: The Reminiscences of Mrs. Theodore Roosevelt, Jr.*, p. 100.

418 Capt. Henry L. Lyster to Theodore Roosevelt, July 20, 1918. (TRC-DSU)

419 Toole, "One of Us: Quentin Roosevelt—A Hero's Journey," *Over the Front*, p. 339.

420 Ibid.

421 Lt. Edward Buford, Jr. to Edward Buford, September 5, 1918. (TRC-DSU)

422 Hamilton Coolidge to Flora Payne Whitney, July 16, 1918. (TRC-HU)

423 Hamilton Coolidge to Edith Kermit Roosevelt, July 16, 1918. (TRC-HU)

424 Cablegram from Eleanor Alexander Roosevelt to Theodore Roosevelt, July 19, 1918. (TRC-DSU)

425 Morris, *Colonel Roosevelt*, pp. 528-529.

426 *The New York Times*, July 17, 1918.

427 Cablegram from General John J. Pershing to Theodore Roosevelt, July 19, 1918. (TRC-DSU)

428 Roosevelt, *Quentin Roosevelt: A Sketch with Letters*, p. 172.

429 Ibid., pp. 173-174.

430 Ibid., pp. 175-176.

431 Ibid., pp. 177-178.

432 *The New York Times*, July 21, 1918.

433 Edithe Normant to Edith Kermit Roosevelt, July 28, 1918. (TRC-DSU)

434 Irene Givenwilson to Edith Kermit Roosevelt, July 20, 1918. (TRC-HU)

435 *Boston Transcript*, July 22, 1918.

436 William H. Crawford to Theodore Roosevelt, July 19, 1918. (TRC-DSU)

437 C.V. White to Theodore Roosevelt, circa October 1918. (TRC-DSU)

438 Theodore Roosevelt to Kermit Roosevelt, July 21, 1918. (TRC-DSU)

439 Telegram from Eleanor Alexander Roosevelt to Theodore Roosevelt, July 21, 1918. (TRC-DSU)

440 O'Toole, *When Trumpets Call: Theodore Roosevelt after the White House*, p. 394.

441 Theodore Roosevelt to Corinne Roosevelt Robinson, August 3, 1918. (TRC-DSU)

442 Quentin Roosevelt to Flora Payne Whitney, August 25, 1917. (TRC-HU)

443 Theodore Roosevelt to Belle Willard Roosevelt, August 11, 1918. (TRC-DSU)

444 Theodore Roosevelt to Corinne Roosevelt Robinson, August 10, 1918. (TRC-DSU)

445 Hamilton Coolidge to Edith Kermit Roosevelt, July 30, 1918. (TRC-HU)

446 Renehan, Jr., *The Lion's Pride*, p. 190.

447 Rickenbacker, Eddie. *Fighting the Flying Circus*, New York: Frederick A. Stokes Co., 1919, p. 193.

448 Hamilton Coolidge to Flora Payne Whitney, July 29, 1918. (TRC-HU)

449 Citation by order of General (John J.) Pershing, 1918. (TRC-DSU)

450 Roosevelt, *Quentin Roosevelt: A Sketch with Letters*, pp. 209-210.

451 U.S. War Department document, September 24, 1918. (TRC-DSU)

452 C. N. Greenough to Edith Kermit Roosevelt, June 13, 1919, available at the Harvard University Archives, Cambridge, Massachusetts.

453 Irene Givenwilson to Flora Payne Whitney, October 23, 1918. (TRC-HU)

454 Theodore Roosevelt to Flora Payne Whitney, August 13, 1918. (TRC-DSU)

455 Theodore Roosevelt to Kermit Roosevelt, August 18, 1918. (TRC-DSU)

456 Theodore Roosevelt to Belle Willard Roosevelt, August 11, 1918. (TRC-DSU)

457 Flora Payne Whitney to Ethel Roosevelt Derby, August 25, 1918. (TRC-HU)

458 Sage, Kay. Flora Whitney Miller papers, Archives of American Art, Smithsonian Institution, Washington, D.C, available online at: http://www.aaa.si.edu/collections/flora-whitney-miller-papers-regarding-kay-sage-10848/more.

459 Richards, Henry Howe. *Groton School in the War*, Groton, Massachusetts: The Groton School, 1925, pp. 51-60. (TGS)

460 C. P. Harris to J. R. Coolidge, March 10, 1919. General Orders No. 37, U.S. War Department, http://www.theaerodrome.com/aces/usa/coolidge.php.

461 Edith Kermit Roosevelt to Kermit Roosevelt, October 29, 1918. (TRC-HU)

462 Morris, *Colonel Roosevelt*, p. 542.

463 Bishop, Joseph Bucklin. *Theodore Roosevelt and His Time*, New York: Charles Scribner's Sons, 1920, Vol. II, p. 468.

464 Theodore Roosevelt to Kermit Roosevelt, December 29, 1918. (TRC-DSU)

465 Morris, *Colonel Roosevelt*, p. 540.

466 Amos, James. *Hero to his Valet*, New York: The John Day Co., 1927, pp. 154-155.

467 Bishop, *The Lion and the Journalist*, p. 264.

468 Ibid., p. x.

469 Ibid., p. 264.

470 Morris, *Edith Kermit Roosevelt: Portrait of a First Lady*, p. 442.

471 Cret biographical sketch available online at www.archives.upenn. edu/people/1800s/cret_paul.html.

472 Friedman, *Gertrude Vanderbilt Whitney*, p. 411.

473 Ibid., pp. 412-413.

474 Ethel Roosevelt Derby to Emily Carow, February 20, 1920. (TRC-HU)

475 Biddle, *The Whitney Women and the Museum They Made*, p. 346.

476 Ibid., p. 50.

477 Ibid.

478 Ibid., pp. 50-51.

479 Biddle, *Embers*, p. 216.

480 Biddle, *The Whitney Women and the Museum They Made*, p. 53.

481 Biddle, *Embers*, pp. 118-119.

482 Ibid., p. 69.

483 Ibid., p. 107.

484 Ibid., p. 71.

485 Flora Whitney Miller to Cornelius Vanderbilt Whitney, circa summer 1942.

486 Biddle, *The Whitney Women and the Museum They Made*, p. 77.

487 Whitney Museum of American Art, *Flora Whitney Miller: Her Life, Her World*, p. 21.

488 Ibid., p. 112.

489 Ibid., p. 113.

490 Biddle, *The Whitney Women and the Museum They Made*, p. 80.

491 Ibid., p. 87.

492 Biddle, *Embers*, p. 44.

493 Biddle, *The Whitney Women and the Museum They Made*, p. 199.

494 Biddle, *Embers*, p. 194.

495 Ibid., pp. 298-299.

496 Biddle, *The Whitney Women and the Museum They Made*, p. 344.

497 Ibid., p. 342.

498 Ibid., p. 345.

499 Flora Miller Biddle in conversation with the author, July 8, 2013.

500 Theodore Roosevelt to General Payton C. March, October 25, 1918, as reported in *The New York Times*, November 18, 1918.

501 General Payton C. March to Theodore Roosevelt, October 29, 1918, as reported in *The New York Times*, November 18, 1918.

502 Trout, Steven. *On the Battlefield of Memory: The First World War*

and *American Remembrance 1919-1941*, Tuscaloosa, Alabama: The University of Alabama Press, 2010, p. 232.

503 Ibid., p. 237.

504 *The New York Times*, May 30, 1960.

505 Library of Congress Biographical Essay, available online at www.loc.gov/rr/print/coll/womphotoj/rooseveltessay.html.

506 Renehan, Jr., *The Lion's Pride*, p. 213.

507 Ibid., p. 65.

508 Attributed to Leonard W. Hall in *The New York Times*, December 12, 1977.

509 Roosevelt, *Quentin Roosevelt: A Sketch with Letters*, p. vii.

510 Morris, *Edith Kermit Roosevelt: Portrait of a First Lady*, p. 516.

511 Biddle, *The Whitney Women and the Museum They Made*, p. 57.

512 *The New York Times*, February 12, 1999.

513 Hale, Richard W. (ed.). *Letters of Warwick Greene 1915-1928*, New York: Houghton Mifflin, 1931.

514 Televised interview, "Serious Jibber-Jabber with Conan O'Brien," September 8, 2012.

Index

N

O

P

R

Y

CPSIA information can be obtained at www.ICGtesting.com
Printed in the USA
LVOW11s1057280914

406234LV00007B/883/P